Walter Gosewisch

Memoirs of student life in Germany and vacation tips in the Tyrol, Switzerland and Austria

Walter Gosewisch

Memoirs of student life in Germany and vacation tips in the Tyrol, Switzerland and Austria

ISBN/EAN: 9783337197988

Printed in Europe, USA, Canada, Australia, Japan

Cover: Foto ©Andreas Hilbeck / pixelio.de

More available books at **www.hansebooks.com**

A NOOK IN THE SULTAN'S PALACE BY MOONLIGHT.

Chap. XIII.

MEMOIRS

OF

Student Life in Germany

AND

VACATION TRIPS

IN THE

Tyrol, Switzerland and Austria

W. R. GOSEWISCH, M. Ph., M. D.

1898
JOHN H. TRAIN, PUBLISHER
LOS ANGELES, CAL.

TO
MY WIFE
THIS VOLUME
IS LOVINGLY DEDICATED.

Off you dond't tole me some shtdory,
    Yah, it is mit sure to be
Dot you hafe some vriendts in glory
    Vot you'd somedimes like du see.

Bin de vriendts vots gone I vondare
    Nodt de vriendts ve holdt most dear?
Vor de scene vay ofer yondare
    Looks much petter as dis righdt here.

Sad de stdrongest oft is dtaken
    Vile de years go rolling on,
Und dare lives de godt forsaken
    Ven dose ghildhoods vriendts bin gone.

THE AUTHOR AND HIS CHUM WITH THEIR TYROLESE STUDENT FRIEND IN THE MOUNTAINS OF THE TYROL.

CHAPTER I.

HERE it was the fall of 1867, and Menton and I were once more back at the University in Berlin, Germany. We had spent the summer vacation touring through Switzerland, the Tyrol, and Austria. We had, on the closing of the past session, student-like, put our knapsacks on our shoulders, taken our staves or eight-foot canes in hand, and, with the exception of a week's stop-over on the Hartz Mountains, had taken the cars direct to the Rhine, up which we went as near to Switzerland as we could, and then leaving the railway became true student foot-tourists for the south.

This custom is general among the students in Germany, to spend their summer vacations in tours about the surrounding countries, and so we had done, now, for four summers. It is called digesting what they have learned during the previous semester or half-yearly session. They are to be met with everywhere along in your trip. You often meet with parties of several, happy and light-hearted; and, again, come across a "lone student" wandering all alone all by himself around the ruins of ancient strongholds and monasteries, the sad reminders of a grandeur of by-gone days ; lurking among the fallen arches and crumbling towers of the castles of old, fondly caressing the historic old stones, and in silence and solitude pondering on the forgotten days of yore ; restoring in fancy the ruins to the perfection of their pristine state ; peopling the abbeys and the castles with the personages of their halcyon and glamour-throwing days, the days when shining suits of mail and gaudy dresses made such picturesque scenes as caught the eye of beholders in wonder and awe.

How many gallant knights clad in the glittering armor of the times came out from behind those now ruined gateways and rode off into the world never to return ; how many fair ladies have sat at those lofty windows, the high outward flanging apertures of the now ruined and crumbling towers, day after day and month after month, watching for the back-coming of the armored knight who had departed, husband, lover or son, and who never returned ! What gorgeous scenes of festivity and gayety must have taken place in olden times within those royal halls ! How many fair hands were promised to brave hearts ; how many false knights there were who loved and rode away; how many scenes of villainy accomplished, deep schemes of atrocious wickedness concocted and dark murders were plotted and consummated behind those massive, old, grim and gloomy walls will never be known. All this the lone student dwells upon, calling up in fancy the gay cavalcades of ladies and knights returning from a successful chase or tournament with gay-colored pennons proudly flying from victorious lances, and galloping in the spirits of youth up to the drawbridge and sounding the horn, chain-fastened to the wall, for entrance.

These lone students, these ponderers of the past, were usually middle-aged or elderly men, wrapped in reflection and contemplation, living for a few hours back in the past ages. A party of several students was nearly always composed of young men, gay, frolicsome, thoughtless, and living in the immediate present, laughing at these old students with the uncharitableness of youth.

Youth is uncharitable, because it has never felt and cannot realize the many ills and weaknesses that the ever-rolling relentless years so surely bring upon us; cannot understand until self-experience stares it in the face; and then, merging into middle life, it begins to comprehend with a pensive sadness the oncoming melancholy loneliness of extreme old age.

Stories, tales, legends and traditions are outgrowths of countries and partake of the diversified characteristics peculiar to and in harmony with the land of their origin. What country is richer in folk-lore than Teutonia, and why? A traveler on going into Germany at once feels that he has entered an ancient and hallowed region. The lay of the land, the position of the mountains, the situation of the lakes, the natural arrangements of the green trees and deep forests, the ruined castles, the dismantled towers, the beautiful clear river Rhine winding like a silver band beneath its grape-covered slopes, past the turreted, crumbling strongholds of the dark ages, all suggest folk-lore. The famed "Schwarzwalder" (black-woods), in the province of Baden, in Southern Germany, with its high mountain-tops covered to their lofty peaks with dense forests of towering pine and cedar trees, and the dark and gloomy recesses of which seem impenetrable, suggest at once to the imaginative mind as being the dismal abode of dwarfs, fairies and hunchbacked wonder-workers. But, alas! the day of the castle is over. Where the plumed, armored, and lance-equipped gallant knight once rode heavily to and fro, now the occidental potato, planted by a prosaic agriculturist, grows to perfection under the dilapidating old walls, and geese and ducks meander among the weeds and in the mud, around about ground that has long since been historic.

On taking the train at Berlin we first stopped off for a visit to the famous Hartz Mountains which lie about one hundred and fifty miles southwest of Berlin and in the province of Saxony, our object being to climb the famous Brocken, a peak of 3,738 feet in height, and witness for ourselves the curious atmospheric phenomenon we had heard so much about, which takes place there on the summit of the mountains just before day breaks over the surrounding country. We got to the city of Hartzburg, and tramped it to the old town of Kleinlesel (pronounced Kline-lay-sel), situated just at the base of the Hartz Mountains, where we put up and made preparations for our ascent.

We selected a night of bright moonshine, when all the sky was clear, and the stars were twinkling and sparkling overhead, and taking nothing along to encumber us, except our staves, which were spiked in iron at the lower ends to assist us in climbing, and with a good, big breakfast of sausage, cheese and bread, well done up in a canvas satchel, the latter loaned us by the accommodating innkeeper, we started out at about eight o'clock, our object being to trail up the mountain and scale the Brocken peak to its summit ere the sun's rays began to touch its extreme top. At about half past one o'clock in the morning we had left the steep sides of the mountain behind us, and at about four o'clock had scaled the Brocken, and tired and panting were sitting at rest —our intended destination, the summit of the noted peak, at length reached. All below us over the land was still shrouded in darkness and gloom; but as the moments wore on the eastern sky began to grow lighter and soon we could see the glimmer of the clear waters of the lake, and a little later on the darkness of the valley, asleep in black shadows, began to turn to a deep, dark gray, preliminary to dispersing altogether before the oncoming sun's rays; and we could indistinctly make out villages as somber spots in the valley away below us. The eastern sky continued to grow lighter, and twilight was now coming upon the top of the Brocken. After our short rest from the overheating exertions of the long, upward climb we cooled off and grew chilly in the cold, early morning at such a lofty elevation, and we shivered, and our teeth chattered as we arose and walked about for warmth on the summit. The atmosphere was also damp and thick with floating vapors which now and again came past, enveloping us, and which seemed to our now cooled bodies, reacting after the warmth created by our several hours of steep clambering, to penetrate them to our very bones. This moisture all at once condensed, a usual occurrence on the Brocken in the morning after clear cloudless nights, and we presently found ourselves in a dense, penetrating, chilly and unpleasant greyish white fog, out of which we could discern nothing beyond about a fifty-foot distance from us; then the first slanting rays of the sun, coming slowly up out of the east, came lightly down from above on to the summit where we were standing; the red rays of its light, having the greatest refractive power, falling upon the mist surrounding us gave it at once a lovely pinkish appearance or tint. This only lasted for a moment, and then the sun getting higher the beautiful color gradually faded away and disappeared altogether, leaving us still enveloped in the thick fog now snow white.

We were walking about, pacing to and fro, east and west, a few yards apart from each other when I sat down, and Menton passed on without observing that I had quit walking. He was turning around to pace back toward the western end of his promenade when a beam of sunshine suddenly broke through the mist and he saw me, as he supposed, also walking backward and forward about fifty feet in front of him. I had now gotten into a reclining posture, with my head on my hand and elbow on the ground and facing the west, and also saw the strange figure at the same moment that he had, and was too surprised at the suddenness of the shadow's appearance to speak, when he addressed the figure in some remark that he supposed I was, as well as he, wishing we had brought heavier coats along with us, or at least that we had some wood with which to build a fire. On me not answering him, he spoke out sharply, "Don't you? Hey?"

Recognizing at once that the phenomenon had appeared and that he had mistaken the shadow for me, in a spirit of foolishness I kept quiet, and he shouted at me again, this time loudly, not even then getting a response from me, although I seemed only a few yards away; he walked toward the "seeming me" in some alarm at my silence;

but the "seeming me" kept ahead of him an even fifty feet as he walked toward it, and it all at once dawned upon him that the form portrayed on the fog was the shadow of himself with his head and neck humped down into his shoulders, and his hands deep into his coat pockets, and not me walking about in a similar humped position. "Here's the old fellow! Here's the boy!" he shouted out to me, not knowing where I was located in the mist and fearing I might have strayed off and thus lose witnessing the curious illusion for the sight of which we had gone to so much trouble and toil. I arose and came up to him, and instantly both of our figures, side by side, appeared projected on the mist. We backed away together to the eastern end of our promenade and our two dumb friends did the same; came forward in even footsteps along with us. A light, glowing, pinkish, prismatically colored luminous circle, or halo, caused by the refraction of light through minute crystals of ice in the atmosphere, appeared to envelop the shadows, making the forms look more distinct in contrast to the bright light surrounding them. We then walked at right-angles to our former course, pacing now north and south, and the specters did the same, steadily advancing on our side, and evenly with us. We stopped, danced up and down, waved our arms and staves about, and the figures contemporaneously with us repeated our movements. We walked to the extreme edge of the top and there both of our figures in colossal size were pictured on the fog away off in the air, overhanging the precipitous side of the peak and in the direction of Gottingen. We stood upon the edge for a moment, looking at the curious and greatly magnified representations of ourselves. As we raised our arms aloft immense arms would rear in answer, and on taking off and waving our hats great hats were taken off and waved in responsive greeting.

The figures became dimmer and dimmer as the sun arose and the early morning grew lighter, and soon the shadows faded out and left nothing to our view but the white fog. This, also, was soon dispelled and we found ourselves standing in a flood of sunshine which was kissing the peak to about a hundred yards beneath us. The lake, far below, was now shimmering in a cold glassy hue, and the valley, dotted with villages, was becoming more and more distinct in the breaking light of early morning.

We stood upon the edge of the summit and watched the sunlight descend the peak and then the mountain, moving downward slowly and lighting up object after object—trees, masses of rock, great clefts, etc.—as it descended, until it finally reached the valley, dispelling the last of its overshadowing gloom; and soon we could see the peasants emerging from their little homes, see the cows come slowly out and wind along to the pastures, and we realized that the surrounding land had awakened to the duties of the day.

An echo is met with at this point of the Brocken, but it is a short one; only about three syllables can be spoken to get them all three back distinctly to the ear. We made the sausage and bread and cheese fly, and hunted through the small canvas satchel (which one of us had worn at the side by a strap hung over the shoulder) for the last few remaining crumbs it contained. Descending from our lofty height we came in time for dinner back to Kleinlesel.

A legend is connected with the appearance of this phenomenon which goes as follows: Many long years ago the inhabitants of Kleinlesel elected a worthy fellow-citizen to the chair of burgomaster, or chief magistrate. On his assuming his elevated office, however, he suddenly forgot the noble and enlightening principles of republicanism and at once arrogated to himself great authority and power from which he would allow of no appeal. In vain did the villagers explain to him that he was merely put in office to make their wants and intentions legal; that they could not, each and everyone, be judge, jury and executor of the laws; that they must put the authority in someone's hands, and vest him with the power of making their desires good by putting his signature to documents, etc.; that they could not all, each one, decide for himself and allow all of their signatures to be held as rightful, but had selected him to be the one who, on hearing their aims and wishes, should carry them out as they expressed. He wouldn't have it, however, but considered himself a great Cæsar, and on hearing a case would at first reflect how it influenced himself, his own well-being, his personal sentiments or purposes, or those of his intimate friends, and would decide not as those who had chosen him from among themselves to represent them wished and requested, but as it suited best what he considered his own welfare. He was petitioned unanimously to resign from his elevated position, but he swore that if he heard more of such an infamous proposition he would imprison the whole town.

At length he grew so bloated at the thought of his own importance that he wanted to extend his yard and own an extended park-like lawn or holding, to be in keeping with his ever enlarging greatness, which seemed to the view of his fellow-townsmen and others to be mainly around his waist. In order to do this it was necessary for him to secure the little home of a poor neighbor, whose modest dwelling on a small piece of ground adjoined his own land. The neighbor whose father and grandfathers for generations had been born and reared upon the place, would not hear of selling his home even after being offered a thousand pieces of silver for it by the burgomaster (and in those days that was an immense sum of money indeed), and the burgomaster grew furious at the refusal and made dire threats against the owner.

They came to hot words on one occasion and the poor villager finally called the puffed-up chief magistrate "ein esel" (a donkey), at which the burgomaster came near exploding at this offense to his lordly dignity.

"What!" he yelled, "you call me 'ein esel'? me! the biggest personage in the town!"

"Yes, I do, for that's what you are," hotly replied the villager, "and even the Giant of the Brocken will say so."

"Oh, he will, will he? If so I will give you half a thousand pieces of silver; here now I will make a contract with you; if he does I will give you the thousand pieces, and if he does not I will take your land; that is fair enough", said the chief magistrate.

"Agreed", replied the villager. And that night he told it around about the contract, and collected together a lot of the most prominent of his fellow-townsmen, who pulled the fat burgomaster along with them up the mountain to the top of the Brocken, where they arrived just before sunrise; and the betting villager, standing out upon the ridge of the peak's summit until the proper moment when his figure of superhuman size appeared out upon the mist in plain view of all, called out loudly, "Was ist der Burgemeister" (what is the burgomaster), "von Kleinlesel?" Immediately came the last three syllables of his question in an answering echo back from the vicinity of the giant, "ein esel!" (big donkey).

At that an immense laugh arose from the townsmen.

"Yah, das sagen wir alle" (yes, that reply we all countenance), drolly called out a joker from amongst the crowd.

At this sally another great shout of ridicule arose, and the burgomaster, thoroughly humbled, awakened to the fact that he was, and had long been, the laughing-stock of the country, and after descending the mountain and arriving once more at the village, he paid the thousand pieces of silver into the hand of the poor villager, took the lesson he had received well to heart, and later became such a model ruler over his little village that he received the loud praises of all.

Late that afternoon we again took to the cars, and striking the Rhine the next evening boarded one of the numerous excursion boats that ply up and down its long course, and, ascending the historic stream, a few days later planted our staves and set our feet amidst the beautiful scenes of Switzerland, among the perpetually snow-capped mountains of that liberty-loving land.

CHAPTER II.

MENTON was from the town of Americus in Georgia. He had been through the first three years of the civil war in the Confederate service, and had lost a hand; he always wore a black kid-gloved false one. The coming session at the University was to be our last. The following spring we would receive our degrees and go our ways in the wide world apart, all life open before us.

This was our last tour together. We met numbers of English in Switzerland, both ladies and gentlemen, tourists of wealth doing the land with guides, climbers, etc., scaling the mountain-tops with all their paraphernalia of ropes, picks, ice-hatchets and alpinstocks along. Many donned the Switzer's garb and cut a picturesque appearance with bare knees, high stockings with a double woven embroidered part at the upper half of the calves, wide and straight knee trousers, and with gaily-feathered, little crusher green felt hats, and with their hatchets hanging from their belts or broad waist sashes worn beneath a wide-sleeved, loose-fitting, cutaway short sack coat; these hatchets were for the purpose of cutting steps in the solid ice of the glaciers in order to enable them to ascend to their summits. The alpinstocks were eight feet long, spiked and hooked in iron at one end, the hook to catch a projection of ice above and pull oneself upward with, and the spike to plant down firmly in the ice in walking to save oneself from falling by a slip of the foot.

These English in speaking use the broad a, pronouncing it as though it were ah. One day we overtook a young schoolmistress on her way up the mountains, along the little paths the people make through the snow, to the small village where she was to teach; her coming had been expected, and an old knee-stockinged forester, who had been at work clearing the path of snow and piling it up on either side, and who now stood resting upon his shovel and talking to a party of English tourists standing at the side of the upward winding road, took off his hat as she passed, stepped back a few paces to where he had hidden in a high drift bank a pink-topped tuberose-like flower about twelve inches in height, and politely presented it to her. She took it, bowed, smiled and thanked him very kindly.

"Ha! that resembles a snow plahnt, a snow plahnt" (snow plant), cried a young Englishman in sudden surprise. Flora are not often seen at these great elevations, as they are not plentiful, growing mostly beneath the snow and usually appearing to sight only when it has melted down sufficiently to allow them. The forester had of course uncovered it during his snow-shoveling work.

The people of the continent all say that the English remind them famously of the Americans, in one regard certainly, in which there is a great similarity between the two same language-speaking nations, and that is, to every question put to them, of giving an answer, "Don't ahsk may (me), mee boy, for I cahn't tell you." In the United States continental foreigners say, on making an inquiry of the inhabitants, the invariable response, accompanied with a shake of the head, is, "Don't know."

On our walk from Interlachen to Luzerne, we met so many men and women affected with goiter, that one exempt from this affliction appeared uncommon. So noted is this region for such cases that a picture hangs in a museum of a more northern city, entitled "The arrival of an Englishman in Switzerland." In the United States we typify an Englishman as "John Bull"—a short, stout gentleman, with a fat, smoothly shaven face, knee-boots, low silk hat, claw-hammer coat, etc. Europe pictures him as a tall, thin, middle-aged man, with half yard long side-whiskers, standing stiffly out beyond each side of his shoulders, a brimless flat-topped cap, with two hanging ribbons at the back, checked frock suit, and carrying a checked shawl hanging from his arm; in the painting such a tall, thin-necked Englishman is standing in quiet dignity on the platform of a railway station in a small village of Switzerland, calmly viewing through a single eyeglass a surrounding assembly of a dozen goiterous men and women who are eyeing him in great surprise; and one of the men with his hands clasped together before his face in astonishment is exclaiming, "Just look! here's a fellow who hasn't any throat."

As one gets into the Tyrol the legends of the people grow loftier, arising probably from their more elevated position. The Tyrol is one of the most exclusively mountainous countries in Europe, having a small proportion of level country; the noble characteristics of the Tyrolese are well known; they are the most patriotic adherents of the house of Austria; their lofty imagination is co-existent with their high-resting habitations upon the mountain sides and summits communing with the skies. Who has not felt the blood go bounding through his veins after ascending a mountain and viewing from a lofty peak the world beneath him? How one's spirits seem to soar aloft and keep pace with the flight of the eagle; thus, while in the deep and dark gulches of the Tyrol and Switzerland into some of the ravines and gorges of which the rays of the glorious life-giving sun never penetrate, one is often shocked at the combined physical and mental deformity he occasionally comes upon among the inhabitants, an unnatural or distorted state of the mind being a condition generally accompanied with congenital malformation of the body, many pitiful, heart-wringing wierd cases of idiocy, spirit-depressing melancholia and disproportioned, twisted shapes are met with; contrawise, upon the mountain-tops the intelligence and physique of the inhabitants are most nearly perfect, and their imaginations and inspirations are as lofty as their own sky-piercing glaciers, and the soaring of their bird of freedom.

The Tyrol is full of beautiful legends of a noble and exalted character symbolistic of lives spent among the mountain-tops, being outgrowths of this people's elevated situation and their consequent high sentiments.

On the summits of the mountains there, just below the line of perpetual ice and snow, there grows a little white feathery flower, shaped like a star, called the "Edelweiss";

it is very rare and hard to find, growing upon the loftiest peaks and in dangerous and almost inaccessible places. In all our Tyrol mountain climbing we came across only one of them, and that we paid for dearly; for after an hour's exertion in the attempt to reach its almost unapproachable location, and just as we secured it, we slipped and fell, and both went down flat upon our stomachs for nearly a mile before checking up. It is about the size of a silver half dollar, the leaves are stellate, there being from five to seven prong-shaped ones, which are of a velvety smoothness and pure white color.

About this flower the legend runs: Once upon a time there was a lady so pure, so sublime, so heavenly-minded, that throughout all the length and breadth of her fair clime no suitor was found noble enough or worthy to win her; so at last she was metamorphosed by the fairies into a star-like flower as white as the snows and placed high up on the loftiest, inaccessible mountain-tops or heights close to the snow she so strongly resembled. Though all men vainly sighed for her, they were, however, partly consoled by the knowledge that no rival had gotten her and reconciled to see the fair object of their deep affections, so loftily placed, there forever to be the type of that womanhood which is most lovely. And because the flower could only be found through peril and toil and an upward struggle, it became a saying throughout the cantons around in defense of it, that he who would win the love of the highest and noblest would be one of the first to begin the upward ascent and be the most successful in plucking the Edelweiss. So at last it began to grow sacred to betrothals as the orange blossoms are to the marriage vow, until at length no fair lady might be won until her lover himself had gone alone to scale the perilous heights, seeking for the precious Edelweiss; and many a brave and gallant lover endured untold hardships or lost his life among the mountain-tops in search of the coveted blossom, and no lady could merit any higher honor than to have the little white flower as her own emblem thrown at her by an admirer, or placed by a lover in her gentle hand. And, like the Scotch white heather, it told in itself the old sweet tale that will still be whispered by brave and bold gallants in the ages that yet are coming; for if the lady took his offering the happy lover knew he might look for hope, and if she placed it in her girdle or on her bosom her lover knew that she was his forever.

Here in the Tyrol we met many of the professors of the Universities of Germany, and numbers of the heavy men of the fatherland — the great lawyers, bankers, manufacturers, etc. Everyone must trip off for the summer, else he loses caste. So at the beginning of warm weather the heads of firms, judges, professors, etc., all accompanied by their ladies, "light out" for green pastures, the mountains, sea-side, or the lakes. Toward the middle of the season less important personages, the clerks, assistant demonstrators, and small merchants, "pull out" with their families; and at the end of the summer the bootblacks, boys who sweep out the banks and offices, the men who pack bundles about and who carry your "grip" for you, and their women folks, all "strike out" for their "reise" or trip — all to avoid losing caste. Back at home again in the fall, everyone talks of their vacation; it is the ladies' chief topic of conversation for two months later — where they have been and their experiences; comparing them with that of their friends, etc. It is a fad of the land, this summer "reisen."

The traveling student is the pet of Europe; he is ever in his journey treated kindly and with the greatest consideration, and all jokes and foolishness of his are looked upon leniently and taken in good nature and humor; all his "dummheiten" forgiven with the remark, "It's a German student; what else can be expected."

Now, at the period of our summer vacation, in the rural districts of Germany and Switzerland, as well as in fact of nearly all Europe for that matter, where stock was expensive to keep, oxen were often hitched to wagons; and the vehicles in general use among the rural inhabitants were large and heavy and made almost entirely of wood — the axle as well as the wheel — and a small pot or bucket of tar was carried hanging behind the wagon; every five miles or so, while driving, the team was stopped and the owner would seize the brush from out the pot and smear tar over the wooden axles. One never saw a farm wagon in those days without its small smear-pot hanging behind; it was as much a part of the outfit as were the tongue or wheels. Here in the Tyrol we met many of these humorous foibles among the wandering students.

One, I remember, at a little village, had a small hand wagon of two wheels which he pulled along with him in his journey by acting horse himself between the shafts; he had his roll of blankets, his drawing materials, lunches, little tent, umbrella, etc., all in this minute conveyance, and had traveled three or four hundred miles in this independent manner. It was very light and strongly built. He was coming from the village as we approached, and was being followed out of town by a crowd of urchins, while behind him at the village could still be heard the laughter and humor engendered by his passage. On coming up to the outfit we saw that he had for his little vehicle a smear-pot on behind larger than the whole wagon itself; so immense in fact as to cause the amused wonderment of every village through which he had passed.

Recognizing each other as brethren, we all stopped and compared notes. He explained to us that the smear-pot was a fake, was the bottom of a large tub driven up to within three inches of the top and an inch of thick tar covering the false bottom gave the appearance of a full vessel; it was a splendidly gotten-up scheme and spoke much for his ingenuity.

This is one instance among hundreds of the plans students work out to create sensations and observation and attract notice to their particular works of art. Much rivalry exists among them to get up the most laughter-provoking and sensation-creating "dummheiten" (foolishness), and in the fall, on returning to their studies at the University, they compare notes and tell the tales of their vacation, their adventures and experiences. We met one student leading a little five-inch high black-and-tan dog with a long, immense iron chain, the links being four inches wide by a foot in length, and nearly an inch thick, which on closer inspection proved to be black paper wound around straw.

Whatever foolishness a German student does upon these vacations is always overlooked; it is expected of him to go to the extreme of nonsense during that period to counterbalance the profoundly deep studies of his previous session at a German University, where thoroughness from the bottom of everything up is instilled into all imbibing minds by learned professors, who, in their special branches, have searched to the lowest depths and are unexcelled.

How often does the German student, while burning the midnight oil, at his books, in his room along with several companions, come across four pages of reading of which he can neither make heads nor tails. There seems to be no connecting link between it all; he reads it over again and again, but with no better success; then reads it aloud to his companions, but they also cannot see the meaning or comprehend what the instructor is driving at. They all read farther on, a couple of pages more, but still the same muddle, and finally give it up. The first student resumes his book and continues, and after reading still another two pages finally comes upon a word followed by a period, at the end of a page, that explains it all, connects it wholly together and makes the entire eight pages of seemingly senseless reading as clear as daylight. "Here she is, boys," finally exclaims the first student; "here's the word, now she's all plain sailing." If the word could only have been gotten in at the start instead of the final, the section of learning might have been a joy forever.

We visited while in this land a fellow-student of ours at Berlin whose home was here, and he took us up the mountains one night to see the fires lighted among the lofty summits all over the Tyrol on some saint's eve, and to hear the warbling signaling of the young men and girls in greeting from the fires of one peak to another. The fires, great piles of flaming forest wood and brush, are lighted at dusk, and one blazes out after another until all over the country as far as flame could be distinguished they were to be seen. From every eminence, lofty peak and towering projection, glowed a fire in the calm of the growing darkness; hundreds of them, some near and bright, others farther away and fainter, and more just discernible as flickers away off over the heights in the far black distance, then the warbling would begin by the men. Living upon the peaks and crags of the mountains their voices are developed from childhood in hallooing or signaling each other, and one of their amusements and pastimes is to sound their voices, exclaiming out loudly and listening to the echo which comes back several or a dozen times, perhaps, according to the numbers and respective distances of the surrounding peaks which reflect back the sound waves, each succeeding echo fainter than the one before.

This night of the fires they had songs, the men of a half-dozen or so fires combining, throwing their voices out upon the mountain air, loud and clear, the echoes answering, and the warblers then continuing the song, often making several different sounds before the previous reverberations have faded away, and combining several echoes together, one recent, one less so, others still older, etc., all different sounds. But the echoes and the true singing blending one into the other and all intermingling in perfect harmony with the Alpine chorus which the less loud and less strong voices of the group of girls about each fire constantly kept up during the young men's warbling, produced a most beautiful musical effect. To be off half a mile and equidistant from several of the groups about the fires, warbling in concert and unison, is to catch the full, lovely effect of it all, everything being so still upon the mountain-tops, not a sound to break in upon the harmonious voices and affect them in the slightest degree, and overhead in the darkness but the moon and stars to be seen silently looking down upon the scene.

CHAPTER III.

WE went clear over the Tyrol and into the adjoining district of Carniola, also a mountainous portion of the Austrian empire, and which lies on the Adriatic sea (the body of water separating Austria from Italy), just east of the Gulf of Venice, which forms the northern portion of the sea. The mountains of the Tyrol shade into those of the Carniola. The latter are generally barren of vegetation, being of a chalky character not favorable to the growth or maintenance of tree and plant life; they are awe-inspiring, however, in their massive, bare appearance, looking vast, desolate, and grand.

We went as far south as the town of Adelsburg, near the strangely acting lake of Zirknitz, about thirty-five miles inland and east of the Venetian gulf. This lake of Zirknitz at certain times becomes perfectly dry, all within a few days, and at regularly known times during the years the mountains appear to open great cavities inside and beneath and swallow the water, leaving the bed of the former lake perfectly dry. After remaining so for some time the lake fills up again; the same water is supposed to return and once more assume its place in the bed it had formerly occupied. The inhabitants can always predict when the next disappearance of the water is going to take place. Streams, the waters of which are strongly redundant in calcareous and metaliferous material, flow out of the mountains from almost everywhere. Our object was to visit the grotto of Adelsburg, the famous underground cave, discovered in 1816, once so renowned as the resort to which flocked pulmonary afflicted humanity from nearly all Europe.

We got to Adelsburg some time before a grand ball was to be given in one of the chambers of the grotto by the younger members of the town, in honor of the day of some patron saint, and we waited about the vicinity until the important night arrived. The town of Adelsburg, containing about two thousand inhabitants, is twenty-two miles northeast of Trieste, and is situated at the base of the mountains, into which the river Poik flows; this stream runs through a part of the grotto and then becomes lost, disappearing in the ground, within the deep recesses of this peculiar geological structure. By floating in a skiff upon the river, one can follow its passage through a low, long, dark tunnel, to where it emerges in one of the interior hallways or galleries leading to the caverns; this, however, only adventurous persons would undertake, so an artificial tunnel to strike the passage way to the interior caves has been cut through the calcareous substance of the mountain some distance above and to one side of the channel by which the river enters; this entrance the men had made years before, the ladies not entertaining the idea of sailing into a cavern deep into a mountain, on the surface of a cold, dark river, in a mere, small, light boat; it looked too alarming. The floating in might have been a perfect success, but the probability of never being able to get back had a depressing effect on their fair ones' spirits; so the aperture by which all now enter the grotto was constructed above the river entrance and runs downward and inward to strike the galleries which lead to the caverns some several hundred feet in.

The night of the frolic we joined the party of merry-makers, some hundred and twenty-five couples, the young men all supplied with torches or flambeaux, and both sexes carrying each a small basket of eatables. At the entrance all fell into an Indian file, one following the other, several young men with their flaring oil lights taking the lead; after getting about three hundred feet in a turn was made and the aperture through which we had entered — the mouth of the tunnel, the whereabouts of which up to that time had been perceptible by us being able to see the late evening sky out of it — became lost to us altogether. At the disappearance of this cheerful looking opening, which had appeared like a faint star on a black night, we felt that we had left daylight and the world behind us, and now every footstep but took us deeper into the blackness of night. The hundred flambeaux of the young men now began to penetrate the intense darkness and lighted up the walls about us. Soon we could hear the rushing and swishing of the river flowing over its rocky bed just beneath and to one side of our feet, now only a thin ledge separating us from it.

The gallery grew wider and wider as we advanced inward until it suddenly enlarged into two deep caverns connected together at the top by an opening, being something like a partition wall in a room that does not reach the ceiling by quite a space, or a chamber divided by a partition that does not reach the top. At the side of this partition we walked along, still in a long, winding procession. The river now breaks into view, flowing out from under its ledge, and we had reached the same spot where formerly visitors alighted from their boats to bring their feet into use in going farther on. The water now rolls swiftly on at our side, looking dark, cold and fascinating in the flickering glow of the lights. On the other side of the partition the chamber is dry, the partition we were walking by the side of being really a natural separating wall dividing the cavern into two apartments, only on one side of which (the side we were on) the river flows, leaving the floor of the opposite one bare of water. At a place near the end of the partition the river has cut through the dividing wall of chalky rock and has entered and overrun the lower part of the bare chamber. When we came to where the river, by passing through the wall to the other side, barred our progress, we found steps had been cut in the rock up to an artificial opening made in the wall, and on ascending and passing through, another flight of steps constructed in the calcareous mass descended, and let us into the bare cavern on the other side of the wall. The river here made no sound, but swept silently and darkly along in its bed, worn deeply in the calcareous rock by the constant abrasion caused by its continuous flow for ages. It cuts diagonally across the lower end of this bare chamber, and again entering a tunnel becomes lost in the mountain at the end of the apartment.

Here some of the young men caught, to show the young ladies, several of the curious looking Proteus which are found in this part of the waters of the river, just before it becomes lost in the interior of the mountains; this cold-blooded and aquatic being is a genus of batrachian reptiles, and bears in science the romantic and very German-like-in-length-name of "Perennibranchiate Batrachia." It is allied to the frogs, sirens and salamanders; its body is of an elongated form, resembling an eel, smooth, and is naked like a frog, with long, flat head, containing very small eyes, which are covered by the skin; its ears are deeply hidden in the flesh; it has four legs which are small and weak, the fore feet have three toes upon them, the rear ones four; between its head and front legs are its very prominent, permanent and external reddish gills. We all crowded around those who had caught them to see the creatures by the flickering glare of the torchlights, and when the boys finally released them, putting them back on the ground, they scudded to the water, and plunging in disappeared beneath an ever-widening circle which they left behind them. We crossed an iron bridge built over the river, to the other side, the deep, dark water glistening beneath our feet as we passed, and ascending more steps entered a large natural opening, the sides of which were jagged and broken into irregular shapes, and passing through this gap again descended some steps, and at length found ourselves in the first of the real caverns, which are the largest in Europe, and are of great size, and lead off one into the other, with often hall-like passage-ways between, deeper and deeper into the mountain for about two miles, in exact measurement 8,550 feet. In groups we followed the grotto all this distance, when our passage was again stopped by running square upon an immense lake, a still, dark, deep body of water. Farther than the lake the grotto has not been explored, although as far as we could see by the light of the torches it extended onward to everlasting depths. The most spacious of all these caverns which open one into another like a chain is the ball-room, which is situated near the lake, just a wide hallway separating them, and four apartments interiorly distant from the famous chamber, so noted as being the resort many years ago of consumptives. This former sick-room does not vary one degree fahrenheit in its temperature the year round, and numbers of consumptive patients were sent to it from all over Europe in the hope that being away from great and varied climatic changes, removed from even the slightest alteration of temperature, would at least stay, if not wholly cure, this scourge of humanity. We inquired how the patients had fared, and what became of them, and were informed that they all had died; a different reply could hardly have been expected, taking into consideration that they lived for months constantly in a damp atmosphere and were totally deprived of heaven's free light, the vital magnetism-imparting rays of sunlight; a potato sprout in a dark cellar will remain white, and should a single beam of sunshine penetrate its gloomy home, the sprout will instinctively grow toward it.

This large lake-side cavern that the revelers finally gathered together in, was the ball-room, and a more magnificent one it would take a fertile mind to imagine. This, then, was the magic apartment we had come so far to see. All the walls are pure stalactite, formed by the crystallizing upon them of carbonate of lime, which salt, in the form of a bicarbonate, is held in solution by the waters percolating through the rocks above and dripping into the chamber. Although carbonate of lime is itself in a slight degree soluble in water, it can be much more liquified by water charged with carbonic acid, of which latter substance, in its ordinary condition a gas, water will dissolve its own volume without pressure. It is an ingredient in a greater or less amount in all rain and surface water which, in soaking from above through the ground to the roofs of caverns, dissolves in its passage as much lime as will make it a saturated solution of that mineral. On slowly dripping into caves the air of the chamber dries the drops, the water evaporates leaving the crystals of lime adhering to the roofs; other drops trickle down, succeeding the first and dry there, and gradually an ever-enlarging pendant cone assumes shape, and thus a hanging stalactite is formed. The particles of water that drip from it, the (in comparison) small amount that runs over and falls off the tip of the descending cone makes the ascending stalagmite which, rising up from the ground directly beneath, eventually meets it and causes the formation of the columns. The young men set their torches around in the center of little heaps of rock which they had built up all about the walls and on ledges at the sides of the compartment; the floor had been cleared free of debris and uneven stones years before and was now almost as smooth as glass. Benches had been made by placing long planks on boulders, heaps of stones, or near the walls of the room from one to the other of the tops of the growing stalagmites which had there been allowed to remain unmolested, and these improvised seats were all about the sides of the chamber. Those of the party sitting down on a board covering a stalagmite were often directly under the corresponding descending stalactite glistening like an icicle in a thousand ever-changing colors just above them. The chamber is so lofty that the roof cannot be seen, only a half-hundred lower parts of descending stalactites, like the smaller extremities of great cones pendant from above can one descry on looking upward, their tapering ends shining and sparkling down out of the intense darkness aloft in all beautiful colors; the stalactites at the sides of the chamber have formed themselves into pillars, sometimes single, round and straight from the floor to as far as can be seen by the lights toward the roof, sometimes twisted around spirally from top to bottom, and again round for the lower half of their visible height and turning like the curl of a shaving from there up to where they become lost in the darkness above; and others of them are in clusters of half a dozen columns each, like a bundle of sticks glued together.

Along the passages leading out of the chamber both of the sides are columned, and it seems to one treading it on the way to the ball cavern as though he were passing along between the piers of a lofty colonnade. The pillars are from two to six feet in diameter, most of them against and a part of the sides of the passages and apartment;

but occasionally they stand out free, so that one can walk entirely around them, their tall majestic shapes rising up and up to disappear in the the deep gloom above. Some of the columns spread out in parts of their ample lengths to wide, thin board-like places, folded and twisted about, and through some of their thin sheet-like curls one could see, by standing in the dark passages, the light of the torches shining. Most of the pillars have bases rounding out often into two or three folds, and many have a fluted appearance, from the material of which they are composed crystallizing in long parallel streaks down their lengths. Some have beautiful cornices and capitals in resemblance of all different ancient architectural styles, and at the sides of the chamber the walls are ornamented in places with the pure stalactite having descended in the shape of draped curtains and large portières arranged as though hanging in folds. Parts of the hanging sheets were opaque, in some places translucent, and in others so thin and nearly transparent that one could tell the exact location of a flame behind them. In places about the sides of the apartment the downward extending stalactite and the ever rising stalagmite it was forming by its slow drip, drip, going on for life-times, were only a few inches apart at a distance of eight or ten feet from the floor, soon to join and become another beautiful solid column, from the floor to the invisible heights above.

The ball chamber is about sixty feet wide by eighty long, and is one of the most spacious of all the caverns. It is, in a direct line, about a mile and a half from the entrance, but nearly two miles by the way of the passage on account of its many windings, turnings, and ups and downs. The walls, being of the purest stalactite, reflect back into the chamber the lights of the hundred or more torches, the reflection increasing the number of lights into the thousands and separating and breaking up the rays, like prisms do, into all the different colors of the rainbow. The stirring of the atmosphere by the young people waltzing and running swiftly around made the lights flicker, and the corresponding reflections danced and dazzled about in all beautiful and lovely constantly-intermingling colors, while the lower ends of the numerous lofty stalactites pendant above sparkled and shown in their background of deep blackness like orbs of fire, constantly presenting new colors to view.

The scene looks very romantic and chimerical; dancing the light fantastic in the interior of a mountain, the young people clothed in all their holiday attire, bright colored ribbons, gold and silver bracelets, and all the women with necklaces of amber, an amber necklet being part of the decoration of each young girl; not a single young lady but what wore one made of amber strung in beads, the center of the string containing a cross of the same material which hung pendant upon their breasts, and from which on each side large amber beads, ever diminishing in size, ran around on the string to the smallest ones located next to the clasp at the back of their necks. A decorated or engraved plate of either gold or silver, of oval form, was worn by the young women above the forehead, and over the front hair, and was held in place by cloth bands attached to its sides and running to the back of the head, the band skillfully concealed beneath their abundant tresses. This decoration is as fantastically formed, as elegant or as rich as the social position or the wealth of the young lady's family entitles her to wear. The young men were all in regulation ancient Carniola festival dancing costume; velvet knee-trousers, colored knee-stockings, soft felt hats decorated with a curved falling feather, braided short jackets with sleeves wide at the wrist, and a colored sash worn around the waist, under the jacket, one end hanging down to near the left knee. The dresses of the women were of ankle length. The orchestra, perched upon a natural ledge in the wall, issued out into the ballroom of the grotto soul-entrancing strains of waltz music, and the whirling couples floated lightly around through the most curious, beautiful and unique ball-room ever seen; dancing with the whole-souled vigor and happiness of youth in the cavities of the earth, on the glassy floor of a ball-room nearly a mile under the top of its roof, and over two miles from its entrance door.

We left Adelsburg the following day, and to Austria's loss and doubtless keen sorrow (?) shook the dust of her dominion from our heels, and returned to Germany over an altogether different route than the one by which we came into the empire of Francis Joseph.

A SECTION OF THE UNIVERSITY, BERLIN, SHOWING THE STATUES OF THE HUMBOLDT BROTHERS.

CHAPTER IV.

AND now we were back from our vacation once again, to the University at Berlin; sun-burned and tanned, hardened to exposure and tough-footed, but with a vast amount of experience of life in its different phases; having met with nothing but kindness and generosity on our way. Many times our offers of remuneration for the night's lodging or for our meals during rainy days were refused by the people of the little cottages where we were obliged to put up for shelter; though often poor and humble in their belongings, their noble good nature was ever to the front. We noticed many little acts of thoughtful kindness on their part for which all recompense was firmly refused. The whole family, and often several neighboring ones, learning of our appearance in the vicinity, would sit up far into the night all congregated about a wood-hearth fire and listen eagerly to us telling of the great outside world and its doings; about distant America and the millions of people who had found happy homes in that wonderfully great and thrice blessed land. The little children would be all eyes and ears, staring at us as though we were enchanted beings, having dropped from that strange and marvelous land we related about — to their minds existing somewhere up in the mysterious clouds; and on the morrow, after bidding them good-bye, on our full stomachs, we had no thought of food again until the noon hour brought around its never-failing reminders — its empty sensations in the region of our belts — and on opening our knapsacks we would find them full of delicious cheese, cut as fresh as the morning dew, loaves of dark brown bread, and savory sausages that tasted like the food of the gods, or like the cooking of our mothers in the days of our childhood.

We were back now and attending our last session at the University. It was October, and already the suicides were beginning. October and November are called the suicidal months in Berlin. It drizzles and rains nearly the whole of the sixty days; is cloudy and damp and gloomy. One gets melancholy and down-hearted, and every day numbers of suicides occur. Each morning finds a long list of those who have destroyed themselves the day before. To add to this, Berlin produces another unique sensation. When a "hard student" imbibes too freely of the cup that not only cheers but also inebriates, during the rest of the year (during the ten other months) he wakes up the next morning with the "Katzenjammer," i. e., has a head on him as big as a court-house dome; but in October and November on arousing from sleep in the morning, after having made a night of it, in addition to and largely on top of this "Katzenjammer," he awakes in all the full force and grasp also of a "Moralischesjammer," i. e., a moral feeling of depression that he has done something awful the night before; he doesn't know for certain just what — probably murdered his grandmother or something of the sort. He can't divine exactly what it was, but the low, dull, depressed, heavy and utterly hopeless despondency he is wrapped in is wonderful, and one must see a fellow in such a state to realize to what perfect depths of despair a student's mind can sink into.

Men in Europe smoke in the presence of ladies, but I have never seen one expectorate. A German gentleman never spits, although he may smoke for an hour in a lady's presence. No one spits in Germany. They have never been so taught, for it is an acquired habit. An American wishing to attract the attention of a compatriot on the opposite side of the street to the one on which he is walking will just give a loud, nerve-racking hawk, whereupon his friend will at once stop, face about and look for the one whom he knows is a sure "United Stateser," and who has employed familiar means to signal him or attract his attention. At the same time a dozen or so Germans behind or in front of the hawker will stop and turn around in bewildered amazement at the curious, strange, and to them unfamiliar sound; and look about from one to another in consternation, wondering what it was and where on earth it issued from. They cannot understand why we have a spittoon to every second seat in our railway cars, and why cuspidors are a large part of the furniture of hotels and public buildings. What pleasure is it to go up to one of the vessels and expectorate? Is it a happiness to do so? and why? they ask. To a foreigner not accustomed to it as we are, from our early infancy, it is one of the most disgusting customs imaginable, and they cannot comprehend how we, holding our womankind in such hallowed respect and admiration, can still be such hogs in their presence in this regard; but it's a custom of the country — it's as you view it.

Well, this last session ended our membership at the "Preussische Adler" (Prussian Eagle) club, the "crack" one of the University. We both had been elected as honorary members at our first session, and a slight mention of this famous association is here proper, for to the manor born is the German student club life to the University. It exists in fact as part of it. The institution was in a five-story stucco-fronted building owned by itself and situated on the "Unter den Linden" street, the widest and main boulevard of the city, and one of the finest streets in Europe, being over a mile long and about two hundred feet broad. The thoroughfare has double avenues or passage ways for walking, its entire length, in the center, flanked by long lines of grass-plots in which grow several rows of the German limes or Linden trees, which give the street its name of Under the Lindens. On the outside of these grass-plots, on each side, are the wide driveways reaching, of course, to the pavements which adjoin the buildings.

At one end of this boulevard is a magnificent, lofty stone structure, erected to perpetuate the memory of some notable event. It has three arched passage ways beneath its corniced entablature, the center one being the largest, the three being the exits from the street and the Pariser Platz into the "Thiergarten," an extensive park of three hundred and seventy acres just beyond, and which it really leads or opens into. This arch, called the "Brandenburger Thurm" (Toorm, i.e., gate, Berlin being situated in the Dukedom of Brandenburg), which is about seventy feet in height and over two hundred feet wide, is adorned and surmounted by the famed group of a female charioteer, driving four fiery horses, the latter in the position of a wild, tremendous gallop. The group was taken down by Napoleon I, and, among other spoils of war, was carried to Paris to grace, after his conquest of Germany, his triumphal return to the French capital. It was brought back and restored to its old place, however, in 1814-15, when the allied armies entered Paris.

The opposite end of this street, so endeared to the hearts of all Germans, and especially Berliners, and which is about the center of the city, contains the King's city palace, i.e., the Royal Palace, having over seven hundred apartments, among the number being the state rooms, all of which are magnificently and very richly adorned; the two finest of all being the "Weisser Saal" (White Hall) and the palace chapel. Situated on the Unter den Linden are also the Royal Theatre, the old and the new Museums, the National Art Gallery, the Arsenal, the Palace of the Crown Prince, the Opera House, the University, Guard House, the Royal Library, having within its solid walls nearly two million volumns and over fifty thousand manuscripts. Here also at one side of the street and close to the pavement is the large mounted statue of "Alter Fritz" (old Fred), the usual familiar title given him, and meaning "Friedrich der Grosze" (Frederick the Great, i.e., Frederick II of Prussia). This grand boulevard follows along a large bridge over the Spree river. The side railings of the bridge are adorned with numerous statues of famous generals, men of science, national heroes, etc.

From the club windows, which are wide and large and usually crowded with sitters, one can look down upon the vast, moving multitude — the ever onward pouring life of a great cosmopolitan city, with the people of all nations wearing their (to us) quaint and curious garbs and costumes passing by. The Turk, in his native dress of turban, curled-toed shoes and baggy pants; the Tyrolese, in his knee trousers and stockings, his feather-trimmed green hat, etc.; the Polish Hebrew, in his heel-reaching black, thick gown, wearing two long, black, pine-shaving-like curls which hang down in front of his ears from his head to his shoulders; the dashing equipages of the nobility emblazoned with their various coats of arms, flying by; the steady tramp, tramp, tramp of the military as a mass of Prussian soldiers go marching past, with playing bands, and flying the Prussian colors— the black eagle having an erect position with wings expanded, upon a silver shield— their officers mounted on prancing horses, looking the embodiment of soldierly grace and bearing.

My chum, Claude Menton, was the perfection of gentlemanship as typified in the chivalric South before the sad days of the great uprising. He was tall, and straight as an arrow, and the image of a sentimental young girl's ideal of a prince. On the night of our election, several years before, he had ascended the little platform at one side of the great room, and in choice language had thanked the assembled club members for the high favor shown him; but he remarked as to his feelings regarding the honor the club did him in his election, that he never felt prouder, except on the day he donned his Confederate uniform and marched out of Americus to the tune of "Dixie," in the presence of all the ladies waving the soldier boys farewell with their handkerchiefs.

Menton had followed the fortunes of the military organizations of the South during the first three long years of the Rebellion. He had then gotten his hand torn off by a canister shot at Spottsylvania in the battle of Chancellorsville, which took place on May 2d, 3d, and 4th, in 1863, in Virginia, while under General Stonewall Jackson, an idol of the Confederacy, who was mortally wounded in the same encounter, being accidently shot by one of his own men; and in consequence of his disability Menton was not along in the army with his two brothers, who surrendered with Lee at Appomattox when the Southerners lost their cause, and with fast falling tears and breaking hearts folded their dear old flag forever.

The club-rooms are richly furnished and are beautifully decorated with works of art, many lovely paintings done by members now living, and others executed by those who have long since gone over the silent river, leaving these evidences of their handiwork to be viewed with reverence and affectionate remembrance by their fellows left behind. All over the walls are stag heads, horns of elk, moose, etc., statues of marble and bronze, mementos of distant lands, that members have brought, such as Japanese carved work, East India figure-cutting on immense elephant tusks, etc., and scattered all about and occupying honored and prominent places are the trophies won through half a century by their oldest and best loved member, mostly gained in contests from other clubs, for this member in his most prominent specialty has never been defeated, and the gold and silver flagons, drinking cups, beautiful clocks and metal-mounted wooden hat and coat racks, etc., that he has won for the club are a sight to behold; but of his exploits more anon.

The students are divided by customs and unwritten laws among themselves into three general classes. First come the "corps studenten", who stand the highest in the admiration of their land, and are especially regarded by their female friends, and by nearly all the ladies in fact, as the very essential comprehension of courage, courtesy, and perfectly lovely manhood. For a girl to have a corps student for a beau is for her to secure the certain envy of all her less lucky friends, and when parading the boulevards in his company one can see by the young lady's looks and demeanor that she is not walking on the ground, but soaring on gilt-tipped white wings through jewel-decorated celestial realms. The corps student is the fighting or dueling student, joins and belongs to the dueling corps of his club, and is always ready for a fight, is continually seeking one in fact, but ever in a gentlemanly manner; is never a rowdy, at least such instances are very rare among them. They can usually be told by the numerous scars upon their faces, gained with the rapier in their hands. Most of these set-tos are of a friendly nature, and no bad blood is engendered among them. Of course there are cases where deadly insults are revenged in the sword fight. Students will be found who take advantage of this old custom to vent their spite and animosity on an enemy, at times in a serious manner. But it is like all countries' usages and laws, which are ever a hiding cloak for the dishonest and wrongly inclined person to work mischief under; a least slight or an accidental touching of them is followed by a challenge to a duel; but of course the insult must be given by a corps student of a rival club or competitor University to be taken notice of. They accept no insults from outsiders or the laity, nor from mild students and neutrals. All these personages do not exist to the corps student. He doesn't know they are alive or have being. All are ignored as even unworthy to be recognized as filling up space in the universe with their miserable anatomies. As far as he is concerned they "don't be." But let a corps student so much as lightly brush against his elbow in passing on the street and an instant apology must be given, or at once cards are exchanged for a duel. The duel is graded; such an offense or insult of so and so, of a trivial or serious nature, must be wiped out with a wound of a certain depth; a slight discourtesy, a slight wound; a graver offense, a correspondingly more serious wound, and for a deep insult a bad wound must be given before the stain is wiped away. Their set of rules govern all this; it matters not which one gets the wound.

These fierce warriors all wear a distinguishing mark on their caps. All students in Germany wear caps of the colors adopted by the clubs of their special University. The valorous ones, on enrolling their names among the "corps studenten," part of a club at once place the fighters' special mark on their caps, so they recognize each other at a glance anywhere. They swagger along the streets, and can always be known at even a great distance by their quick strutting walk, but they are never bullies, are never disagreeable in their demeanor. One of them wanting to get his name up as a furious and desperate fellow who sticks at nothing to get a fight, will pick quarrels with his compeers of other clubs and Universities wherever he may meet them. One manner of doing this is to go into a café and order refreshments, sit down in a chair by one of the many little marble-topped tables the place contains for the accommodation of guests, and look about the room until he sights somewhere among the assembled customers a similar corps student; then he will fix his large single eye-glass in one eye and sit as erect as a post, as silent as a mouse, and as immovable as a statue, with set, wide-open eyes fastened upon his rival dualist in a firm, true, unwavering solid stare; this attitude is kept up until the rival happens to see him ogling at him, or else has his attention called to it by the crowd about looking around to see who the gaze is leveled at. This usually produces a sensation among the guests, deep silence at once intervenes, all conversation ceases as one after another, feeling the gradually lulling noise, turn around to see what is the matter, and finally the whole room is looking at the gazer and the one gazed at. At this moment the insulted one—for this is one of the direst of insults among them, indicating the fact that the insulted was so small, so insignificant, so contemptuously beneath notice that the insulter has to put his microscope to his eye or his telescope to his visual organ and level it in his opponent's direction, and even then has to hold his eye staring wide open focused for great lengths of time before he can even see him or find where his contemptible figure grovels about among the other specks of dust and dirt upon the floor, etc. — at this supreme moment of silence from all onlookers, when every eye is turned upon them, a moment the insulted has been waiting for all along, he suddenly turns around and in much surprise and well feigned astonishment finds a rival in the room with concentrated gaze leveled upon him. "Donnerwetter!" he says, hauling his own glass up to his eye and sighting it at the insulter. There is a fellow who "fixirt mich" (focuses me), and instantly arising goes over to the other, hands him his card and gets one in exchange, the duel is then fought at the club of the one challenged.

A corps student sometimes in passing a rival on the street will remark as he goes by, for the other's ears to catch, "this is a very dumb looking fellow." Then the dumb fellow will, of course, challenge him on the spot, and the insulter will have the fight at his own club ; but if he is a very high minded gentleman he will scorn to take such an advantage as to have, after insulting a man, the fight take place at his own club, where he is at home among friends and surrounded by a general aspect, amid the scenes of which he is so familiar that it cannot distract him and unsteady his nerve as it may his rival's. So he does what is called going the insulted man "one over" in gentlemanship. He turns on the student he has insulted by calling him a dumb fellow, and who has in response challenged him, and insults him again, deeper and in a greater measure than the previous one, by calling him an infernal "hundefuss" (dog-paw); then a second challenge given, although by the same man, entitles the duel to be fought at the challenger's club, by right of two insults received and resented; but if the twice insulted one is also a very fine, high minded gentleman he will doubly scorn this patronizing offer of the insulter (for it assumes or presents the imputation that the insulted is so poor a swordsman that his opponent offers him the option of having the fight at his own club), and he will not challenge him for the second insult but in place go him one still "higher over" in lofty gentlemanship, and insult him most terribly in return by calling him a "verfluchter schweinehund" (cursed pig-dog). This is one of the most terrible insults that can be offered, and an extremely serious wound has to be received by one of the participants to obliterate it.

So, often you will hear upon the street, on seeing two ferocious corps students approach each other and come in contact, "dummer junge" (stupid youth). Then a passage of cards, or "stupid youth" from one voice, an answering "infernal hundefuss" followed by exchange of cards ; or, more rarely, "stupid youth," "infernal dog-paw," and "cursed pig-dog," follow each other in "quick, fleet, rapid" and hot succession; and then vicious glances threatening danger, along with the transferring of pasteboard. If a corps student does not take the insult, being, perhaps, on the way to his stage station or his train depot for a visit home, or has friends in town for a few days whom he is escorting about to see the city, and a wound be the means of curtailing their pleasure by causing his confinement for some days, he merely, on the reception of the offense, says, "bitte" (which means that he assumes that the affronter has said "schul's mich" (excuse me), in apology, and his own reply is intended to be one "higher over" in begging him not to think of mentioning it, and passes on, that being understood between them all, that it is inconvenient for the recipient to resent at present. He usually, however, if he recognizes the offender at all, remembers him, and bears the offer of a fight well in mind, and at the earliest future opportunity seeks him out, or lays for him around his haunts and presents him with an affront in return.

Some of these men come into the clinics of the Medical University to have their wounds dressed specially by some professor; a serious blood-vessel, a nerve or gland being injured or severed and needing extreme care in dressing or skilled services in treating; a divided nerve must often be re-clipped, i. e., the two ends again freshened by trimming, and then once more sewn together to allow them a new chance to adhere; cuts through the salivary glands, and their ducts are always serious and demand extremely careful attention while healing, so not to leave an unsightly drawn pucker in the cheek or let remain behind a salivary fistula, necessitating during mastication the constant use of a handkerchief in wiping away the saliva as it runs down the cheek. Some of these corps students would come in for attention, upon whose faces one could not place the tip of a little finger anywhere without touching a scar, while others had received, as shown by long-healed wounds, a single, terrific swipe, reaching from the top of the head to the chin. Donnerwetter! often exclaims the chief surgeon at a clinic, as some fighter comes in for the dressing of a new wound before a former one is half healed; or one appears for attention with deep cuts in all stages of healing on his head and face. Donnerwetter! Sie werden bald nicht zum ansehen sein. (Thunder-weather, you will soon be not lookable at.) Such is the "corps student," the gladiator of Germany, the admiration of his friends, the glory of the ladies, and the Greek god of the young girls. Next, in a general class, are the mild students, who attract notice to themselves in a humorous manner by some curious fad, or by some uniquely thought out dummheiten (foolishness or nonsense). Their jokes, however, are never of an unliked or unwelcome kind; they never do anything of a mean or harmful nature, is why their amusing conduct is so much countenanced; they never run their liberty, allowed them by the populace in this matter, into the ground, and abuse the confidence the public place in them. No young German gentleman of a mild student will lower his esteem for himself, will degrade his own self-respect by doing or lending his assistance to disgraceful or injurious tricks or mischief that would be costly and hurtful to others : such behavior as pulling down signs, tearing off and carrying away gates, breaking gas lamps, etc., is an unknown trait of the mild student's character. Such as that displays no high-minded development or art in agreeably entertaining the community; deeds of that style are not jokes, show no remarkable intellectual attainments to produce fun, but exhibit a sort of meanness that is far from the German mild student's style of deporting himself. These are the students one meets so often during the summer vacation tours, creating sensations in the small towns and villages that lie along their routes.

In Berlin, at the time of our attendance there, their fad was mostly big dogs, vying with each other in the endeavor to own the largest one, always decorating him with a beautiful collar, and never going about without taking him along. All Europe had been brought under tribute to furnish a sufficient supply of dogs; great, shaggy, black, oily-coated, ever-faithful Newfoundlands, natives of the island of that name, with lengthy tails, thickly covered with long, hanging hair, majestic in appearance, with their benevolent expressioned faces ; huge, broad, flat and full-headed English mastiffs from the British

Isles, with small, downward-hanging ears, and their mild, brown eyes and massive square jaws; immense Dutch doggers from the near surroundings of home; giant Saint Bernards from the regions of the dreary Swiss Alps and the mountainous portions of the Tyrol, differentiated only by their remarkably unsimilar hairy coverings into rough and smooth-coated animals; colossal Danes of bluish and of brindle colors from Denmark; and now and then a mild student appeared on the streets who had somewhere run across a canine of no special breed, but so vast a specimen of dogdom, indeed, that he put nearly all of his brotherhood to shame and made them feel small in their boots. You see large numbers of them all over the streets led by chains of silver.

Sometimes a crowd of several hundred of these mild students, each with his dog, will congregate in the suburbs, and sending in and hiring carriages, will occupy them with their dogs, each two-seated carriage containing two mild students, everyone with his enormous gaily-collared dog on the seat beside him; they will then form the carriages in a procession, often four or five miles in length, and come into town and drive slowly through the principal streets, to the admiration and wonder of the beholders, but to the inexpressible annoyance of the police force, for they blockade the streets, create jams of vehicles, and as one student carriage closely follows the preceding one, often cause, when the procession goes down a prominent boulevard, the entire stoppage of traffic in all the side streets until the last one of the miles of carriages has passed, by which time the police officials are using language fearfully grating to one's auditory nerve. All the while, however, the students are sitting quietly and calmly in attitudes of careless elegance, fixedly staring through their monocles at the surging, excited, swearing, raving and threatening crowd of blocked vehicle-drivers, with set, expressionless faces as vacant as though utterly oblivious of anything but perfect silence and quietude being present, and as though lost in far-away thought, or wrapped in deepest contemplation of the great distance between suns, or in the profound effort to grasp the meaning of eternity, or something else equally beyond the mensuration of science. Welcomed for the laughter he creates, and forgiven all the trouble he causes by his nonsense—for the public feel flattered that he goes to such risk and troublous work, takes such pains to ingenuise some quaint and curious method or device to tickle its humor—it has its "eitelkeit geschmeichelt" by him (its vanity flattered). Such is the mild student, the pet of Germany.

Lastly, in a general class are the neutrals, who never become members of fighting corps or belong to the band of the ones who court fads, but apply themselves to their studies and attend strictly to their own business, join the clubs for the amusement and recreation they offer, and, as the fierce and mild students express it, are formed merely for the purpose of throwing their own respective valiant and mirth-exciting exploits out into a grander light by contrast. Such is the neutral student, to which class belong all those from foreign lands, whom, together with their German colleagues in the same designation, form a great part of the attendants of the University.

A fad among the whole mass of students, however, and something which everyone effects, no matter to which club or what section of it he belongs, is to own a "trink horn" (drinking horn); this is a steer horn of as large a size as can be had, and is highly polished by the owner himself during his leisure moments. It is then mounted in gold or silver, as follows: A piece of either of the two metals, about like the top of a baking-powder can, is fitted over the large open end, a funnel-shaped tip or ferrule about two inches in length is placed over the point, at equal distances apart between these, two inch wide bands are fitted on, each having a ring at the top or concave side of the horn, to which is attached a thick colored silk cord in a loop of about a yard in length; two tassels hang from the attached ends of the cords. Each student has his horn, and takes great pride in it, carries it about the club-rooms hung over his shoulder, or hangs it upon the walls or chandeliers as he sees fit; it is never taken, however, beyond the club apartments except to a club picnic or gathering. The custom is in allusion to olden times, when the making of glass, one of the lost arts which was not re-discovered until the seventh century, was still unknown, and metal goblets were costly and rare, and the barbaric Germans used horns for drinking-vessels on account of the ease with which they were to be obtained and the numbers that could be gotten; these old timers also carried water about in them on their long trips, and, of course, when empty, kept them to dip up drink from a passing stream and refill for future use. Our hunters here a century ago had great use for horns as shot and powder flasks.

CHAPTER V.

OUR club had its share of all kinds of these three classes of students, and all were in the best of feeling and comradeship toward each other. A feeling of brotherhood pervaded all. The Prussian eagles dwell together in perfect peace, good fellowship and harmony. As regards our members, first in size, first at the wine and gaming tables, and largely first in the hearts of his club, stands Baron von Vielbeer. Vielbeer in appearance is something so extraordinary as to excite wonder and astonishment in all those who behold him. He is about sixty-eight years of age, is extremely stout, has blue eyes, gray hair and mustache, and has such an enormous stomach that it extends his waistband out several feet in front of him. He is not very large standing up, but when lying down on his back is an exceedingly tall man. As a passionate gambler Vielbeer stands at the summit of greatness, and is a marvelous success, for as far back as the recollection of any member of the club reaches he has never been known to lose a single cent at play, which startling statement might lead one at first to suppose that he possessed some occult power or hidden ability which enabled him to know the secrets of the minds or read the thoughts of his fellow-players; such a conjecture, however, would be far indeed from the true facts of the case, which really are that he sits down to the table where a game is starting up, absolutely and completely "busted", without so much capital as a halb silber groschen, or even a pfennig (one-fourth of a cent) in his possession, and consequently nothing on this round earth is more dead certain than that he will not lessen the pile he starts out with in his venture upon the expansive sea of chance, and with his perfect freedom from nervousness or anxiety on account of the large stake he puts up, with his great skill and long years of accumulated experience, he always manages somehow or other to come out ahead a good deal at the wind-up. He is the owner of a pretty dilapidated old castle on the Rhine, standing in the midst of a small number of acres of land still belonging to it, up in the kingdom of Aufberg adjoining that of Baden in the highlands of Southern Germany, the neighboring state of Baden containing the celebrated dark-wooded mountains with which in long past days he and his ancestors have been extensively associated. Much to his regret, often deeply expressed, he is unable to keep a carriage and a pair of horses, he being of course very weighty, and it is something of a hardship for him to get about over any great distance. He often sits at the windows of the club-rooms and looks out longingly at the smart turn-outs going past with their lively high-stepping horses and soft and comfortably cushioned vehicles; it seems as though nothing on earth has the charm for him that a carriage presents. "If I only had such", he will mournfully and sadly remark at times, as a prancingly drawn barouche glides by over the smooth street before his yearning eyes, "my old age would be filled with happiness and content."

From the source of his castle grounds, rented to surrounding peasants, he receives an income of about twenty-five dollars a month, and were it not for his much more extensive income derived from his great business capacity displayed in the matter of games of chance, he would be in dire stress indeed. He has an enormous prehistoric looking meerschaum pipe with a long weiksel holtz (a kind of German cherry wood) stem, and an immense bowl in the shape of a Turk sitting cross-legged on a small square cushioned mat, which it is his chief delight in the late evenings to fill, sit and puff by the hour, watching the members at their games of billiards, chess, dominos or athletics, the latter of which he never takes part in for obvious reasons; or when surrounded by an appreciative audience, which is nearly always, telling stories of his house's former grandeur by the hour. He can trace his ancestry back way beyond two thousand years, and is never weary of relating the heroic deeds and valors of his forefathers; indeed, he often gets so far back in the narration of his reminiscences that his ever large crowd of eager listeners sometimes get nervous in the fear that the remote centuries will play out before he is quite through with the tale. He matriculated at the University years and years ago, has never dismatriculated, which one must do to leave a German University before graduating, and left it, but has been hanging on ever since with a tenacity worthy of a better cause.

Second in the esteem and regard of the club stands Count Luft von Schweffelsblatter; he is a young man about thirty-five years of age, tall and handsome, a blonde, an officer in the Hussars, but at present suspended on account of some trouble between him and his brother officers; he is of a very fiery temperament, and of an exceedingly excitable nature that, however, does not cool as soon as it flares up, but unheats slowly; he is immensly liked and is very popular for he has a good sound judgment, but in several ways is what some might see fit to call peculiar; for instance, insults that others would think he should resent at the peril of his life, he pays no attention to whatever, never even awakens his interest, while some slighting small cut that no ordinary person would heed for two moments, sets him wild for days.

The fact is he is very generous hearted, and on receiving a direct insult goes home and ponders over it; finally finding it effects no one but himself, he thinks, "poof! the dog can say it again a dozen times if he wants to, who cares" etc.; but the slightest offensive remark or insolent action of another that he broods over and imagines was directed at his family, his sisters, etc., gets his ire up, and it may be days before he meets the offender; still he does not cool until an apology is offered or the matter explained, to the surprise of everyone else who had long since forgotten the occurrence and supposed it something of the past. He would occupy a high position in the army on the merits of his military capabilities alone, were it not for this ungovernable temper which so often masters him. We two accompanied Count Luft one night to a state ball and recognized on that occasion to the fullest extent how nothing on earth exists that will knock a woman's eye out quicker than a man in uniform; there were none but civilians there at first and they were enjoying themselves hugely and whirling the young ladies of a dozen different nations around at a lively rate; they gave one the impression of young men who were making hay while the sun shone brightly. We shortly saw why: the military soon began to come in, the elegant figured officers with boot heels four inches high, plumed hats, braided coats, epaulets, sashes, glittering swords, and equipments, waxed mustaches standing straight out like pencils from their faces, etc. They were entering in all their soldierly bearing and the reign of the civil fellows was over; no more ladies would dance with them now after the officers had arrived, and they all skulked around after their hats, stuck them under their arms and silently slunk away just as their late partners started in the dizzy mazes of the waltz, whirling in the seventh heaven of bliss on the arms of one of their country's defenders one moment, the representative of their land's bitterest foes the next.

"Did I enjoy myself?" one fair creature was overheard to say among the flowers and plants of the conservatories adjoining the ball room. "Did I? Why, I just let the officer put his manly arm around me, clasp me to his brave, medal-decorated chest, hung myself on his broad, epauleted-shoulders, and, as the orchestra started, stepped out into the golden-lined clouds floating over paradise." Who, after hearing that, would not wear the uniform of a German officer, or that of a United States policeman?

Next comes Berthold von Felderstein, a young man of twenty-two, just in all the glory, strength and pride of youth; tall, of handsome physique, and the very image one thinks a lord should be emmodeled in. He is one of those magnetic men who are born to be leaders; live to command in whatever they undertake; immensely popular with all he meets. He has the organ of intuition so marvelously well developed that you can feel him reading your deepest thoughts and soul on his first look at you. In a minute after meeting him, it seems to one as though he had known you for years. He reads your innermost nature at a glance, and treats you accordingly; and of course he treats everyone differently, as each one's nature varies, or just as you would be acted toward by your oldest and dearest friend. He is one of those whom nature intended "the thoughts of conquering thousands to command." He has bluish gray eyes, and is a brunette; slightly built, but very muscular. One feels an assurance of safety in his presence, a feeling of security when near him, a consciousness of protection when he is in the vicinity. He is the seventh son, however, of an old illustrious nobleman, standing high at the Prussian court, and will have to, as the saying goes, win his fortune or spurs with his sword. He is the best swordsman in the club, and his skill in handling the dueling rapier is a sight to witness. He is metal to the center, and as brave as can be. It was feared, on his entrance as a member, that he and Count Luft would soon clash, but they are the best of friends.

Felderstein is of a temperament not usually understood, not generally recognized; he is one of those natures it is impossible to pick a quarrel with unless he wants to, and in that case a saint could hardly escape an altercation.

Lastly among the members, but by no manner of means least, comes Booblely (pronounced Boobuley, i. e., puppy) Schnurkelyah (snoor-cle-yaw), an exceedingly fat little German dachshund (badger dog), widely bench-legged and broad backed, with stomach nearly reaching the floor and with tail long and slender and projecting horizontally and in a straight line with his long spinal column, his foreknees bend in and overlap each other and his toes turn away out toward his sides, as fine a specimen of knock-kneed dogdom as is extant; and how he manages to walk his ungainly rolling gait no idea can be formed until the sight is witnessed; the shorter and crookeder the forelegs of his race are the purer is their blood considered; and one can see from a glance at his legs that he, as a natural consequence, surely must be a sample of the purest breed out; he possesses great strength in proportion to his height, and by reason of his remarkable obesity also great weight; has a long slightly arched wide head with lengthy drooping soft ears and a short thick neck; as a digger in the ground to unearth badgers, hares and foxes that have taken to their holes, he has a reputation that is unequaled and a record that is unsurpassed east of the celebrated six hundred year old hunting tree at Verden an der Aller; his admirably arranged forelegs and paws are set in such a position that the way he can fling out the dirt in going down a hole after game that has run into the ground is a caution; his dark brown or nearly black eyes are deep set and rather small and have a look of almost human intelligence, as though understanding the very words addressed to him. He comes of an illustrious race of antecedents also. His long line of ancestors have followed the fortunes of Vielbeers and have clawed and chawed the soldiers of the enemy in innumerable engagements in which their respective masters were involved. He is the last of his line, and, as Vielbeer says, is now dutifully resting on the glories of his forefathers. He was always showing his military blood by perpetually skirmishing around under our feet at the lunch table for any stray piece of waste pretzel, wurst or pumpernickel that might chance his way; but no matter what amount of forage he managed to collect of an evening he was never known to exhibit signs of regretting it, his stomach thus proving his pure teutonic genealogy as nothing else could. He took a great liking to me, and I often spread a small rug over my lap and lifted him on to it, where he would lay for half hours at a time listening to Vielbeer's reminiscences and now and then wisely blinking his eyes as though punctuating his revered master's remarks.

One evening as a number of us were sitting around Vielbeer and watching his curious pipe as he slowly and silently drew the smoke therefrom, and sent it into the air, seeing us contemplating it, he remarked that the pipe had been in his ancient and honored family for many generations; and, indeed, it looked it.

"It was captured," said he, "from the Turkish Grand Vizier by one of my ancestors at the seige (by the Turks) of Vienna, at the time King John Sobiesky of Poland came down with a Christian army, and, joining the Austrian and German troops, made the Turks raise the seige. That was an important time for Christianity. The Mohammedan scimetar had conquered everywhere, and the children of the Orient had come so far westward as to attack the capital of Austria, the last stronghold separating them from the Christian countries. Had it fallen, the invading hosts of Moslem would have overrun the whole land, stamped out the teachings of Christ, and Europe would today have been Mohammedan instead of Christian, our Christian religion would have been swallowed up, and as entirely lost and forgotten on earth today as thoroughly as many others in the far East have been after their adherents have gone down before some all-conquering invader. But Christian Poland and Germany rallied to the relief of the sore pressed and overwhelmed Austrians at Vienna, and compelled the wave of Mohammedanism to roll back eastward, and sad indeed has been the fate of Poland in recompense for the saving of Christianity.

"Europe will yet pay dearly for the manner in which it has treated that intensely patriotic land. The Grand Vizier made such a hasty retreat before the onslaught of my ancestor and his body of cavaliers that he left his tent with all its belongings and baggage behind; my ancestor took this pipe as a memento of the fight and left the rest of the plunder, the rich silks and laces, tobacco, fine Turkish shawls, rugs, carpets, and sashes and Damascus swords, etc., to his brave troopers as their share of the spoils. The pipe was once lost for twenty years near the famous chasm in the black forest at the time of the sad death of my uncle at the young age of twenty-five years, but was finally found in the dark woods, and King William learning of it had it returned to me, the nephew of the loser, then a young man also. You may wonder what our beloved, thrice high, holy Prussian King had to do with it, so I will have to explain that in the early part of this century, in the year 1813, an exceedingly youthful and handsome prince, then but in his seventeenth year of age, fleeing from the enemy became lost in the dense interior of the black forest.

"The enemy was in full possession of our country; fair and historic Germany's white-winged angel of peace had buried her head in grief and sorrow beneath her snowy pinion. Prussia's king had been driven from his throne and exiled. His sainted queen, Louisa, after flying with her two young sons from one refuge to another, from the desolators of her beloved country, had but lately sickened and died broken-hearted, with the remark, 'We are asleep on the laurels of Frederick the Great' upon her lips. The royal family was scattered to the four winds. Germany, separated into thirty-two different kingdoms, all quarreling and fighting among themselves, was all united in one particular at least, and that was in lying prostrate, her neck beneath the heel of the triumphant Napoleon. The prince, the younger son of Queen Louisa, wandering in the dark woods, was at that moment a fugitive from the soldiers of the ever-conquering Emperor. Weary and foot-sore, his way was stopped at length by him suddenly coming upon a wide, yawning chasm, the gulf reaching down to seemingly endless black depths below; overhead the wind sighed through the deeply clothed branches of old oaken monarchs, hoary and grim, that had silently watched the suns of a century rise and fall over their sublime and towering stateliness, their outstretched densely foliaged arms thickly clothed with the gloomy old grey hanging vines of the black forest. The bank of the chasm was covered with verdure and fallen leaves, and he threw himself down on the green carpet, in hiding behind a large rock, and being worn out he closed his eyes while the songs of fair-plumaged birds soon lulled him to sleep. He was suddenly awakened by the report of a gun, and seizing his weapons and jumping up to defend himself, perceived a young mountaineer slowly approaching with bowed head, with a smoking gun, and carrying a large wreath made of the black moss which hangs so profusely from the dark forest-tree limbs to the ground.

"The prince recognizing the new-comer as being no enemy, awaited his slow and solemn approach; suddenly raising his head, my young uncle—for it was he—observing the delicate and weary figure before him and the impression left in the verdure where he had been reclining, paused, and asked what it was that had brought him thither to rest beneath the fairy Elfrida's rock. On the prince making himself known to my uncle, the latter immediately went down on his knee before the son of his own ruler's ally and explained that he was his Prussian Majesty's devoted servant, Thorwald von Vielbeer, a younger brother of the Baron of the ruined castle of that name upon the Rhine in the kingdom of Aufberg, which was one of the few provinces that had remained through all the disheartening war, firmly true to the Prussian monarch; that he was just lately commissioned lieutenant in the Aufberg cavalry, and had come to the chasm to cast into its depths the wreath of mourning in memory of a remote ancestor, Baron Crusadus von Vielbeer, who had lost his life by reason of the chasm, in the eleventh century.

"Once every ten years since, the descendants had made a trip to the yawning gulf to construct a wreath from the hanging moss in the vicinity, and place it upon the rock of Elfrida, the head of the house ever doing so if able; if not, then the next in succession. He had selected the present time for his coming, as he was preparing to join his command and ride with their united swords to the help of the Prussian patriots who were trying to rescue Germany. On his arising, the prince asked him why he called the rock Elfrida's, and placing the wreath on the ground, the stock of his gun within its center, and folding his arms over the weapon's muzzle, my ancestor informed the prince that, many long years ago, during the days of the crusades when the knights of all Christian Europe had joined forces in the attempt to rescue the Holy Land, the birthplace of Jesus of Nazareth, from the hands of the infidels, Elfrida queen of the fairies came with her court one day at earliest dawn, to the great rock to wash their faces in the dew of the morning. The queen wore a beautifully decorated crown of gold, having around the head-band a row of large pearls, and standing up above the forehead, part by its two lower points, was a golden star, its topmost prong supporting an immense glittering diamond, the rays of which outshone the sun. The fairies all washed their faces and hair in the dew, and while drying her tresses the queen laid her crown upon this rock when a sudden gust of wind blew it down; it fell with such force that it rolled to the edge of the chasm and went down to darkness and oblivion, to the great consternation of them all. Although the beautiful fairy queen was capable of doing wondrous good upon the surface of the earth, her influence did not extend to realms beneath the ground, and she was unable to recover it. Elfrida was a woman, and although the loss of the crown could be repaired, her grief for the big diamond was inconsolable. She wandered over Germany, and with prayers, tears and promises endeavored to get one brave and bold knight after another to recover the crown for her; but as the deep, gloomy and mysterious chasm in the depths of the somber woods was reported to be the summer residence of the Evil One, the brave and bold knights had more important affairs to attend to elsewhere. At this period, while the fairy queen was disconsolate, a far-back ancestor of my uncles, Baron Crusadus von Vielbeer, who had been one of the first to unsheath his sword and join the Crusaders, returned from his victories over the Mohammedans in Palestine. On getting back to our castle from the Holy Land, he heard of the visit to the stronghold, during his absence, of the fairy queen and of her unavailing endeavor to secure there and elsewhere a champion to recover her priceless crown. Crusadus von Vielbeer, fresh from conflicts where the element of success was ever present with him, determined to offer his services; at once sent word to the queen; and he, she and her court, all met one day on the brink of the chasm; my ancestor had provided a unique method to make the attempt to secure the coveted crown; he caused to be brought along with him, by his retainers, two ducks, two geese and two hens; to the legs of all of these he tied stout cords about as long as himself and fastened them together at the ends to a single rope; the wings of one duck, goose and hen he had tied by means of a band about their bodies, and taking the latter three in his arms and seizing firmly the rope above a large knot at the extreme end, he advanced to the edge of the chasm, kissed his hand, that had ever been so successful, to the fairy queen who was watching his proceedings from the top of the rock, and picking up and flinging the three free-winged fowls into the air, sprang far out over and into the gaping fissure; the flying and fluttering of the fowls so buoyed my ancestor's weight, that he sank but slowly from view down in the gloom of the engulfing darkness; here accounts very much differ about what occurrences succeeded; events followed each other in such marvelously rapid succession, that of all my ancestor's retainers awaiting his appearance at the top, no two could give the same account nor state what they did perceive, with any degree of accuracy or clearness; the best that we were able to glean, however, was, that after waiting some hours (in that great length of waiting, of anxious suspense, they all concurred although the fairy queen reported that it was but a few moments), fearful shouts, clacks, squeaks, quacking, rustling of wings and demoniacal howls arose from out the depths of the chasm; their blood curdled in their veins, and they were all too paralyzed to move, but stood with wide starting eyes staring in blank amazement at the cleft, when amid terrific noise, straight up, soaring high aloft into the air came the six fowls, all wing-free and making a dreadful clattering, while holding on to the extreme end of the rope that secured them all together was the devil, black as night, horns, cloven hoofs, spiked tail and all; laughing and yelling like the fiend that he was, with fire flashing eyes, snapping teeth and flapping ears, while to his tail clung my ancestor holding on with a grip of grim fastness, and shouting down to those below him as he sailed upward, some information about which they could only catch the words 'crown', 'seen' and 'there', out of which they could construct nothing; they soared upward and upward, higher and higher, and finally they seemed to swerve south and to be going in the direction of Geistplatz, a German town on the border of Switzerland; my ancestor's retainers watched them in awestricken wonder till they were out of sight, and at once hurried back to the castle and reported so many conflicting versions of what they had seen that it was some days before the family got at the true state of the affair; but my ancestor was never more seen; the story was noised abroad and great search and inquiry made, and even the province made a special investigation into the matter, but nothing was ever gleaned about him; not the vestige of a trace ever discovered until seventy-five years later, when a very old woman living south of the forest disclosed that in her youth she had seen the flight of the trio, the fowls, devil, crusader and all, had seen it when a little girl, but had been so terrified at the time that she said nothing, fearing evil might befall her parents and brothers, etc.; then later numerous other reports began to arrive; other aged women were heard of, who also had seen the flight in their youth; and then the trail was taken up by our family, aided by the surrounding knights and burghers, and was connected link by link, by the statements of old women all the way, who had seen the flying spectacle; some of them minutely described the fowls, their cackling and squeaking, their yellow bills, etc.; others remembered it all as plainly as though they had seen it yesterday, describing the Evil One, his arrow-shaped spiked tail, his cloven hoofs, and told how they had bowed their heads and shuddered as he had looked down in his passing rapid flight, and grinned so fearfully at them, while others depicted my ancestor, minutely portraying how they had seen him holding on to the tail with both hands, etc.

"So there could be no doubt of it. Thus he was traced by the evidence of old women who had seen it all, clear to Geistplatz, which, as you know, is on the river Irren, that separates Germany from Switzerland, and on arriving there in a body, lo and behold, on the old stone bridge which spanned the river from Germany to the Switzerland side, on the high stone wall railing that ran across on each side for the safety of vehicles and passengers, mounted on the top at the entrance, one on either side, were the stone figures of the knight in his garb of a crusader, and the devil, horns, tail and all, while behind each one, equidistant apart to the far side of the bridge, were the stone figures of a duck, a goose, and a hen, also on the summit or capping of the high stone railing. Inquiry among the inhabitants could elicit no information as to how and when the figures came there; only the oldest inhabitant could shed any great amount of light upon the matter, and he stated that they were there surmounting the stone railing when he played about the bridge as a little boy seventy-five years before; this was all we ever could gather on the subject. The supposition was that my ancestor had seen the coveted object of his adventure, and had freed his three bound fowls, preparatory to seizing the crown, shewing them to upward flight and ascending, when the devil rushed out, frightened the fowls to wing, and grasping the rope from the hands of my suddenly startled ancestor, was sailing aloft, when the crusader, realizing his position at the bottom of a hopeless chasm, made a desperate jump, clutched the devil's tail, and upward from intense darkness to the glorious light of day they all came together; the fowls flew so plumb upward in arising from their start at the deep chasm's mysterious lower end that they were some distance in height in the air from its upper surface before they turned and flew southward, and my ancestor probably awaiting to relax his grasp till his fall would be free of the chasm, found when the fowls turned south that he was then too far from the ground to do so with any degree of safety, and doubtless resolved to hold his grasp until a better opportunity arrived, and was soon out of sight

"There our knowledge of the mystery ended, and it is all explained at the bridge of Geistplatz certainly, but in what way may probably always be wrapped up in the dark secrets of the almost impenetrable history of the past.

"Elfrida, the fairy queen, shocked at the fate of her champion, a few months after the disappearance of my ancestor, returned with her court to the spot where the crown fell, stood upon the summit of the great rock, and it being no longer enclosed by the crown, 'her beautiful golden hair was of course hanging down her back,' and weeping pearly tears, and waving her wand over the chasm, made a vow that the first prince who should get a sight of the crown should raise his country to an unparalleled prosperity and rule over Germany entire. She then threw her wand down after the crown and disappeared forever.

"All this my uncle related to the prince in response to his inquiry about the name given the rock, and after he had completed his narrative, a shudder passed over his frame as he gazed down along the stock of his gun to the wreath, and then cast his eyes at the chasm.

"'To bring under one rule our disunited fair land, to secure a United Germany!' exclaimed the prince. 'To obtain such an end has been the cherished dreams of our patriots for centuries. O, Thorwald, assist me to secure that crown and you shall be rewarded far beyond your wildest dreams.' My uncle of course consented. The lives of the Vielbeers were always placed at the disposal of their sovereigns, and through them at the service of their allies. Together they made a long twisted rope of the climbing vines from the neighboring trees, fastening knots and loops among its strands at short spaces apart; securely fastened one end to the rock and let the other down the chasm. The prince threw off his coat, and eagerly grasping the rope was about to descend. 'Let me but see the crown,' said he, and 'my country! my country! all may again be well with thee. I will take a torch, and should the vine not be of sufficient length, I may yet be able to descry the fairy's jeweled circlet by the aid of the torch light, down in the deeper recesses of the chasm.' My uncle Thorwald looked at the prince's slight figure, worn and weary from privations, anxiety and flight, and said, 'Let me go; your strength might fail. I have been reared among the mountains,' continued he, looking down at his own stalwart limbs, used from childhood to scale the harsh rocks and steep cliffs of the lofty eminences — inured to endure hardships, etc. 'I will bring it up to you.' My uncle then removed his coat, in which was this pipe that he ever carried with him, and depositing it, with his hat, gun, and wreath, on the safe side of the fairy's great boulder, at once lighted the torch, stuck it in his girdle, and seizing the vine rope began the descent, soon disappearing downward in the gloom, to the view of the eager watching prince, who, lying face downward, hung his head and body over the precipice as far as he dared.

"Every few moments a faint halloo from my uncle in greeting to the prince that all was well with him, would come smouldering to the top, which grew fainter and fainter until the sound ceased altogether and finally only the swaying of the speck of light remained to show the prince that the gallant mountaineer was still descending. Then the light grew dimmer and dimmer, until it faded out altogether in the far deep distance. The moments to the anxious watcher above seemed hours. After a long time the rope slackened, at which the prince knew that the intrepid venturer had no longer hold of it. Had he fallen? Had he released his grasp from sheer exhaustion, or been overcome with faintness and swooned, or had he descended safely to the bottom? Soon, however, the rope became again taut and the prince then knew that the adventurous mountaineer was ascending. Had he found the crown? Anxiously he looked for the spark of fire, but it never came to view. His torch had been extinguished. After a long time a faint halloo came again smothering up, and soon afterward the prince, with eyes now grown accustomed to the darkness down into which he had been all this time so intently peering, could distinguish the dim shadowy outlines of my uncle's form away down in the gloomy blackness. My uncle stopped in his ascent and waved something in his hand which the prince could not distinguish in the deep obscurity. 'Hurrah! Hurrah! I have found it! I have found it!' shouted the young mountaineer, clinging with one hand to the rope, and waving the object in the air with his free hand. He then slipped it once more down over his arm and again took up his ascent. Suddenly a few strands of the vine rope parted with a loud snap, a few yards above him. Attracted by the noise he looked up, at once perceived his danger, and rapidly strove to get above the breaking section ere it was too late. Before he reached it, however, another loud snapping sound from the same place told him he was lost, and once more clinging with one hand he seized the crown and patriotically threw it far up toward the overhanging face of the prince; made several desperate clutches upward on the vine, and had ascended to within a few feet of the breaking section, when the last strand gave way, and with one long wild shriek of despair he went down to the dark unfathomable depths below. The crown thrown forcibly upward struck against the stony side of the chasm in the darkness and gloom some distance below the prince, the large diamond coming full against its rocky wall a bright flash of fire flew out from the sharply struck flint, lighting up for an instant to the view of the prince the coveted, long-lost and fateful crown in all its beauty, and then it went back down, down, following my intrepid but unfortunate uncle. The young prince had seen the fairy Elfrida's crown, but the future greatness that getting a sight of it meant to him, was effaced from his thoughts in the shocking ending of the adventure, and stricken with horror the young prince fled from the fatal spot. Swiftly flew over his head the ever-revolving silent years, but that the events of that unfortunate hour never grew dim upon his memory I am certain, for twenty years later the pipe was found among a few shreds of clothing, many miles from where left in his coat by my uncle at the time of descending the chasm. The garment had been carried off by savage beasts or wild animals, and torn and dragged about, and finally left where found years before. The prince, hearing of the find, which was noised about, secured the pipe and returned it to me—then a young man and succeeding my lately departed father, the head of our noble family. I was a young boy at the time the accident happened, and well remember the sensation caused by the news being carried to the castle of the awful fate of my uncle, and the overwhelming grief of my sick father when the rumors were at last verified, and he was sure his favorite young brother had met death at the fatal chasm. So far, the fairy queen's vow seems to be correctly interpreting itself.

"The prince's elder brother, Frederick William IV, our former Prussian king, died six years ago, without leaving a direct heir, and our present king, the younger brother, who was the prince mentioned in the adventure with my uncle, came to the throne in 1861. The country under him has been getting very prosperous, but he is now past seventy years of age, and is becoming old, and all our German kingdoms would have to unite and proclaim him Emperor William I of Germany, to fulfill in its entirety the fairy queen's vow ; a general danger threatening our States would go far toward causing them to enter into a union and becoming a great confederation under our Prussian monarch, Prussia being by far the largest kingdom and the dominant power among all of the provinces of the fair land of our fathers. Still, our people have hopes that by means of some peaceful intervention of again becoming what we were formerly, long ago, a united fatherland."

CHAPTER VI.

AFTER the conclusion of Vielbeer's story of the curious pipe, Menton got upon the little two-foot-high platform which stood against the side of a wall and sang a song of the backwoods portion of Georgia, which went as follows:

> Thar's signs ez goes back on thur oldest uv men,
>   Thar's omens ez furever fail,
> Thar's sayens ez fishy in word an' pen,
>   Ez Joner wot swallered thur whale.
>
> Freg 'zample, th' cows ez hev lost thur cuds,
>   Air ther cows thet ur never seen;
> En th' frost-killed apples ez told by thur buds,
>   Guv th' biggest crop ever hez been.
>
> In thur front rows at thur ballets so fair,
>   Never a bald head* will yer see;
> An' wen the big an' little man start a fight square
>   Ther small un ull pulverized be.
>
> Thur beautiful formed girls in scant bath-suits dressed,
>   Thet in summer newspapers yer see,
> Disporting about in old ocean's breast,
>   Frocked in tissue paper en glee.
>
> In the editor's brain they exist at most;
>   This delusion 'tis sad ter dispel;
> Fur most women's figures resemble mud posts,
>   As seaside sojourners ull tell.
>
> Th' summer of th' year thet th' moon hung wet,
>   Wuz th' dryest ever wuz seen;
> En th' fall thet th' shuck on th' corn wuz thin set,
>   Brought a hard winter cold en keen.
>
> Th' findy-sickle woman who wants ter dig coal,
>   An' man's unmentionables fill,
> We'll never meet her this side uv our goal,
>   Fur its 'gainst godle-mighty's swill.

---
*They all wear wigs.

> Thur shoe box top plank druv in at thur head
>   Uv the young wife's rich old husband's mound
> Uv which you en I hev so often read,
>   Hez so fur never been found.
>
> Young gal's fathers who put lovers ter flight,
>   Hev vanished all too soon;
> But th' man who did Billy Patterson smite,
>   Is unyarthed, he's th' man in th' moon.

As an answer to the encore this evoked, he read an original poem of the author's, entitled "A Reminiscence of the 'Historic City.'" Dorsey was a free negro barber in the writer's old home in 1845, and about that year went to the negro settlement in Liberia, and came back after a stay of some months in that country. All the old citizens remember him well. He was a superior darkey; had a roman nose, and was almost the equal of a white man in intelligence; and his report on Liberia, which he gave out by conversations about the streets of the town, was listened to with much eagerness by the people at that time, the slave colonization scheme being much agitated in 1845 to 1847.

This was as follows:

> His mustache was acoming, his pretty brown hair curled,
> Excelsior! on the banner he high and proudly whurled.
>   He had just come out of college,
>   With his head jam full of knowledge,
> And he braced himself right firm to shake the wurld.
>
> He declared that on the earth he'd make a noise,
> That the town would honored feel one of her boise
>   Had been raised to such high fame,
>   So lofty'd stand his name
> That the Senate and the House would be his toise.
>
> Though of beard upon it, there wasn't much to speak,
> To colored Dorsey quoth he, razor thou my cheak,
>   And for souv'nirs let me tell ye,
>   Save the hairs, for cash to sell ye,
> When this wealthy nation with my mighty name doth reak.
>
> Said Dorsey (as he shaved him), ambitious men I lub to see,
> Dey strike a 'sponsive chord, sah, in de pulsing heart ob mee;
>   To Liberia I went and expected, sah,
>   As king to at once be elected, sah,
> But found dat ebery niggah dah wanted king to bee.

I went wid dat 'spectation, sah, my merits were so deep,
Dat lofty honors on my head I would by showers reep;
  Unnoticed long around I squeaked,
  Den out de land one night I sneaked;
Since den, in my opinion, sah, I hab come down a heep.

But my aunts all tell me, Dorsey, on my hat should rest a plume
Because I am so handsome; and that certainly does lume
  Up in the mist before me,
  My sisters say the presidency;
Why, the universe wont be in it if I once get standing rume.

For a corset "manufack" for years he drummed.
Only in one house in ten was he welcummed;
  He did many miles of walking,
  And yards on yards of talking,
But his finances remained always bottummed.

The years had passed, not few had been his woes;
Hard luck he'd seem, not singly, but in roes;
  But he told them on Main street
  When his old time friends he'd meet.
He just took the job to wear out his old cloes.

Time flies, still things seem to go wrong,
And his world noise he would not delay too wlong;
  So his vow he now makes good,
  As he said he surely would,
For a railroad eating-house he beats the wgong.

This was also loudly applauded, although the quaint pieces of poetry and humorous tales, current in the United States, delivered in the vernacular of the backwoods and of the Southern negro, seem very funny at times to us, and are always roundly applauded abroad when gotten off at a banquet, reception, or before a club, as was the case with the above; still, one can see that it is done as a mere matter of politeness; they don't see the humor of it, not having lived among the inhabitants, and not educated to appreciate its ridiculous or laughable departure from the correct speech of the land. Spanish students state that Don Quixote, in its native language, is the acme of mirth-provoking reading, that on first perusing it they rolled on the floor over and over again shrieking with laughter, but on reading it in its German translation it lost the greatest part of its charm. So may peculiarities of Spain and the Spanish people that the work has reference to that are foreign to Germany makes a translation but little more than a curious tale about the days of old. It is like the songs of our Southern blacks commencing with, "O, dem golden slippers." A foreigner would not grasp at all the meaning about the slippers being a part of the dress of the celestial land, or that the very words "golden slippers," when spoken by a black, meant existence in the realms above, and expressed their ideas of the hereafter state. And so it is with our English translation of Don Quixote, even far less funny than in German, we being much farther removed from the customs and peculiarities of Spain than Germany and therefore much less capable of appreciating it. No English or American boy rolls about the floor in laughter on reading the book; indeed, it is only appreciated by older persons after years of experience of human nature, then they come nearer to the Spaniards in enjoying it.

Menton had finally got so proficient in his German as to have in his repertory a song in German of his own composition, which he now gave in response to the flattering encore, one verse of which here follows. Berlin is pronounced in Germany Bareleen, e being a, and i being e, but the Berliners themselves pronounce it Beahleen, and so it is intended to be in his song:

> In jugend war einer sehr lean,
> Er wird immer so bleiben by jinks,
> Aber austrinkt sein flaschen sixteen,
> Bis sein maul-thier shaut ihm an links,
> In Beahleen, in Beahleen, in Beahleen,
> War das ein ganz anders dings.

He accompanied it on the banjo, upon which he was an expert. It was the height of ridiculousness and nonsense, and evoked roars of laughter and deafening cheers, to all of which he politely bowed and then got down from off the platform. Menton showed that he was an apt pupil and was imbibing largely of German high gentlemanship, by thus going them one over in flattery (in presenting a German song of his own construction) in return for their highly flattering encores of his first pieces.

Then O'Brien, a resident of a large city in Ireland, and who was one of the handsomest men and one of the most perfectly cultivated gentleman it has ever been my good fortune and to my advantage to meet, arose, stepped upon the little platform, and in his rich, clear voice recited in English the later-on following beautiful verses of Thomas Moore, first stating that he would give a short account of the history of the poem's hero:

"Mononia," he said, "was the ancient name of what is now Munster, the most southern one of the four ancient kingdoms into which Erin was formerly divided. Brian Boroihme, or Brian Boru, born about 927, was first ruler of Mononia, succeeding to the throne as chief of the Dal Cais in 976 on the death of his elder brother, who was murdered at that time, and reigned from the year 976 until 1002, and afterward, at about the latter date, backed by the knights under his unexcelled leadership, he became, after much fighting, Ardrigh na Erenn, king of entire Ireland, having reduced, in the year 1001, Malachi, the king of the northern half of the country, under his dominion. He was one of the greatest military generals of which history gives any note.

"The Emerald Isle reached its highest pinnacle of prosperity and eminence of ancient times under his famous reign. In twenty battles, subsequent to his assuming the control of the government, in which he was contested with the Danish invaders, his troops, with himself at their head, were victorious in every one, without a single exception. In 1014 he had united against him a large army of Danes, Scandinavians, Saxons, Flemings, and a number of Maelmorda's, Leinster and Welsh troops, under the leadership of Sigurd, the Earl of Orkney and Caithness. Malachi, the former king, who had been deposed thirteen years before, with the forces of Meath, joined the bands of Munster and Connaught which Brian had mustered. When the king was advancing to the attack, on his way through the plains of Fine-gaill, north of Dublin, he was accosted by a beautiful young Irish girl, who sprang forward and grasped his horse's bridle-rein and who stated that it had been related to her in a dream to caution him not to linger near his tent during the battle. He paid no attention to her admonishment and attempted to waive her aside, but she persistently clung to his horse's mane and told him that if he paid no heed to her warning and remained in the vicinity of his tent during the progress of the conflict he would not live to see Saint Venerdi's Eve (Holy Friday's evening), nor would there be a coronach (an Irish weeping funeral dirge or lamentation for the dead) sung over him. She was finally hustled away by his men, and the king proceeded. The battle took place on Good Friday, April 23d, in the year 1014, and the ground was so desperately contested on both sides that nearly all the leaders fell in the conflict.

"Brian was then an old man of eighty-seven years of age and unable to lead his troops into the fray as he had in former years always done in person at their head, but directed the course of battle by couriers from his tent; toward late evening, and against the protests of his bodyguard, and unheeding their fears for his safety, he dispatched all but a score or so of them, to lend their aid to their sore pressed fellows in a certain far away part of the field, where the now defeated enemy were still stubbornly resisting; after their departure to the assistance of their gallant comrades, the king standing before the entrance to the royal tent, saw a large body of soldiers in the distance rapidly advancing toward him and surmised that it was a party of his men coming for more orders or with farther news of victory, of the repulse and flight of the enemy. Suddenly the banshee (a supernatural being of Ireland, which always gives notice to the members of the royal house of their speedy death) appeared about six feet from the earth, floating backward and forward and from side to side in the air before him; a caped and long dressed slender womanly figure, with unbound waving hair, the end of her long dress fading away into nothingness beneath her. 'King of Erin! King of Erin! Prepare to die!' issued from between her lips in a long, mournfully chanting wail, as she desparingly kept waving her clasped and wringing hands up and down from her waist to above her head. Brian fell upon his knees, dropping his sword upon the greensward between them, and held out his upraised arms appealingly toward the apparition, who only slowly and sadly shook her head from side to side in answer and repeated, as she continued undulating about in the air before him, the doleful wail, 'King of Erin! King of Erin! Prepare to die!' And then with a final lament of utter hopelessness disappeared as though absorbed into the surrounding elements. Brian bowed his head; he knew that his hour was come, arose, and soon the oncoming party getting sufficiently near to be recognizable, he saw that they were enemies. After the battle had been won and the enemy defeated, the troops spread out all over the field in pursuit. The king, save by a score or so of men bunched about the back of his tent, was left alone, and was standing before the entrance with eager eyes watching the ebb and flow of the distant tide of battle, when the Danish viking king Gutring (sometimes called Brodir), with a large party of followers, all of them fugitives, hastening from the scene of the now decided conflict, happened to come across, in his flight, the royal tent, which he recognized immediately, as well as the person standing before it, the king himself, now left all but unprotected by his victorious forces. They saw at once that the royal personage was but feebly guarded and immediately rushed toward and attacked him.

"Brian, although an old man, seized firmly his weapon, and at the head of his little band, who leaped to the fray in the defense of their king, met the onset, and all his own men and most of his attackers were slain ere he was finally pressed backward into the interior of his tent by overwhelming numbers; and disputing every foot of ground was at length slain by the Viking king. Thus, with his weapon in hand, face to the foe, and surrounded by his own dead men and the dying and slaughtered of the enemy, and with blood flowing like water all around him, a king and a general who was without a superior in his time, at last sank to the earth ere yet the dying sun had removed its final beams of light from off the bloody plains of Clontarf. And thus the girl's foreboding dream and prophecy came true; for neither lived he to see Saint Venerdi's Eve, nor was there a coronach sung over him; for when the conquering forces bore his body home, bleeding from a hundred wounds, the knights contended that no single weeping outcry should be made over him, and all with one accord declared that he had killed enough that day for the women of the enemy to wail his coronach from the land's end to the green banks of the Shannon.

"He had seats of government also at Tara and Cashel, but 'Kinkora,' the home mentioned, to which he was taken for burial, was the main palace of Brian, and was situated in Mononia, in the section of country that is now County Clare."

O'Brien then ended his preliminary statement of explanation, and recited the verses as follows:

> Remember the glories of Brian the brave,
>   Tho' the days of the hero are o'er;
> Tho' lost to Mononia and cold in the grave,
>   He returns to Kinkora no more!
> That star of the field, that so often has poured
>   Its beams on the battle, is set;
> But enough of its glory remains on each sword
>   To light us to victory yet!
>
> Mononia! when nature embellished the tint
>   Of thy fields, and thy mountains so fair,
> Did she ever intend that a tyrant should print
>   The footstep of slavery there?
> No, Freedom! Whose smile we shall never resign,
>   Go tell our invaders, the Danes,
> That 'tis sweeter to bleed for an age at thy shrine,
>   Than to sleep for a moment in chains!
>
> Forget not our wounded companions who stood
>   In the day of distress by our side:
> While the moss of the valley grew red with their blood,
>   They stirred not, but conquered and died!
> The sun, that now blesses our arms with his light,
>   Saw them fall upon Ossory's plain!
> Oh! let him not blush, when he leaves us tonight,
>   To find that they fell there in vain!

At the conclusion of this, he got off the little platform and resumed his seat, and to the ensuing applause merely arose from his chair and bowed gracefully; but they would not let him off, and he finally had to get back and respond before the cheers and clapping ceased. This time he also gave a poem of Moore's, entitled "Let Erin Remember the Days of Old." A mouse's squeak could have been heard during its rendition:

> Let Erin remember the days of old,
>   Ere her faithless sons betrayed her,
> When Malachi wore the collar of gold,
>   Which he won from her proud invader!
> When her Kings with standard of green unfurled,
>   Led the Red-Brauch Knights to danger:
> Ere the emerald gem of the western world
>   Was set in the crown of a stranger.
>
> On Lough Neagh's banks as the fisherman strays,
>   When the clear, cold eve's declining,
> He sees the round towers of other days
>   In the wave beneath him shining!
> Thus shall memory often, in dreams sublime,
>   Catch a glimpse of the days that are over,
> Thus, sighing, look through the waves of time
>   For the long faded glories they cover!

Then a Russian student from the far ice-bound lands of the north got upon the little stand and gave a selection of poetry in his native language; a translation of which I made into English as follows, although it loses much of its beauty in being changed into a foreign tongue, especially by the author of this work:

> Thou still seem'st the girl I used to take sleighing,
>   In the days of our youth, when the future looked bright,
> With the handkerchiefs waving and the proud horses neighing,
>   And the curved runners cutting the swift air of night.
>
> How fast through the suburbs we used to go flying,
>   Then out to the far wastes we sailing would go,
> The silver bells jingling, past the lurking wolf lying,
>   Over the wild steppes of ice and of snow.
>
> Will th' remembrances of those days ever perish,
>   To banish them often though we might strive?
> Never! Those memories we will ever cherish,
>   Ever while life lasts to keep them alive.
>
> Combined with these roses I send thee a blessing,
>   And to you may I hope 'twill as welcome be,
> As the whistling winds of Cossack Land caressing
>   Were to the flowers ere I picked them for thee.

"Would you believe", said Vielbeer, getting the memory of his youthful days stirred up by the sentimental song, "that I was once in love?"

"Impossible!" inadvertently said several of those sitting in the ring of chairs nearest to him, and half circling his front, surprised out of their self-possession by the incongruity of associating his contour with the tender passion. At this he glared about, but meeting only respectful, attentive faces, continued:

"Yes, fifty years ago I fell in love with a young girl, an angel on earth, an angel, truly, although without wings, of course. Ah! how my old heart beats and thrills with emotions I thought long since stilled as I again call up her sainted picture to memory's view.

"My, my! how deeply I was in love with her only those of you who are aware of the depth of my nature can realize. I can close my eyes now, after the lapse of over half a century, and see my darling as plainly as though 'twere only yesterday walking up and down the paths of her father's garden in the fair summer days, all clothed in gauzy white, looking like a fairy from the realms of enchantment. How I used to envy the pink and blue ribbons that at times encircled her waist—the waist I would have given kingdoms (if I had had them of course) to clasp with my arm. How I viewed her from afar; how at night I would have gotten into the garden and kissed the walks her dainty feet had trod (if I could have scaled the big wall of course); how I spoiled reams of paper in sending her poetry and prose, declaring my life was wrapped up in her; how I caught colds by the wholesale, and once almost the galloping consumption, under her windows at night, singing solos to the accompaniment of a guitar (which I continually carried in my pocket to have handy for that special purpose), expressive of my undying and life-engrossing love for her. All this I need not tell you, as most of you young 'suckers' can realize my plight from your own experiences. That I have never been able to look at any woman since, but as a sister, is evidence sufficient that the flame of affection that flared for her then was so deep and fierce that naught but ashes has ever since occupied the place in my heart where affection is supposed to exist. She was indeed a lovely girl, weighed two hundred pounds, had flaxen hair most abundant, light blue eyes, a face very fair, and her arms at her shoulders were fat, round, lovely and large beyond my powers of description. In addition to these charms her father owned the only brewery for forty miles around. In spite of my furious and 'take her by storm' kind of passion—for I was very much in love with her you may believe—neither the girl nor her father seemed to look with the least favor upon me. But I was young then, and you can imagine that such trifles as that did not bother me in those days. Seeing that my progress in her affections from the time of my first meeting her was very decidedly stationary, and remembering that faint heart ne'er won fair lady, and that to the brave belong the fair by inherent right, and all that sort of thing, I resolved on a bold stroke, considering any means, fair or foul, perfectly appropriate and justifiable to secure possession of this dainty pearl beyond price.

"So one day I got out and polished very brilliantly my Sunday garment. I must remind you that in those old German days, that outside of our shirts our clothing consisted of a single garment made of leather, which we now call pants. The waist-band was very large, covering our stomachs up to our necks; and the boots were also sewed to and were part of the legs of the pants, so it was all in one piece. German gentlemen, in those days, continued Vielbeer with a smile lurking deep in his eyes, first donned their shirt, then put their lower limbs in the legs of this garment, the waist-band of which came up to the arm pits, and it was fastened at the back of the neck. Thusly clad, with a feather of our soaring eagle in my cap, I grasped a stout and heavy stick, mounted my steed Groszfitter, and rode off to the deeply-timbered regions. After winding about, I finally surmounted an elevation from which I could see the chapel of the old hermit priest, who, for years, had made his home in the dense, somber woods, in the obscure recesses and secret depths of the black forest mountains, and whom all held in reverence, and the superstitious in great awe—as his only known associates, except on Sundays, when the peasants flocked to his chapel, were the mysterious mountain gnomes and kobolds of German legendary lore.

"Seeing smoke issuing from his stone chimney, and knowing from that that he was at home, my spirits began to rise. Fate seemed propitious; ere long my peerless Gretchen would be mine, mine own forever! for well I knew that as soon as I got her alone with me, away from her villainous father's influence, she would not be able to control her feelings of affection that I felt she certainly must have for such a handsome young fellow as myself, and would put her arms around my neck, lay her soft cheek to mine and say, 'I love you, O my adored; let us hasten to the priest ere some mishap befall you, my beloved.' By all this manner in which I had her sentiments toward me worked out in my own mind, you can see for yourselves that in olden days I did not differ materially in self-esteem from the young men of the present. I meant to abduct my willing bride, and knowing the hour she always passed in the garden, I turned Groszfitter's head toward her father's stronghold. It was the partially restored building of an old castle which had been blown up by the French under Louis XIV; was on the bank of a river, surrounded by a wall, had a draw-bridge and portcullis-like gate, and was approached by a large stone bridge running over the river. On arriving there I rode down to the bank, and seeing the river flowing away into the distance, calm and placid, winding like a silver band to the far away sea, I saw in the river's motion an expression of my own happiness awaiting me. After she and I were married so would our lives be — lovingly meandering down the stream of life, adoringly going along the path of existence, calm and placid like the silent-flowing river; no ruffles, no ripples, no unsmoothness — all the days and years just love and happiness. So many things in nature seemed to be doing their best to urge me on that my elation reached the highest rung. All nature was showing me favors, and conspiring to aid me.

"So I tilted my cap over my left eye, rode lightly over the bridge, up the paved roadway and raising aloft my stout stick, thundered heavily at the gate, which I did so lustily that echoes returned from the lofty pine-covered mountain peaks of the Schwarzwalder (black forest) seventeen miles away. 'Potts donnerwetter, sapperment, schwearnote, blitz carrambo!' I heard her father swear in astonishment and awakened awe, inside; doubtless thinking, by the assurance conveyed in the summons at the gate, that the king and his whole retinue must be seeking admission. The gates of these old fortified places slid up and down in groves like a guillotine blade or axe; and suddenly there arose the noise of clanking chains and then up went the gate and I rode my horse in quickly right under the overhanging, bottom spiked, heavy oaken door, so that he could not drop it without a serious breach of etiquette, as well as damage to my lordly and well-thought-of self. Her father glared terribly at first on seeing me, but suddenly his eyes taking in my fine attire, supposed I was now flush with wealth and had come to settle for the many kegs I had soaped him for all those years gone into the past, and asked me quite civilly to come in. I read his thoughts like a flash in one of those intuitive moments we all have at times of great anxiety and peril, and my own thoughts at once leaped to the occasion. 'No!' I replied, 'I have not time to dismount and enter; bring my account, I would like to pay all my bills in full' (which was the truth). 'I would also like to be able to do the same this day.' I caught a glimpse of my darling fair one, my sainted Gretchen, in the garden, sitting under an aged overspreading linden tree, reading; so puffing out my cheeks and swelling out my chest and reaching my fist down into my empty leg pocket and holding it there in a suggestive 'paying-up' attitude, I said, 'Make out my rechnung' (statement), 'I will await here your speedy return.' He went into the house, and I galloped toward the garden and up to Gretchen, and said, 'My angel one, my swan of the air, fly with me and reign queen of the world forever.' She was quite taken by surprise and startled, like a sweet gazelle in the meadow, out of her composure; and before she recovered I reached down from my horse and grabbed her, enfolded her lovely being in my clasp, and although I was young then and had the ardor of love in my heart, the fire of youth in my veins, and my lovely maiden in my arms, still it was only by the most strenuous exertion that I managed to lift her in front of me upon the saddle.

"Gretchen, however much she may have loved me, however deeply she may have sighed all the past months at the omission from her presence of my charming company, however longingly she may have dwelt on my name in her prayers for my success, and in admiration of my persistent meritorious firmness in the endeavor to overcome her father's infernal obstinacy, did not, it seems, approve entirely of my desire to make her queen of the world. Great heavens, how she fought and struggled and screamed and scratched my hands and face! I marvel yet how such a lovely angel could so suddenly transform into such a terrible wildcat.

"I finally grabbed her arms down tightly to her waist, turned Groszfitter's head toward the entrance, gave him a baste with the stick, to which he responded nobly and went like the wind out of the gate, over the bridge and into the country beyond, just as her father, hearing her screams, came tearing like a sore-pawed bear out of the house. Terrible indeed was the language he wafted after us as we rode away. I tremble to this day when I think of his words. I turned around in the saddle and shouted back that in a few hours I would surely do him the honor of recommending myself to him as a son-in-law, threw him a merry kiss and gayly galloped on, for well I knew he had no horse to follow, and I felt so safe that as I entered the outskirts of the black woods I checked my steed and turned to look at my bride; she was overcome at the joy, at the exquisite thrilling sensation of feeling herself at last secure in my arms and had fainted away. I rapturously squeezed her to my breast, calling her my precious sugar plum, my onliest own honey girl and other saccharine terms of endearment, and then bent forward and my lips touched her irresistible and coyly tempting ones in a loving endeavor to revive her; then I acquired mental cognition of the extremity of happiness and felicity, for that was the divinest, most blissful, moment that I ever experienced in all my life. The pearly gates of paradise opened, celestial wings of snowy whiteness were wafted through the air in rhythm to heavenly music, the nectar of the gods was given me in abundance to quaff, all the delightful blessedness in the universe showered over me. All, all this occurred during the second of time in which I kissed her. The ecstasy that was mine at the thought of how soon I should now possess her was too great for me to tell you. In a few moments we would be married; soon be joined into the most hallowed of all friendships; soon be united in the dearest of all associations, the sweetest of all companionships. My rapture was absolutely beyond the bounds of a human breast. I had supposed that no reasonable being would be imbecile enough to think of pursuit on foot for fear of being made the sport of ridicule in attempting to dream of 'foot pursuing horse,' but I had forgotten for the moment our thundering German persistency, for on suddenly hearing shouts and cries in the distance I looked back and saw her father and his infernal hirelings in hot pursuit. I had also forgotten that although I had ridden Groszfitter for years, still I had never tested his bottom farther than from home to the brewery, where he always rested and nourished himself for several hours while I refreshed myself, and then the return to my tumbling old castle. Now I discovered to my dismay that although my two hundred pounds of beautiful girl sat very lightly upon my loving heart, her weight soon began to set pretty heavily upon my gallant steed's back, for he began to puff and blow terribly. I urged him on, but he began to get wobbly. This did not tend to increase my hopes; besides, I could see that the pursuers, coming with giant strides, were gaining upon us. I cut through the woods, over hill and dale, at all angles, but made the great mistake of always keeping headed for the priest's chapel, and they ever and anon got a glimpse of us through the trees. Had I coolly reflected, I would have thought that they surmised my destination and would at once make for the chapel, and I should have hidden with Gretchen in the forest until the hovering, angry clouds had rolled away. But I was excited, and all my energy and mind bent on arriving there first, and, I still hoped, in sufficient time. I was already in sight of it; saw the welcome smoke ascending from the chimney and the aged priest, clothed in his peaked hood and long waist-roped gown, standing in meditation near by; the goal was in view, but I was too late.

"I can now realize what the feelings of shipwrecked mariners must be, after days of fighting for life on the storm-tossed ocean, to sink beneath the cold, dark waves, to go down to the bottom just as their vessel approaches a harbor, with crowds of willing but unavailing helpers standing with outstretched arms on the shore. Indeed, that must be an affecting experience, only second to what I felt as they finally caught us.

"All the blood of my noble and illustrious ancestors rose in my veins; I raised my heavy stick high in the air; my hair rose in rage and fury from my head, and my noble self roused to conflict rose in my stirrups. I clung to Gretchen and made a desperate resistance, my heart's delight lending me every assistance; she clawed and scratched and bit me with all her strength in order to urge me on in the fray and to keep my ire from lapsing into languor; and so I used my stout stick upon their thick heads with all my power, but I might as well have been hitting butcher's blocks for all the impression it made. My horse was soon pulled down; and in the furious struggle of passion and resentment that ensued was rolled over us four times. My peerless Gretchen, the darling of my heart, the light of my soul, was torn in a terrible heart-broken, hysterical state of streaming tears from my arms. Her father's cussed hirelings seized me in a lump, and by his directions I was swung around in the air several times, and then fired six hundred feet away into the Clammer river, which resembles," continued Vielbeer, looking squarely at me, "your American Missouri, in being more mud than water. Three weeks later when

I had gotten the last of the mud scraped off of me and appeared once more in cultivated society, I heard that her father had made her marry some infernal hundefuss whose possessions adjoined his own. I decided that if she would pine away to a shadow, and die in some early summer time with the sweet smile of lost affection held out to me still, that then I would consider that the loss of his daughter as being sufficient punishment for an obstinate father, and forever hold my peace; but to the contrary I heard that she was getting fairer and fatter and more lovely as the months went on, so I swore terrible vengeance on him, which later on I carried out, so fearful was it, indeed, that it would crack the roof of this building even to mention it here," concluded he, looking around over his shoulder as though he feared some lurking danger.

As he ceased speaking we all shuddered, our hands trembled, teeth chattered, and our knees shook.

"Let's hear it, Vielbeer," said several, finally.

"I cannot," replied he.

"Oh, yes; do now," we all urged.

"You all won't tell?"

"Never!" came in a chorus from everyone.

"Well, then, I moved away for a while into the next county, and the consumption of his beer by that means having fallen off two-thirds, great quantities of it began to sour, and daily he would have the satisfaction of seeing many more barrels spoiling for a consumer, and each morning calculate his loss; the daily losses so preyed upon his mind that he got sleepless, grew thin, sickened, and, finally, on his physician stating that only a disordered liver was ailing him, gave the medical man a volley of round curses, turned his face to the wall and died. When I heard of this last occurrence, I realize in my extreme youth what so many of us in the wide experience of after years see, how and where we missed our happiness or our fortune, by not taking advantage of some slight circumstance, or by the lack of a very little forethought. Had I but had the noble foresight to move away a few months sooner and had let his beer sour a half a year earlier, you can readily see that the soon orphaned girl would, or at least could, if she so wanted, have rushed into my arms without my having to meet a parent's cursed pig-headedness with resolute staunchness. Ah, me!" ended Vielbeer, sighing retrospectively. "Ah, me! it might have been. But for the lack of a little forethought it might have been, and yet it still is better to have loved and lost than never to have loved at all."

"Another song, Vielbeer," came from several.

"No, no. No song," replied he.

"Yes, yes; just another," they said coaxingly.

"No, no song; I can't bear to think of a swill song as long as such hallowed memories of my loved and lost one remain in my mind. I will, however, tell you about the exploits of my great grandfather, who was such a famous wine-drinker, and who was renowned all over the lands north of the blue Danube for the great quantities that he could consume, and who seemed never to show the least trace that he had absorbed a single drop; always appearing at the end of a convivial bout as cool, collected, clear-headed and thirsty as at the moment of starting in, while his contesting companions had, long ere he ceased, given up the fray and been snoring like hippopotamuses in their sleep.

"My ancestor, Baron Marverdt von Vielbeer, commanded a regiment of eleven hundred men under 'Friedrich der Grosze' (Frederick the Great), to which belonged five cannon of staunch, stout make, but of very heavy build. These pieces of ordnance were the pride of the command, and the men vied with each other in their care of them.

"In those flush days of our illustrious and noble house such a mean drink as beer offered to a gentleman of my ancestor's standing would have been considered a deadly insult. Ah me! Would that the situation of his somewhat less illustrious great grandson were in keeping with the high position once maintained by our race. So goes the revolving wheel of time — the men of one generation up, those of the next down. Who knows but what my nephews, the heirs of my house, may, in the not distant future, raise the luster of our line again to its former place — second only to his Imperial Majesty's family. One thing you can rest assured of, and that is the fact that if the wheel of fortune is still turning, whichever way it moves, will certainly bring results immensely to the betterment of the finances I draw from the few acres still surrounding Vielbeer castle.

"Well, my ancestor enjoyed the deepest confidence and bosom friendship of the immortal Frederick during all the Seven Years War; and after one of the many brilliant exploits of my great grandfather on the field of battle, witnessed in person by the king, he publicly embraced my ancestor before the whole army, and showered on him such high honors as to awaken the envy and animosity of Commander Vielbeer's numerous enemies within the ranks. This particular brilliant exploit of my ancestor was something about the commander, alone and unaided, and with a broken sword at that, putting a whole brigade of four regiments of the enemy's to flight, in full view of all the army and the king. There were later rumors, emanating, doubtless, from the envious persons who endeavored to belittle his achievements, stating that the commander ran ignominiously, and caused the enemy's whole brigade to take flight in pursuit, but they only related part of the occurrence.

"No military man will, for an instant, believe that so large a body of soldiers would pursue to capture a single officer; nor that a king in the presence of an army would honor an officer for simply flight, for merely a glorious retreat; though all soldiers will admit, that had my ancestor only a broken sword, a hasty falling back before armed men would not only be considered allowable, but also perfectly justifiable and sensible; many soldiers would not entertain the idea of flight for merely the saving of their own lives; no! perish the thought; but might do so after considering that they had no right to lessen their army's strength by the loss of their individual selves; but the great are ever subject to malicious attack, and so we will let it go at that, and I will tell you the facts related by my ancestor as they truly occurred. Just at dusk in the end of November, about a month after the great victory of Eindorf, which had taken place the middle of the preceding October, and which reflected such credit on the Prussian arms, and in which the Bombazeunt cavalry rode through a hail of shot and shell, right up to the enemy's fortifications, sabered the gunners, captured the outworks and compelled the evacuation of the last fort held by the enemy on Prussian soil; well, just at dusk — it was the very end of the month of November, during the drizzling and rainy season — and immediately preceding the battle of Kremzburg, in which the army and Great Frederick sent all the united allies flying in wild disorder—from which they never recovered and which made them sue for peace—beyond the border, leaving all their arms, cannon, supplies and twenty thousand prisoners in our hands, and losing the flower of their army by shot and saber, and which success was the ending of the Seven Years War, and beginning of the greatness and ascendency of Prussia over the German-speaking States of the north, and which convinced the world that King Frederick was invincible—well, as I said, it was the end of November of that year, and still drizzling nearly every day, when my ancestor with a couple of dozen brother officers of Frederick's standard, were all agreeably and comfortably sitting together around a large table in one of the wine cellars of the Black Raven, in Gerbstadt, to refresh themselves for the coming campaign—for King Frederick was planning an attack on the enemy's entrenchments, the last stronghold, the last position that they held in Prussia, and which they had retreated to and now occupied in force at Kremzburg, fifty miles away. The wine cellar was in the foundation of an old monastery which in medieval times had been strongly fortified; it had fallen to ruins, however, after being taken and held by first one side and then another, and eventually razed by the purchasers to the massive foundations, which, being beneath the ground, were left for cellars, and the Black Raven Inn erected upon them, from the fallen stones that were lying scattered all about. The large room in which the officers had congregated was beneath the ground, except the extreme upper part, from which two windows, heavily barred, admitted a faint light from the stone-paved street; the walls were heavily built of stone, were six and eight feet thick, and the room ended upward in an arched stone ceiling; only a dim light was admitted by the high windows to the lower part of the cellar room at the best of times, and even in broad daylight flaming candles were needed. All the officers were known to each other except one, a stranger, who was a sparelooking man, with a thin face and palid countenance, with jet black hair and eyes, with a small, stiffly waxed mustache, and a small pointed goatee on the very tip of his chin, and who had a satirical expression, at some times more perceptible than at others, playing about the corners of his mouth. None of the officers seemed either to have met him before or to know anything about him, or how he came to be seated among them at the table, and just opposite my ancestor, the commander; for all had come in a body to the door with an attendant who had unlocked it and admitted them, and who, upon lighting the candles on the table and ordering his underlings to carry in the lunches and the liquors, had retired; however, there he was, that was certain, and the officers wishing to welcome him to their company, all saluted him in a military manner after seating themselves; at which the stranger arose and gravely bowed in acknowledgment.

"His dress betokened a high military commander in some extremely northern country that no one present could designate, or recognize from it or its decorations. That he was an officer from a frigid zone all mentally agreed, as his exceedingly tall cap, made in the shape of an inverted bell, was composed of thick woolly and longhaired black bearskin and had a yellow and white rosette on one side of the top, from which decoration arose, towering above the cap's flat summit or crown, a tall black plume.

"The bottles were opened, the glasses filled and emptied, and the officers fell into discussing the oncoming battle, the probable results of the previous victory in influencing the army in an assault on the enemy's works, the amount of stores and supplies the enemy still had, etc. Soon all were getting garrulous and becoming wine-heated, flushed and red-eyed from their deep potations as the night wore on, and as dozens after dozens of bottles were drained and flung aside. At length the assembly grew noisy, songs were sung, toasts were made, their military hats waved about and swung around over their heads in their exuberance of spirits, and to emphasize their remarks. 'Let us uncover ourselves all together and drink to the king,' said one finally. This met with instant, unanimous assent; was regaled with immediate, loud and joyous approval. The goblets were again filled, and all removed their military head-dress with one hand; raised them altogether high in the air, and giving in loud concert responses to the health of the immortal Frederick, lifted their glasses, clinked them one with another and then all in unison and with a last deafening cheer raised their 'bumpers' to their lips and drained them. Only the stranger said nothing, never spoke a word, never opened his mouth in speech, and never even touched his tall bearskin covering which all along he had kept tightly upon his head; but sat erect, silent, pale and calm, though he had slowly and coolly filled an immense goblet, held it up and touched with all the others in responsive greeting to the officers in their toast to their king, and quaffed it off in company with the rest. It was now getting far into the night; the large quantity of wine consumed began to have its effect. 'Vengeance *is* mine; I will repay', sayeth the Lord. Voices grew thick, glassy eyes dull and heavy; heads after nodding awhile sank upon breasts; deep breathing emanated from all parts of the room, and at last one by one they lowered their heads in sleep upon folded arms on the table before them, fell with limp necks and back-hanging heads backward in their chairs, or dropped off their seats to the floor and rolled under the table until all were deep in stupor—and an intense silence supervened, broken only at times by the heavy sighing and breathing of the unconscious ones—all except my revered ancestor the commander, and the stranger, who were still occupying their seats at the table as at the first of the evening, just opposite each other. Then for the first time the stranger spoke, and in a clear, thick, round, cutting, peculiar, musical voice, addressed my ancestor and said:

"'Now, since these worthy gentlemen have seen fit to withdraw their highly entertaining conversation and extremely pleasant companionship from us, and have, snail-like, shrunk into themselves, withdrawn into a reserved stand-offishness seemingly; in this gathering, peculiar to only those who are now deeply enfolded within the arms of Bacchus, depriving us of their agreeable and interesting songs, and dispossessing us of the sight of their warlike figures and handsome countenances; and now that we have a clear field before us, and as I am exceedingly empty, distressingly dry, and very thirsty, indeed, and would like to open a few more bottles, if you are samely disposed, and it is agreeable to you, we will quench our thirst in a flagon or so of the famous vintage of 1612, than which no finer nor better bouqueted wine has been seen in all Germany north of the peerless grape-raising banks of the Rhine for two hundred years.'

"The commander nodded to him in acquiescence, of course; he was never the one to offend a strange guest or not make him feel perfectly at home by refusing to accept convivial hospitality from him. Whereupon the stranger seized the large brass bell, raised it and rang a furious peal, and on an attendant entering ordered several dozen bottles of the famous vintage of the year 1612. 'And be sure and get it from the south or sunny side of the cellar', continued the stranger as the attendant was leaving. After his departure the stranger explained to my ancestor that the vintage of 1612 had been casked in the deep cellars of the 'Rath Haus' (town hall), and stones, timbers, and other rubbish, had gradually accumulated about the door leading to the vaults until the passage-way was finally blocked up and its existence eventually forgotten for over a hundred years; until about thirty years since on cleaning out the cellars the passage-way and the door were disclosed to view, the cellar broken into and the casks discovered containing the wine, which was at once drawn off into flasks. The bottles were finally brought, being carried in in immense topless oval-shaped baskets by the attendants, one carrier at each end being necessary to convey each of them, and all placed on the floor by the side of the stranger. 'Now,' said he to my ancestor, after the attendants had retired, 'kindly do me the favor, as you are the nearest, to close and bolt the door, so we may not be interrupted by some disagreeable fellows tumbling in upon us.'

"The commander arose, went to the door, and being under the impression that he heard someone knocking, opened it and looked out into the stone-pillared and high-vaulted passage, but seeing no sign of life anywhere about, except that suggested by the lights streaming from under the doors of opposite cellar chambers all along the wide stone-paved hallway, and that expressed by the clink of glasses and the gay songs of revelers emanating therefrom, withdrew his head into the room, and at once closed the massive and heavily ironed great oaken door, shot its two large bolts firmly and securely, and returned to his seat at the table just in time to witness the stranger lovingly brushing the cob-webs of over a score of years from off the necks of a couple of dozen bottles, which he had already lifted up to beside him on the table.

"The stranger filled the glasses of both my ancestor and himself, and together they drifted into conversation; and the commander found him a gentleman of marvelous education, widely learned, and who conversed on all subjects as familiarly as though he were intimately and personally acquainted with them. They finally, quite naturally, got to speaking of the recent battles, and the insight the stranger displayed in regard to all the tactics of the army, the position of every army corps, the knowledge of the actions the commander's own regiment participated in, etc., was so true that it perfectly astounded my ancestor. From the last topic of conversation they gradually came to the discussion of former battles and wars, great leaders of earlier and ancient date; and all the time emptying glass after glass, bottle after bottle, until when the stranger got to explaining the movements of

Xerxes in the year 480 B. C., in conveying his vast army over the pass of Thermopylæ before and after overwhelming Leonidas, the commander's head was so muddled and giddy that he could barely make heads from tails of it. The sides of the compartment wavered backward and forward to his gaze, the table and chairs seemed to whirl about the room, the plates of lunch, bottles and glasses were dancing the lanciers all over the table, and my poor ancestor's head felt so big and heavy that he thought sure it was about to burst or else topple him over by its great weight plump upon the floor.

"The stranger, however, still sitting in the chair opposite him, as he had done all evening, calm, cool, collected, erect and pale, was continuing his explanations in which he seemed to be deeply and retrospectively interested; he had taken strings of pie-crust in illustration of his explanations of the line of wheeled or movable wooden fortifications behind which Xerxes' legions advanced to the attack, and which were finally found too heavy and cumbersome to scale the heights with; his battalions he had constructed out of rows of bread crumbs; the mountains he made by piling up a number of the twos' now sleeping companions' tumblers; the pass of Thermopylæ represented by the space between the necks of two upright wine bottles placed close together; a large puddle of wine with small pieces of cork floating in it, indicating the Ægean sea and the Lamian gulf with the fleet of Xerxes upon it; a long streak of the liquid that he had drawn on the table toward his left from out the Gulf of Lamia, showed the Spercheius river at which Xerxes swore so, etc. The stranger moved his legions from one position to another about the table, explaining the movements minutely, bringing up a battalion to the front at one place, spreading it out in a skirmish line at another, embarking a legion on the sea at one part of his position, carrying it around by water and disembarking it at another, and marching it up to the scene of strife; showing the projecting eminence on the Saromata Mountains, an uncomfortable looking sitting point on the glasses, indeed, where Xerxes sat as he viewed his vast armed horde strenuously striving to scale the mountain heights down which Leonidas, the heroic king of Sparta, and his brave band were rolling great stones, giant boulders and immense masses of large rock upon them in floods. Five glasses, two standing upon top of three, and a single one capping the two upper ones, all in the shape of a cone, representing the distant heights which Xerxes finally gained by leading a body of archers in person, and from which eminence they eventually so shattered the forces of the handful of brave defenders by shooting heavy arrows from their mounted colossal bow-guns upward into the air, and at last getting the exact range, making them drop from above down upon the unprotected heads of the three hundred, which destroyed so many, that with a final rush the enemy's myriads overwhelmed the few remaining defenders, and Leonidas went down to death and never-fading glory with the last of his immortal warriors just as the setting sun was taking his dying rays from off the lofty peaks of Thermopylae.

"All the time the stranger was absorbed in his recital he was emptying bottle after bottle and talking as coolly and collectedly as though he had touched nothing but water for months, while the commander could barely keep his head off the table, and the room, stranger, fortifications, glasses, bottles, chairs, sleeping companions, table, pictures, and candles, were all swimming around and around in a great rapidly-moving swirl before his eyes. But I see you are losing interest,' finally remarked the stranger, shutting one eye and drawing his mouth around to the ear under it. 'So let's drink perfect success to the Prussian arms of the immortal Frederick in the coming battle, and quit.' Saying which he seized a bottle, filled a glass for my ancestor and then one for himself, put his own to his lips and at once drained it off. The commander, in order to respond to the stranger's offering toast of drinking the military success of his beloved captain, made a last convulsive effort to pull himself together, and with his head whirling like a spinning-top, made a wild spasmodic grasp at where he supposed his goblet to be sitting, by good luck managed to seize it, raised it to his lips and making strenuous exertions, gulped it down. Just as he threw his head back in patriotically draining the last drop, however, he observed the stranger run his hand up over his ear and under his great bearskin busby, (a movement he had made several times during the evening) and a second later saw a cloud of yellowish fumes issue out into the air around about the stranger's head, from beneath his shaggy head-dress. 'You have brushed against a candle-flame, your cap's smoking,' shouted out the commander; and then his head, being much heavier than all his body, overbalanced him to one side; however, he caught the top of the table with both hands to stay himself, and just the few seconds before his head, toppling over sideways, went beneath the table-top, as he was about tumbling off his chair, he shot a final startled look at the stranger and perceived that he had for the first time raised his cap from off his head and placed it upon the table, and with his long, pale, white hand lifted up to his brow, was calmly smoothing with a slow, meditative stroke the hair back from his temple, and ascending straight upward into the air in the shape or form of a cornucopia or horn, with small end downward, as though from out a small, rounded aperture in the very summit of the stranger's head, and just midway between two short black horns growing out the sides at the top, he perceived a faint greenish fog arise, widen, and grow dimmer and more vaporish as it dissipated itself, and gradually mingling with the surrounding atmosphere grow mistier and fainter and disappear altogether in space, and all the time also perceived the stranger staring straight at him with an inquiringly quizzical knowing gaze.

"'The commander, losing his hold upon the table, sank out of his chair plump upon the floor, alighted on one shoulder, rolled over and settled squarely on his back upon the stone flags. The stranger jumped up with a bound from his seat, whirling the chairs out of his way in some mysteriously dextrous manner as he rushed around the table, his footsteps making a noise as of a two-footed horse running over the floor; and coming to where the commander lay on his back, with wide staring eyes and intense astonishment expressed in his look, he stopped and again fixed his curious gaze on my ancestor; the commander gasped out with an effort, 'Frigid zone forsooth! He's from an extremely hot zone, or else am I much mistaken, for I now greatly bethink me that he wore that warm cap to conceal his horns and so that they might be more in keeping with the temperature of his own native clime; frigid zone indeed! I believe it's the foul fiend himself, who has been our guest the whole of the evening.' 'You never made a truer guess in your life,' said the other in his strange musical voice; and unstopping a small vial, which he drew from his pocket, he bent over the commander and held it under his nose. The commander, thinking it was intended by the stranger for him to swallow the contents, closed his mouth tightly and gave several suspicious sniffs at it; what was his surprise on inhaling the fumes emanating therefrom, to instantly find all the effects of his conviviality disappear; the stranger immediately pocketed his vial, and retiring to his side of the table resumed his former seat; and the commander at once arising from off the floor, smoothed his clothing, pulled his chair up to the table and again seated himself, feeling as empty, cool and lightheaded, as though just back from a campaign in which he had drank nothing for weeks. 'Your power of acute observation, your aptitude of deduction and deep insight into affairs is perfectly marvelous,' said the stranger, arising in his seat just opposite my ancestor, and with his handkerchief, which he drew from an inside breast pocket, sweeping the table clear of all military display of crusts, crumbs, cork, puddles of wine, etc.; and after drying it, by a few seconds holding over a candle, laying it down at the side of his glass. 'And centuries back I determined to richly reward every one, who, in a friendly drinking bout with me, could keep his penetrative or perceptive powers clear, under wine, long enough to perceive the smoke coming out of my head, by which means I instantly eliminate all the bad effects of drinking; and if you will allow me the honor, I will do so now.' Saying which, he again arose from the seat he had resumed while speaking, and leaning over the table tapped my ancestor on the left temple with his long, lean right forefinger, at the same time informing him that whenever he was deep in wine and wished to rid his brain of the clouding and befuddling effects, to search among the hair at the side of his head with his left hand, and, on finding, gently twist the little thumb-screw he would feel deeply concealed there above his ear, and he would instantly discover that all the muddle, whirling and heaviness of his mind and senses would be dissipated as though by magic.

"The stranger then took up his handkerchief, which my ancestor noticed was in the shape of a half square, and seizing the commander's glass and then his own, wiped away from the external part the sticky gaum that had collected there from the liquid's drying, and polished the outsides of them until they shone and sparkled so brilliantly that my ancestor's eyes were dazzled, filled both glasses again, and, taking up his own, once more resumed his seat, and with up-raised glass nodded at my ancestor to respond.

"'That must be a wonderful handkerchief,' said my ancestor moving his eyes from the dazzling reflection of the goblet he was just raising, to where the stranger had laid it again beside his bottle.

"'It is, indeed, and has many historical associations connected with it, or rather the other half of it has, for you see but half remains; and your company is so very agreeable that if you don't mind I would like to prolong our companionship to the extent of my making you acquainted with its history,' said the stranger, emptying his glass.

"'Nothing could be more perfectly to my taste,' replied my ancestor, following his example.

"Again filling both goblets, the stranger spread the handkerchief flat upon the table before him, and smoothing it with both hands, continued:

"'You are the only gentleman since several thousand years who has witnessed my method of effacing the brain-clouding effects of wine. I was a guest, many centuries before the coming of Christ, of Cheops, one of the grandest Pharaohs of remote times, and who reigned during Egypt's highest civil and military power. He, considering himself the greatest personage on earth and almost a god, was most anxious to out-drink me at the banquet table in the presence of all his court, not liking, naturally, for it to be known that there was a single merit extant in which he did not excel. In order to test his capacity and to sound the depths of his determination I always so regulated the evaporation of the fumes from my head at these matches that the king, after drinking until he dropped, did so just about a goblet before it seemed to the assembled guests that I myself would have to give up. So each succeeding evening the Pharaoh would stretch himself, and be able to conquer a few goblets farther than the previous one, I would pretend to be just able to keep pace with him, but still to seem when he was overcome to be able to swallow one more. The king made strenuous efforts, indeed, to overcome that mysterious one more goblet; but at length one evening, after prodigious efforts on his part, he succumbed, saying as he was being carried away by his counselors, 'I give up, I acknowledge my first defeat, there is no beating the fellow, he's from the infernal regions I am sure. See, he's afire now; there's bluish smoke pouring out from under his head-dress.' 'I wore of course the Egyptian costume of that day', continued the stranger. 'The assembled guests all looked at me in answer to his remark, but seeing of course nothing unusual, accused the wine of causing phantasies in their monarch's mind, and Pharaoh, lapsing into unconsciousness, was borne to his apartments.

"'Some days later, as I was standing upon the brow of an eminence overlooking the Nile, I saw the imperial barge approaching on its way up the ancient river. On arriving opposite, the king perceived me and directing his oarsmen to land, stepped ashore and bidding his retinue remain in the vessel until his return, picked his way alone up the slope and ascending the prominence to where I stood, his imperial form and mine were finally outlined together face to face in relief against the sky, in full to the view of his attendants. 'Mysterious stranger', began the king of kings, 'my friends and counselors all declare my words the other night arose from the overheating of a fanciful brain. Let me ask you in all candor, and despite the fact that all my guests saw nothing, did I not perceive at the last banquet, just prior to lapsing into unconsciousness, and at the moment you stroked your hair from your left temple, vapor or smoke ascend into the air from under the covering on your head?' 'Truly thou speakest, Oh mighty king', replied I, 'and a resolution long since made and never broken by me shall be placed at thy service—a vow I made to reward the man who retains his intellect under wine long enough to perceive in what manner I prevent my mind getting under its influence. Make your wish, Oh noble Pharaoh! think long and well, mighty Cheops! ponder upon whatever is dearest to thy valiant heart, for its granting shall be thine.'

" 'That will need no waste of time, not one moment's deliberation,' answered the king in return, ' for there is one desire of mine that stands so paramount as to dwarf all others to insignificancy. Far-famed is my country's greatness; renowned above all else upon earth is my land's magnificence; the kings of the world bend to me in submission and obeisance. But all is transitory. Of the epochs of civilization that have appeared and departed, following each other in brief succession since the advent of man ; of the eras of monarchial-like governments that have come and gone since the world began ; of the series of kingdoms and empires of royal splendor that have arisen and fallen in the gone-by ages, all are forgotten— all have crumbled to oblivion amid the wrecking tramp of ensuing events, along the effacing march of succeeding consummations ; everyone has passed into obliteration adown the long vista of the departed aeons of years. Between the far past then and the present now all have been lost in the engulfing swirl of time, in the revolving wear of the periods of enlightened man's existence; not one enduring record remains ; they have come and gone e'en like the waves of the deep sea, and as each foamy-crested lave is swept upon the shore and drawn back again, as much impression rests upon the sands as remains of ancient empires and their rulers after a few miserable hundreds of years. What is left of them to awaken wonder and inquiry; what denotive of their influence; what suggestive of their power, skill, glory and opulence; what to excite investigation or call forth the antiquary to delve beneath the surface, uncover and bring to light evidences of the civilization of past and forgotten ages! My desire—and how oft I have pondered upon it and bewailed the incompetency of puny mankind I need not dwell upon to thee, to such an one as thou, who hast walked the realms of endlessness, beyond the threshold of mathematically considered infinity—is to leave behind me an unalterable record of my reign, something of more permanence than written rolls and plates of metal that war and years obliterate; to bequeath a memento of Egypt's greatness while I ruled it; a monument expressive of its wealth, art, high civilization and power of accomplishment, an unperishing memorial that could never again be paralleled, such to endure for all the countless years to come, to last for all immeasurable futurity, a wonderful structure of awe-inspiring dimensions that should never cease to be, and over the majestic grandeur of which the suns of centuries shall rise and fall until time shall be no more; something to remain for all eternity, in witness for nations yet to come, as evidence of my magnificence, power and skill. Our people mummify the dead; and when of royal lineage, or of illustrious name or eminence gained through merit, are enclosed for their last limitless rest in mounds of stone of greater or less cost and beauty, according to their standing, wealth or the love of their descendants or of their fellow-men. I shall follow the custom of my race; but for my sepulcher— for the king of king's sovereign mausoleum—I would erect a monument of stone so vast and enduring as to continue unconsumed into the boundless ocean of forever; to outlast all the universe's aggregation of cycles, and be a record in itself to succeeding empires and races of the glorious and wonderful reign of Pharaoh over a marvelous and all-conquering people. I would build my monarchal tomb of stone, an uncostly substance, so not to excite the cupidity of possible future conquerers of this land and cause its destruction for plunder. I would erect a pyramid of wondrous proportions, rear it aloft with blocks of stone of size so large no army of vandals, no nation of ruthless destroyers, could ever move in their barbarous endeavors to mutilate for the base human pleasure of injuring a work of art exhibiting the original ideas, labor and accomplishments of others. Such is my desire; but of such huge dimensions, so immense and weighty must the separate stones be to prevent wanton tearing down, to avoid envious despoliation, that mankind's strength does not exist sufficient to move and place them in position. My wish is a means to succeed in this, if thou wilt grant it, O mystic stranger.'

"'Nothing easier, mighty Pharaoh,' replied I, and taking from the pocket of my Egyptian dress my handkerchief, the same one of which only the remaining half you now see, or anyone else has seen for that matter for several thousand years,' continued the stranger retrospectively, smoothing his hands over it as it lay still outstretched before him on the table. 'I tore half of it away, touched him on the lips with the half I then gave him and advised him that whenever he wished any great weight lifted to blow the cloth full of air in the shape of a bubble about as large as a closed hand, tie a stout string around the end so that it would appear as though enclosing a ball, tie the string to the heavy object, and the ball ascending would lift within a few pounds' weight the heft of whatever it was secured to.

"'I see you do not quite grasp my meaning,' said the stranger, noticing a blank, incomprehensible look on my ancestor's face. 'You see, whenever Pharaoh wished to lift any object, however heavy, all he had to do was to attach the ball to the top of it; the ball straightway went upward like a balloon, and such was its curious power that if an object weighed a hundred pounds, the ball lifted ninety of them, leaving but the force needed to lift ten pounds necessary to be exerted; the same with

UNIV. OF
CALIFORNIA

THE SPHINX AND PYRAMIDS OF EGYPT.

any immense weights, no matter how heavy, on being secured to the ball they would weigh but the ten pounds mentioned. So you see, by means of the ball fastened to the bung, a child could have carried in the hollow of its hand, held over its head, the Heidelberg tun, plumb full, and that cask is so large, as you probably have seen, that it took the entire vintage of three years to fill. Pharaoh thanked me kindly, not, indeed, as a king, but as a child securing the toy of its dreams—man is, as you know, but a grown-up child, with but larger and more complex playthings—descended the hill and returned to the shore, where, entering the barge, he stretched forth his arm, waived me a dignified and respectful farewell and departed.

"'Urgent affairs requiring my immediate and particular attention elsewhere prevented me from again visiting Egypt until years after, when happening to be on the west bank of the Nile, around in the vicinity of Gizeh, I noticed that the Pharaoh Cheops had the pyramids and Sphinx well along in building, and then I saw that my gift was working like a charm; immense stones had been cut and dressed at the quarries, the ball attached to the top of a chain fastened around them and each one conveyed to a flat-boat in the Nile, and when the boat was loaded with them to the height of its carrying or containing number, to the limit of its holding capacity, the two ends of mighty chains fastened to the sides of the barge were joined over the tops of the heap of stones, the ball fastened to the summit of the chains, where all were brought together, and then you see, as the whole caboodle (vessel, load, men in it, oars and all) only weighed ten pounds and sat like a plank on the river, practically displacing no water, that the boat was rowed very swiftly to the place of disembarkation, where they were taken in bullock carts to the pyramid's site, a very appropriate level space of the Libyan chain, in the same manner as from the quarries to the Nile. You can also see that it was no trouble at all to pull them up slides and troughs of wood to their places in the growing monuments; and if a mighty block of stone did not quite fit its place a man at each end took hold, lifted, and held it up while numerous stone-dressers worked at the sides and underneath to smooth it.

"'So skillfully, industriously and faithfully worked these artisans at their craft that when the enormous stones were finally set in their places, so nicely were they approximated and finished off that one could not discern where they were joined. As soon as one was in its final resting place the ball was released and sent down for the next, and immediately another stone was in the act of ascending, and I assure you that after the Sphinx and the great Pyramid were completed, sand-papered and polished off, they looked for all the world as though they had been carved each from an immense mountain of solid stone,' concluded the stranger again filling the goblets.

"My ancestor cast covetous eyes upon the remaining half of the handkerchief, and wild schemes of future renown whirled through his head, and his hand made an involuntary motion as though to grasp it, but he suppressed the movement almost before it was perceptible; not liking to take more of the stranger, and soon feeling that he had already been favored so greatly, was quite ashamed that for an instant his deep interest in the story and his excitement had gotten the better of his lofty sense of honorable conduct and gentlemanship, of both of which he was ever the height.

"'I see by your countenance', remarked the stranger, 'that you have some desire you wish to accomplish, and I noticed a moment ago that you would fain possess yourself of the remainder of my handkerchief. What is it you wish? In this life you are as well aware as I that one who does not ask has faint chances of receiving.'

"'I have a great desire, indeed', replied the commander, 'of as long a standing as the length of my connection with the army, the army of my own ruler of Aufburg's firm ally, King Frederick, and the knowledge of being able to accomplish it—an achievement reflected upon for years—by means of the handkerchief flitting through my mind made me make an uncontrolable movement to grasp it. I have long exhausted the resources of military science in endeavors to promulgate a plan by which I could quickly move my ordnance along with my troops, for should I engender such an invention, my regiment would at once be singled out by the sharp eye of the ever-watchful Frederick and become the pride of the army. When after heavy rains the roads are muddy and cut up by a marching army, most trying indeed it is to the spirits and strength of my soldiers to pull, push, and shove, and drag their five big heavy cannon through miles on miles of deep bog, slush and sticky mud. Could I get the means of transporting my artillery without trouble, thus relieving the men, what an appearance they could cut on parade, plenty of leisure to shine up their uniforms, arms and accouterments, instead of plenty of hard labor and toil getting them dirty. Our victories are always neutralized by the enemy in retreat moving as fast, if not faster, than our pursuing victorious army, as disorderly bodies generally out-travel orderly ones. Although the pursuers have the elation of success to carry them on, the fugitives have the strong sentiment of fear and the incentive of terror to lubricate their knee joints and urge their forward movements. The fleeing also cast away their arms and accouterments, and even all clothing that is superfluous, to lighten their footsteps, and our cannon being stuck in the mud, and usually of course at the rear end of our pursuing army, are ineffective.

"'If I could get my artillery to the fore and open with shot and shell on the rear of the flying mass I am sure I'd give the miserable hound invaders of our land such a lesson that they would see how soon they could be able to collect themselves and come at us again. A victory is but half won if a vigorous and energetic pursuit of the defeated does not follow it to disorganize the enemy. Frederick has never been defeated, though such overwhelming numbers of the allies are so often pitted against him. Should our ordnance be captured it would of course be only after the last man was slain; but so used are the allies to flight, and so much do they expect it as a part of their combats with Frederick, that they always keep a bunch of files tied to each cannon to spike it in case of having to flee (which latter is, by the way, the usual outcome). Frederick's soldiers had to have this explained to them on capturing cannon, that the enemy just before flight drove the pointed end of a file deep in the cannon's touch-hole, and then broke the end off in there to prevent us turning their own heavy guns to instant use against themselves.'

"'The handkerchief alone would have been but of little use to you. However', said the stranger, 'here it is.' And grasping my ancestor's right hand tightly with his left one, with his other he pressed the cloth firmly into it. 'Now, first make a well-cooked apple dumpling, using the handkerchief for its cover, and whenever you wish to move your five pieces of ordnance, strap their wheels together, tie the dumpling firmly on top of the barrel of the center one, and you will find that a single horse can draw them all with perfect ease and comfort over the deepest and thickest mud in all the fatherland, which is saying a great deal, as you seem well aware.'

"My ancestor placed the handkerchief carefully and securely away in his deep inside coat pocket, and while his attention was distracted from the stranger in doing this he suddenly heard outside in the quiet night of the street, the sudden swish of a spiked tail against the side of the building near the high windows, and then a clatter of cloven hoofs galloping over the paving-stones of the street, flying away and dying in the distance. My ancestor put his hand to his temple, and on actually finding a screw there, turned toward the stranger with outstretched arms to thank him, when behold he was gone— had utterly disappeared, to my ancestor's deep wonderment, for the windows were barred so closely and heavily that not even a rabbit could have escaped that way.

"After examining the door and finding it still strongly bolted, just as he had left it, my ancestor took a light and searched every nook and crevice of the room, but no aperture large enough to admit a mouse could be found; the cellar being, as I told you, in one side of the foundation of an old fortified monastery, with walls of stone, six and eight feet thick and having been in use during its peaceful days for storing the vintages of the surrounding fields. My ancestor could scarce believe his senses for quite a time, and upon reaching across the table and out of curiosity seizing the stranger's goblet, finding a pale bluish vapor arise therefrom and a slight smell of brimstone becoming perceptible in the air, he had his suspicions of the stranger's identity pretty well confirmed; resolved to keep his own counsel, hailed the attendants to care for his still sleeping compatriots and took his departure just as a faint light in the eastern sky showed that the darkness of the night would soon be dispelled.

"He was ever very reticent about the subject, as you can well see from the very little we could ever glean from him about it, and when questioned thereupon by any of his descendants always became very pensive and thoughtful, much to our regret, for more particulars would have been very interesting. But the commander was ever glad that the stranger had not asked his name, and disliked to relate much of what had occurred for fear the stranger might get to know who he was and take revenge for a shabby trick one of the commander's ancient ancestors, Baron Gustavus von Vielbeer, had played on the stranger just six hundred and twenty-four years ago this very year.

"Well, it was after this event that the commander achieved such military glory that his name resounded all over Germany. The commander did about the apple dumpling as he had been instructed, and prepared it carefully the very next day on joining his command, which he lead at Kremzburg a few days later, and during the night before that famous battle (it was a night fitting for his purpose, dark, rainy and mud to your waist) tied the dumpling to his artillery in the manner he had been informed to do, and moved it without the least inconvenience along with his regiment to a woody heights on the left flank of the allies.

"The commander then went alone as near to their campfires as he dared, to spy out their position, and ran suddenly right against the enemy's wagon that contained the demijohns of wine. The commander immediately attacked the two soldiers in charge of it, deeply wounding them both and breaking his sword short off at the hilt in the encounter, took the dumpling out of his pocket, quickly tied it to the front of the wagon, got alongside the tongue, took firm hold and made off afoot like the wind toward his own men and would have escaped in the darkness without the following commotion and all the subsequent glory it occasioned had not just then the clouds moved away and daylight breaking discovered him to the enemy.

"The enemy's whole brigade of four regiments recognizing in an instant their refreshment conveyance, seeing it rapidly disappearing, and realizing the fearful disaster its theft would cause to fall on them, as well as the depressing effect its loss would occasion on the spirits of their whole army, at once pursued with loud cries, fearing to shoot, else their bullets would work irreparable damage to the wine vessels, in which I can commend their prudence," soliliquized Vielbeer. "Each one strove to be first at the rescue. The commander of course made for the woods where his regiment lay concealed and which point the enemy's own artillery commanded, but well they knew that no cannon of ours could by any manner of means be there, as all ordnance had been stuck fast and immovable in mud for days.

"My ancestor was fleet of foot and in order to awaken the zeal of his soldiers shouted as he came running on, 'Hurrah, refreshments! refreshments! hurrah!' to inform them of the substance of the load he was attempting to convey into their midst. This had an immediate effect on the alacrity of his command, and berloom-blungboom-berloom! opened our artillery over my ancestor's head, carrying havoc to the pursuers, and sweeping the enemy's left flank like wild fire. Then a loud, joyful and exultant hurrah! from the eleven hundred deep beer voices of the command, as my ancestor pulled in with all his capture safe and sound, was mistaken by the pursuers of the commander for the whole army of Frederick being in the woods, having executed a flank movement, and they turned and fled in the wildest panic straight back to their army which caught the contagion.

"As the day getting brighter, great Frederick, ever watchful, and quick to see a situation, opened on them with all his available cannon. Disordered, confused and appalled they wavered. Frederick's cavalry immediately took advantage of their plight and charged their cannon so suddenly that they fell back from them like chaff flying before a blast. The king's infantry at once crossed the space between the two armies in pursuit, seized the cannon and turned them on the enemy's center with fearful effect. The cavalry went after and cut down the the right wing, while my ancestor's artillery played on their left, and in a complete rout they were sent flying away beyond the border. The stores captured, arms taken and prisoners secured were immense. And that was the end of the Seven Years War, for the allies never recovered and at once sued for peace.

"It was three days later that the immortal Frederick, in the presence of the whole army, made the commander's regiment his imperial bodyguard, and calling up my ancestor in view of all, embraced him, and with tears in his eyes said, 'Take away the whole of my brave and unparalleled army; take away the last ship of my brilliant and glory-covered navy; take away all I have, everything I possess, but leave me my commander, the noble Baron Marverdt von Vielbeer, behind me with a cannon, plenty of powder and sufficient balls, and I will strike a warlike attitude, draw my sword, wave it in challenge over my head and defy the world.'

"That is what Great Frederick said. My ancestor also, after peace was declared, became renowned throughout the land as far south as the Danube river for his capacity for drinking wine. I believe that he made a bet once that he would out-drink the whole Potsdamer council of seventy-five burghers at a sitting, and captured the bet without getting the least sparkle in his eye; and all the other ventures he ever undertook were prosperous and successful beyond his wildest dreams, so much so that he was just swimming in wealth all the time; and on being invited to the court of Komwecht, fell deeply in love with my great grandmother of sainted memory, then the young Princess Christina Marienchen Hedwig Wilhelmina, of that royal house, married her, and as I never heard anything to the contrary, I suppose lived very happy with her.

"One night, however, there came a fearful thunderstorm over Germany. The wind blew in hurricanes, lightning flashed and thunder crashed as though the very heavens were being smashed against each other in contention; immense forest trees that had stood for ages were uprooted and thrown far away; the rain fell in floods, and vast sections of the black forest were laid low and washed to the valleys all over the lower provinces. Well, that night, during this terrific thunderstorm my ancestor disappeared and was never seen afterward — not the least trace of him could be found, nor was he ever heard of although minute search was made in every wine celler in all Germany, from Memel to Saarbruck, until thirty years afterward in one of the deep vaulted cellars of Vielbeer castle there was discovered a glowing light in one of the distant dark recesses. On close inspection it was seen to be a moldy decaying ball about the size of an apple dumpling, which gave forth a faint phosphorescent glow that lighted up a grewsome object lying alongside, which object on investigation proved to be a skull, in the left temple of which was a hole in which was skillfully fitted a small silver thumb-screw. On attempting to handle the ball it crumbled at the first touch to dust which seemed to melt away on the stone floor and disappear, emitting a faint sulphurous odor. Although the whole castle was searched and all my ancestor's papers and archives carefully and thoroughly perused, we never could get any more information or light upon the mysterious occurrence," said Vielbeer, showing by his tone of voice that he had concluded.

"But about that shabby trick, Vielbeer, how was that?" we all asked eagerly, let us hear that.

"That has nothing whatever to do with the narrative I have just completed," replied he.

"Let us have it anyway," we all answered in unison.

"No; I'll sing a song now, I have such a beautiful one in my mind. It goes:

"Was ist das leben ohne bier,
　　Alles hangt daran,
　Sehr wenige yahre sind wir hier,
　　Ich sage oft, Herr Mann.

"Nur einmal kommt's zu jederkerl
　　Die schoene herz liebe treu,
　Und der wo nicht * * * *"

At this juncture Schnurkelyah raised his head into the air from off my lap and elevating his nose toward the ceiling emitted two or three prolonged, mournfully resigned wailing howls, as he always did on hearing his master begin singing.

Vielbeer with much good humor showing from his face looked down at Schnurkelyah in my lap and teasingly continued:

"Who loves not smoke, beer and song,
　He stays a fool his whole life long."

"Song be cursed," said several; "let us hear that other story."

"No," replied Vielbeer, "I am much like my ancestor in that regard, quiet, close mouthed and taciturn, and I never like to put our family's former splendor forward, nor like their valiant and heroic deeds to recount; it isn't gentlemanly like."

"But give us a short outline, Vielbeer, like you have of the others," said all together.

"Well, that little I will of course do, as you all request it. You all well know that in the fourth century one of my very ancient ancestors, Centavus Vielbeer, assisted Monk Monastus in an interview with the Forty Saints, which was productive of so much benefit to the dwellers in the small hamlet of Koln (Cologne — the Colonia Agrippina of the Romans), on the western bank of the Rhine, that the village built the worthy monk a chapel of stone. The building which stood for nine hundred years, or until the thirteenth century, contained in front a large prayer-room or service chamber, and at the back numerous stone cells for the monk and his worthy associates, in which to make their devotions, alone and unseen, or to reflect in silence and tranquility on the fleetness of this life, and prepare themselves, and with their fervent prayers others, for the one to come; or from which they could be summoned by the inhabitants at all hours to go forth on their charitable missions of mercy.

"When the holy monk finally died he was laid to rest in the little garden adjoining the building, among the flowers and shrubs in the midst of which he so loved to wander in his moments of leisure and recreation. Some day in the far off years to come I may find time to tell you all a little something about the monk, to give you a short account of his times as laid down upon the skin tablets prepared during the fourth century by my ancient ancestor Centavus Vielbeer, now among the very early records and archives in the vaults of Vielbeer castle. But for the present it has but little to do, and that little in a somewhat indirect way, with the shabby trick my ancestor, Gustavus Vielbeer, played on the devil now nearly seven hundred years ago.

"Well you must remember that in the year 1242, the wealthy burghers of the city of Cologne, at that date grown into a large, important and properous town, meeting in council, decided unanimously to tear down the old chapel—erected nine hundred years before for the monk, and which had been occupied by his sect ever since, a structure representative of a by-gone and rude architecture, now fast falling to pieces—and replace on its site a lofty building for worship, a cathedral which should be of a design entirely new and original, differing from any edifice in existence, and a work of great perfection, which by its beauty and grace should be the admiration and marvel of the world and attract men of learning and science to the city as the seat of an art culture showing itself capable of engendering such a production, a structure that would be, on the site of his grave as well as that of his old chapel, symbolistic of their love and veneration for him, and that would be worthy to commemorate forever their gratitude to the holy monk, whose bones had been dust for nine hundred years.

"The burghers caused the report of the council's decision to be spread far and wide, asking for plans for such a building as they wished for, setting the day to receive and inspect them a good year off, to allow all architects to compete who were willing; and the greatest in all the surrounding land, as well as those of distant countries, exerted their talents to the utmost, and many were the plans sent to them. At the expiration of the year, on the day set for inspection, the worthy burghers met again in council and opened the many rolls received. All were good and of worth; many meritorious and beautiful edifices were depicted; but of them all not one was entirely original. All of them were in some parts copies of already existing structures. One architect had taken a nave and its carved arched columns from the church of this distant city; another had copied the front from the abbey of that foreign land; another had drawn the windows and steeples from so and so, a remote towns minster, and his beautifully interlacing arches and his flying buttresses from a monastery of a certain other far off country; and still another had used the spiral-columned arcade of such and such a distant cathedral, the cornices of this convent, the towers of that way-off castle; and some had mingled Doric, Ionic, Corinthian, Gothic, Tuscan, and other styles of architecture all together, and so on; none were in their entirety new, and as the greatest architects of the world had competed, the worthy burghers despaired of ever getting better.

"Supposing that all architectural ideas and science inherent in mankind in building had long since been exhausted, and nothing new or different could be brought to light, they decided to examine the plans received thoroughly, weigh them deeply in mind, and select the one found most appropriate to met their city's wishes. One night, during the weeks the deliberation among the council was going on, some hours after midnight, all outside being as black as pitch, or even blacker, if such could be, the abbot or superior father of the ancient chapel was awakened from his priestly and refreshing slumbers by a loud rapping at the door, and on opening it admitted a young man of pale face and delicate mold whom he recognized as a young architect of the city, who asked to be closeted with him in secrecy for a moment. The priest, after closing the door, led the way to a deep cell, and on setting his light into a niche in the wall turned in inquiry to the young architect who began:

"'Father,' said he, 'this midnight, when passing through the deep, dark woodland, being attracted thither as the gloomy surroundings seemed in keeping with my present spirits, lowered in melancholy and dejection at the knowledge that my plan, on which I have labored diligently and earnestly for the year, being numbered among those the council this day refused to consider farther, while walking in the dense woods with slow steps and bowed head, I was suddenly accosted by a stranger in a long, black-hooded cloak, which reached from his neck to heels; all parts of him were concealed save his face, on which a sardonic grin was portrayed; he carried a flaming pine torch and a roll of parchment as long as himself. I noticed, also, as he politely requested me to step back with him to beside the body of a giant oak, that he left cloven tracks in the ground he passed over; on arriving at the oak he unrolled the parchment and exhibited to my astonished eyes a plan of an immense cathedral, something so new, and of such original drawings and ideas, of a design so beautiful, of such noble, graceful and enchanting proportions, that I stood gazing at it with outstretched hands, unable to speak, almost perfectly deprived of mind in wonder and admiration. It was such a marvel of perfect loveliness and shapely elegance that I was rooted to the spot and speechless. Seeing my attitude toward the vision, the stranger's very eyes seemed to emit light, his sardonic grin deepened, and he said, "'Tis thine, for thy and thine posterity's souls for a thousand years."

"'No offer would he entertain in any manner, shape, or form, although I exhausted the resources of my linguistic capabilities in the endeavor. No other compensation would he listen to. I, even, finally losing hope of securing it for myself, spoke of the gold the burghers would give for it; he would none of it; would hear of nothing else but an acceptance or rejection of his proposition made at the start. So I asked for time for deliberation before paying such a price, and he granted it for a sun's turning, agreeing to meet me again at the oak at midnight of the morrow. I have come at once to you, father, for the price is too much to pay, although most anything is worth sacrificing to gain the plan. Being the architect of such an edifice as was shown me would cause my name and that of my posterity to be remembered in glory forever. Undying fame shall be mine. On leaving him I at once hastened to you.'

"'And well you did, my son, ere agreeing to such an unholy and nefarious scheme. It smacks of the infernal one, or much I am mistaken. But outwit him we will', observed the wily priest. 'Do but hold thy tongue and meet him as appointed tomorrow night. I will give thee a charm along to counteract his evil ways and render thee safe from harm. Ask again to see the plan, to inspect it more minutely, and when the chance offers and he holds it lightly, tear it quickly out of his hands and make swiftly off with it. With the charm he cannot harm thee. But stay, he may pursue, and attacking thee, recover it; alone, and appalled as thou mayest be, awed by the silence and darkness of the forest and by his affrighting presence. Take along some stout friend with thee', craftily continued the priest, 'some one thou knowest and can rely upon; who would not meanly lay claim by reason of his help to a large share of the gain and glory, the profit, fame and renown that will be thine should the venture succeed', continued the intellectually deep and far-seeing successor of the ancient monk; 'some one of courage and bravery who would but love such an adventure tasting of danger and deviltry. Canst call to mind such?' asked the priest.

"'That can I', replied the young architect. 'I will take along my friend Baron Gustavus von Vielbeer, a roistering young blade who would jump at such an adventure, particularly as it speaks of dangerous complications, something he chases after. He has been going to the devil as fast as he can the past few years, and I will now bring him to his Satanic majesty all at once and thus save my friend Gustavus much future troublous search. And should his Satanic majesty, after losing his plan as well as his prospective souls, wax wroth, I will set Vielbeer at him, and much I warrant that the Evil One will soon find his hands full. I misdoubt not that he of the sardonic smile will, soon after coming in whack with Vielbeer, offer me still another plan to call my champion off.'

"'Tis well', replied the priest. 'Vielbeer, since thou mentionest him, I now call well to mind, and although sad do I feel at the much I have long heard of the young man's ungodlike ways and carryings-on, still safely does it beseem me that with him thou goest in good hands for such an occasion as this one.'

"The priest then took up the light from the niche in the wall and opening the door of the cell was followed by the young architect to the chamber of worship; and ascending the steps leading to the altar, on reaching the holy place, took therefrom a bone of the little finger of Saint Ursula.

"'Take this, my son', said the priest, dismissing him at the front entrance, 'and when in the presence of the Infernal One, and you come to strife, hold the sacred relic far out at arm's length toward him, and all the powers of evil cannot harm thee or e'en come within the guard of the consecrated memorial thou holdest.'

"So at dusk the next evening two briskly stepping young men, the architect and my ancestor, might have been seen making gallant strides in the direction of and toward the forest. On arriving at the great oak my ancestor drew his blade, cut a few slashes in the air, that made the wind whistle, to feel satisfied that the suppleness of his wrist was in proper trim, and hid himself among the thick underbrush behind the forest monarch, while the young architect paced the ground to and fro in front of it, to while away the slowly expiring moments and calm his anxious soul and eager appearing demeanor, for the stake was great; its gain or loss meant all in all to him. The moments sped on, the moon fell and intense blackness supervened. Punctual to the second he of the cloven foot appeared, again with his flaming torch and giant roll, and seemingly in much good humor, foreseeing in the return of the young architect the acceptance of his proposition.

"'Let me view the plan once again', asked the young architect, 'to see that my vision of yesternight was not all fancy. I would look once more after a day of cool comparisons turning in my judgement.'

"The stranger again politely unrolled the great parchment and the young architect made as though minutely examining it. At this moment my ancestor ready to spring out to the relief of his companion, rustled slightly by accident the underbrush among which he was concealed, and this attracting the instant notice and attention of the stranger, the young architect suddenly snatched the plan from out his grasp and backed away just as Vielbeer rushed from the thicket and made to his companion's protection. The stranger, on perceiving the oncoming new-comer, threw his torch to the earth where it remained brightly flaring, drew from his girdle behind him an arrow-pointed, four-pronged, great iron fork; whereupon Vielbeer drew his blade and at it they went, the stranger's grin broadening to his ears as he contemplated his easy victory; but as the weapons flew faster and faster and struck from each other showers of sparks which soared upward all about and lit up the surrounding deep shadows, and overhanging boughs and dense foliage, his grin lessened and lessened until finally having received a wound in his right hand he transferred his fork to his left one, and his smile disappearing entirely his face took on an awful and deeply profane expression; his eyes rolled and flashed in hatred and he used language so fearfully terrible that the young architect's very bones shivered, and having no weapon of offense or defense he hastily and involuntarily moved some distance away.

"Vielbeer played so industriously that soon the stranger's hood and gown were cut to shreds and fell from him entire, leaving him revealed in all his satanic blackness, horns, spiked tail, cloven hoofs and all, until finally, by a dextrous masterstroke and expert twist of the wrist, Vielbeer sent the stranger's four-pronged fork flying

away out of his hand, it alighting some distance off, almost at the feet of the young architect. The stranger then brought his tail into play and tried with it to get within my ancestor's guard and puncture him with its spiked, harpoon point-like end, but my ancestor at once gave it such a whack with his sword as made the sparks fly and caused some exceedingly uncultured language to emerge from his antagonist's lips. This last weapon of the stranger's then being returned to where it belonged, behind him, my ancestor, at the sword's point then backed him to the body of the giant oak and ran his blade through his stomach and well into the tree and thus pinning him to the sturdy monarch, with his free arm he then spun him around on the blade like a whirligig or revolving wheel until the fire shining from his eyes and mouth looked like a complete flaming circle, and until the echoes awoke with his terrific fiendish howlings. Eventually withdrawing his sword and allowing his antagonist to drop at the tree's foot in a heap, Vielbeer said, 'Now hustleth! get ye gone at once and let's no more of ye.'

"The cloven hoof picked himself up and emitting blood-curdling oaths, rushed as swiftly as lightning to where his fork lay near the feet of the architect, picked it up and made for the unprotected young man still standing some distance away from my ancestor. The young architect perceiving his swift-footed oncoming had just time to raise his arm and hold out toward him the Saint Ursula's finger bone, on seeing which the cloven hoof grew furious; his mouth emitted bluish fiery vapors to such an extent that the whole forest smelled of sulphur, and he danced in fury up and down, gnashing his teeth, and waving and charging with his fork, running around and around the architect looking for an opening; but the young man kept turning around with him, constantly facing him, letting him whirl around him, like the hands of a clock, many times in a circle, but always keeping presented to his front and holding out to him at arm's length the sacred relic.

All this happened as swiftly as a whirlwind and occurred

during the time Vielbeer, heavily booted and naturally slower of foot than his Satanic majesty, was rushing to his friend's rescue. Just as he arrived to his companion's succor the Evil One made a last desperate grab for the roll. The young architect drew it instantly aside, but not before the cloven hoof had seized hold of the end of the plan, and the young architect pulling it backward had caused to be torn off the extreme top of the parchment, which remained in the cloven foot's hands; then backing away from the two companions he cursed my ancestor loudly, rapidly and thoroughly, vowing he would haunt him and his descendants to the thousandth generation; vowed that the cathedral should never be completed, and finally vowed that the young architect's name should, at his death, be forgotten and remain forever unknown, ran and picked up his shreddy garment and still flaming torch, and with a last terrific, demoniacal, wailing howl disappeared in the deep forest.

"The two companions at once betook themselves to the city, and at daylight, on investigating the plan, found that the Evil One had torn off the upper part of the two beautiful towers, which were of course positioned at the top of the roll and which part he had secured hold of as he grasped at it. When the plan was shown to the burghers in council that very day, as the work of the young architect, they were absolutely astounded that anything so beautiful could be engendered in and emanate from a human mind, and perfectly captivated at its beauty, and trusting to the young architect's promise of replacing the drawing of the upper portion of the towers, which, he explained, he had lost merely through a sudden and unforseen accident the night before, they immediately and unanimously decided to adopt it, and at once ordered its erection. The old chapel, fast falling into ruins, was vacated by the priests and demolished, the stones used in making the new edifice's foundation, upon which ground-work, as the years rolled on, one of the noblest specimens of Gothic architecture in Europe, and the most beautiful and graceful edifice in the world, the Cathedral of Cologne, arose — all finished entire except to where the upper third of the two large front spir-

CALIFORNIA

THE CATHEDRAL OF COLOGNE.

ing towers began, and there the architect, now grown old, stopped; he could go no farther; had never in all those years spent in the construction of the building since his youth been able to devise a design to complete the airy, graceful and lofty towers that would at all agree or be in harmony and keeping with the part of them already completed and with the lovely grace of the rest of the cathedral; and no one could help him out with any idea or plan. There the work on the beautiful world-famed edifice ended. Designs and plans and drawings by the many had drawn the aged architect in all the by-gone years; ever trying to search his memory of the spires as he had beheld them on the roll in the cloven hoof's presence. But in vain.

"All work was suspended, the whole land awaited his untiring efforts. Years rolled on, until finally the Huns threatened an invasion into Germany; there was an instant rush to arms, and into the southern countries to forestall it, and during the long wars and dissentions which followed, the architect died, the archives and records of the building were lost or destroyed by the many ransackings and plunderings the town and its cathedral were subjected to, by first one enemy or set of conquerors, and then another. And when peace again entered the land, after years of turmoil, strife and devastation, accounts came of great reverses to the armies of the Soldiers of the Cross in Palestine, and at this news the knights of entire Christendom, German, Huns, and all, dropped their private quarrels and united again in the attempt to retake the Holy Land from the grasp of the infidel; and at the close of the great struggle and return of the vast armies, and tranquility settled once more upon the land after a space of nearly a century, all records had been long lost and forgotten, and so the Cologne Cathedral has stood as it was then left the day work was stopped, and so it stands today; never has been completed, and the name of the architect is unknown. And the devil, as all of you are well aware, has hung to our family with great persistency and tenacity ever since", concluded Vielbeer with a proud, grandiloquent and slowly waving flourish of his old pipe right before our attentive faces.

CHAPTER VII.

AT this juncture a confounded rumpus was heard at the front door, and soon in at the entrance came a noisy crowd of young men, all wearing the uniform caps of the Maikaefer club (pronounced my-ca-fer), the body of the cap a dark green, with a band of yellow around the rim. They carried with them a long, slender, yellow-trimmed green leather rapier case, and also a little leather satchel of the same colors containing the protective dueling paraphernalia, and it was evident that a duel was on the tapis.

In Germany, where the whole nation is of a military stamp and soldierly cast, nearly everyone is uniformed. The country resembles a vast arsenal, or does so to us over here where uniforms are so rarely seen. Everywhere over the Teuton nation you hear the tramp, tramp of the military. Even the school-boys have their military caps, and each grade a different one in shape or colors, so that one can tell at a glance which school a boy attends, and what grade he is in. This takes the place largely of discipline for an untractable or indolent youth. He is merely lowered in grade and has to stand the jokes of his companions, and endure the shame of appearing among his town-folks as a big lubberly fellow in a baby grade or class; and the incentive among the whole school is by industry and application to secure for wearing as high a grade cap as they can. This method of degrading has been found to answer better than any other plan yet devised. So all the school-boys, wearing uniform caps, are added to the rest of those of the nation in military dress.

The Universities, assuming their students are men and gentlemen, exercise in consequence not the least supervision or control over them, hold no roll-call and no recitations, and of course have no uniform. The members of the faculty lecture and demonstrate as their several hours come according to the curriculum, and the lecture goes on if but a single student is present. Some professors are popular, and their lecture-rooms are crowded with eager, ardent, attentive faces, while other lecturers have ever but a sprinkling of listening ears and absorbing minds in their amphitheater while holding forth. This plan is necessary in a great city like Berlin, the seat of so much science and deep learning. Many thousand students attend the University, great numbers from foreign and from distant lands, every nation on the earth being represented in numbers more or less large; and many students, some of them aged men, white-haired and bent, are attending but two or three professors' lectures for special purposes of their own.

To an American mind the word student usually conveys the meaning of a young man at an academy or college. Far different in Germany; many gray heads attend the University; one, while I was there, came to take his degree from some place in the south of Africa. He was seventy-five years of age and came back from where he had lived for fifty years to get a diploma from the University. The professors addressed him as "worthy colleague," and the students as "Papakin," a word indicative of respectful and reverential endearment. Many literary men, whose names are already famous, deep in their coming books, take but one or two lectures to gather the material necessary to complete their works, and so on. The younger members of the University coming fresh from these boy schools and endeared by custom and long association to these colored caps, usually form themselves into clubs and again wear their beloved distinctive head dresses, or join an old club and adopt its colors. Their "colors" designate their caps. Asking a student in Berlin to "Name thy colors," is equivalent to requesting the name of the club to which he belongs. Of course all the young men know the colors of each and every club by heart; they learn that to perfection long before they absorb the first month's teaching, and great rivalry exists to be known as the first or second, etc., in standing among the clubs, to be known as the one containing the most distinguished members, or the one of greatest exclusiveness, or as the one having the highest general standing, etc.

It can readily be seen that our club, the Prussian Eagle, in its possession of Vielbeer posed on the summit of fame and occupied as high a position compared to the rest and stood out as prominently in the opinion of the city in contrast with the other clubs, as the name of Washington does among the other patriots of 1776 here in America.

No club has ever dared to question the Prussian Eagle's claim to supremacy since Vielbeer joined it fifty years ago. But the Baron's fame does not rest alone on his rich powers of story-telling, not by any manner of means; perish the infamous thought, that is the least of his many meritorious accomplishments. He has the eye of an eagle, and in the duels which so often take place among the members of the rival clubs, is chosen the umpire as often as he can be had, on account of his quick eye, which is so sure, and his marvelously good and true judgment, which never fails to satisfy all; and in all truth has never been known within the memory of the clubmen to have been questioned. No one has ever asked an appeal from his decision, so sure has always been his sight. In addition to the above highly esteemed qualification, he is the greatest beer-drinker in all Berlin, and the quantities of lager he can absorb at a sitting is a marvel to behold; glass after glass can be poured down without him ever showing the effect of it, and one wonders where in all the world it goes to. A heavy bet was once made by some members of our club, who had sized up Vielbeer's capacity pretty thoroughly, with some Asiatic fresh arrivals at the University, that the Baron could drink two great hogsheads of beer, containing a quantity many times his own cubic space, in an hour. The bet was, of course, eagerly taken; Vielbeer was located and approached with the subject in hand. The whole party adjourned to a brewery on the outskirts of the city, and the full hogsheads pointed out. Vielbeer demurred for a while on seeing the size of the vessels he was expected to empty, and not liking to risk his friends losing the bet, but finally asked for an hour's leave of absence to deliberate in and promising he would then return and decide.

In an hour he was back, told his friends to go ahead and close the bet, saying, "Yes, I will put myself at your disposal, for I can do it," started in and really got away with the very last drop of the lager long before the last minute of the hour had gone into the past. When asked, after the bet was paid, by the astonished assembled crowd, what had led him during that hour's deliberation to decide that he could do it, replied, "Oh, I didn't want to deliberate, that was merely an excuse to get away; I went right across the street to a rival brewery and tried it first, so I would be sure we would win the bet. Since that achievement any club dreaming of reaching the eminence held by the Prussian Eagle with a ten-foot pole would be liable to examination by a commission as to their sanity. The best club of Magen (pronounced mah-ghen) once sent a challenge up to the capital city to send down their best beer-drinking club for a match between them, the losers to pay for and present to the winners a golden cup, a tall vessel, the cup part being upheld by two draped female figures, a beautiful work lately finished by a Magen goldsmith. The challenge was naturally turned over to the Prussian Eagle club, which sent word in return that the matter was too small for them, as a body, to consider; that if that was the best offer the Mageners could make to the champion club of Berlin, it was almost an offense, and they had better have held their breath and saved it from useless waste. Had they said all Magen would drink against them the club might have considered it, but for just the club of Magen alone they would send one man down, a single member of the Prussian Eagle, to compete alone against them, and, of course, Vielbeer was shipped thither accompanied by Count Luft and Felderstein as his body-guard and matched alone against them, and long before four o'clock the next morning he had drank the whole Magen University under the table and was calling loudly for a keg or two more as a night-cap.

The joy of the Prussian Eagle at the depot, where all the members went to meet the victorious and triumphant return of the triumvirs, covered with glory, and by reflection covering the whole club and even the city of Berlin, and best of all, with the golden cup, the emblem of success in their possession, was a sight to behold, and welkin ringing was the shouts, and furious the demonstration. The champion, however, did not return in the palace car surrounded by all the comforts and luxuriance of ease that the defeated Mageners had placed at the three Prussian Eagles' disposal, but instead, on a dirty old flat-car, where he had to sit with his two friends and a large sack of sand on each side of him to prevent him rolling off, the whole way, not having been able to squeeze through the door of the elegant railroad carriage, and time being up the railroad officials at the last moment hauled out an old flat-car which the three took to and made the best advantage of they could.

Vielbeer's temper was by no means of the sweetest on being lifted down from his stiffened position by half a hundred willing hands, and let out the suppressed spleen of his long uncomfortable journey, and emitted his opinion of soulless corporations in no mild language. "The black, thundering devil take these infernal car-companies" said he, "they make plenty special cars for sleepers, plenty special cars for smokers, and have plenty special cars for ladies; they can also have a special car for fat people too, and be danged to them, the infernal apes; the next time they get fourteen thalers from me for a round-trip ticket to ride back home in the dust, cinders and hot sun like a stuffed pig they will know it, I tell you. No, not if they present me with a ticket and fourteen thalers beside," etc.

The golden cup has, of course, an honored and prominent position in the club-rooms, but not more so than many other unique trophies that Vielbeer's merits have brought to the club from victories during half a century. "My family always talk about my drinking," says he, "but no one thinks about my thirst. What a blessing from heaven is water," is one of his sayings, "for if we had no water we could make no beer."

The Maikaefer fellows crowded in at the door, talking and singing, and as it was about three o'clock in the morning by now, and they all were more or less gay and frolicsome, they had probably been having a night of it somewhere.

"Hello, there, Vielbeer! Hey, old boy! Whoop! How are you, old sod?" cried several rushing up and slapping him on the shoulders, much to his good-humored disgust.

"What do all these sheepsheads here and at this hour?" inquired he of his surrounding friends, every one of whom bewilderingly shook their heads in reply.

"I am on for a deadly duello with Hecht and Brun of the Maikaefers," calmly remarked Felderstein.

"How is that?" asked Vielbeer of Felderstein, who answered, "They both insulted me grievously on the open street the other day, and I challenged the two of them."

"Both for a single time?"

"Yes, both tonight, one after the other."

"That is bad," replied Vielbeer, "they are both seniors of their club, and I hear are the best swordsmen there."

Felderstein shrugged his shoulders, at the same time saying, "I'll take my chances."

Although this cutting and slashing of each other, and usually the breast and face, by the German "corps studenten" is looked upon in America as a species of coarse, low brutalism, it is viewed far differently in Teutonland. It is a long standing custom of the country, and an outgrowth and the remains of feudal days; and a country's custom, no matter how it may be looked at by outsiders, is an expression of its interior conditions, its surroundings and old 'associations, its people's natures, and of its soil. Like our present American cattle-herding cowboy —he is no part of the wooded East; he is a product of the treeless plains of the West.

The scars of these fights on the face are not viewed as a disfigurement in Germany; far from it. They are greatly admired by the ladies. Sentimental fair ones have been known to cry because the students fight protected by leather and not in armor as in the days of old, for the duello is all that remains of the days of chivalry — the long-past good old times of ribbon-streaming lance and glittering armor, when the new woman was unknown, and the olden time ones so conducted themselves as to be considered goddesses on earth; and brave knights, armed in suits of mail from head to heel, rode forth on gallant, prancing steeds to battle for their fair ladies' smiles. The duello is a degenerate relic of all this former gallantry. A student having two scars on his face is prouder than he who has but one, and one whose face is covered with scars struts and swaggers about the streets, the admiration of all his lady friends; and let a student but get his face to resemble a butcher's chopping block and he can, with perfect confidence, aspire to the hand of almost the highest daughter of the land, being reasonably trustful that to the girl at least he will appear as though surrounded by a halo.

In the photographs of the corps studenten or dueling students, of profile view, the side of the face, usually the left of course, containing the most scars is invariably taken. In America here a few scars on the face would be considered by the generality of the people as having been gained in some disgraceful manner, such as a low drunken brawl, etc. It is as you view it; it is the way a country's usages run.

Contrariwise, to strike a man a blow, to come to personal physical combat, which is prevalent even among the highest gentlemen of the United States, is, in Germany, held to be a kind of vulgar, barbarous rowdyism, excuseless except among the very lowest classes when besotting their cares and poverty in liquor; but a blow among German gentlemen is something almost unheard of, and its dust left on the clothing is only erased by apology or blood. Among the first things you hear from a compatriot in Germany is, "If you ever get into a fuss with any of these fellows over here just politely knock him down; they don't any of them know how to hit—don't know a thing about striking." It is all as you view it.

The Hindoostanee belles laughed immoderately on seeing the Christian ladies of our touring parties visiting their country wear rings in their ears. It was so funny to them; they had never seen the like; yet all their lives they had worn rings in their noses—a matter of course to them, but a method applied only to hogs and cattle among us. The Moslem thinks it sacrilegious to uncover in his house of worship, and remains with his head-dress on while at his devotions—while preventing his veneration for the prophet from getting rusty. What! bare his head in undignified arrogance before his Supreme Being's altar? Never! and considers us profane for removing our hats on entering church. All the same, before entering his mosque he takes off his shoes, while for all our American gentlemen to deposit their boots in a heap in the vestibule at the entrance, and enter church in their stocking feet would be regarded by us as a desecration of our house of worship, not saying anything about the chance that the foot-gear might all be stolen by some passing unchristian-like inclined or ungodly minded fellow; and those paying homage to the Divinity not only go in that way, but discover, on the conclusion of services, that they would also have to return home still in the same gentle and soft-shod manner.

Something like this only occurs among us amid the jack-rabbit, sunflower and prairie-dog lands of our West, when a bridegroom standing up at his marriage, and being requested to produce the wedding ring and on fumblingly searching his pockets learns that it has slipped through a hole down into one of his tight boots and on stepping aside and nervously removing the wrong one first and then the other, finding that he cannot get them back over his swollen feet, goes to the conclusion of the interrupted ceremony with them under his arm.

The wild Indian on swooping down into an unprotected border town and killing half a dozen women and children, and bringing back their scalps to his tribe would receive high honors from his people; it is the custom of his land; it is as he was reared to do. While let a white man do the same at a neighboring village of an unfriendly state and return with the scalps unto his people and he would also receive high honors, but at the end of a rope, in quite a different manner than that accorded his red brother; it is as you view it.

"What was the insult, Felderstein?" asked several.

"Hecht shoved Brun against me in the street, nearly pushing me through a show window."

"Was he intoxicated?"

"No, not in the least; neither was Brun. I told Brun that I had nothing against him as he was an innocent cause, but for Hecht's outrageous offense I challenged the latter right there. But Brun at once spunked up, called me 'zwei lumpen' (two rascals) and replied that he indorsed Hecht's procedure to the utmost, and I of course then could do no less than offer him satisfaction also. I know it was a put up job between them, the two cowards; they are the best swordsmen of their club and think themselves my superior, I am confident, else they would never have taken the means to draw out my challenge. They also made me challenge them so that over my defeat they could crow at their own club what a dressing down they gave a young Prussian Eagle upstart who dared to have the face to challenge them. But let them watch out; they don't know me yet, and the battle is not yet over."

"You challenged them?" asked Vielbeer. "Then why was it not fought at their club?"

"Because they are in repairs there."

It was characteristic of Felderstein that he had all evening made not the slightest mention of, nor the least reference to, his coming fight; had been quiet and calm listening to Vielbeer and joining in his companions' games, and not a ruffle had he shown on account of the desperate combat he was due to enter into in the early morning.

"What's that I hear from some one, Felderstein?"

asked Hecht coming up to us, "that you call me a coward. I shall remember that at the duel."

"It's what I wanted you to, coolly replied Felderstein," turning his back on him and walking away.

"Did you fellows bring an umpire along with you?" asked Luft, who was to back Felderstein, of the two seconds of Hecht and Brun.

"No! but we'll accept Vielbeer," replied they.

Whereupon Vielbeer, hearing this, arose from his chair, went over to one side of the room, reached up and took down his trink horn from where it was hanging upon a bracket on the wall and swung it on his left shoulder as a badge of office or authority. At this juncture the whole number of students still in the building at this late hour left the big room we had been in all evening and congregated in the large front hall on the ground floor, the hall that was decorated with the antlers of deer, elk and moose, the swords, sabers, scimetars, armor, shields, lances, etc., arranged about the walls. A case of dueling rapier blades and the necessary trappings were brought and placed on a table at the side of the hall.

The length of the blades used in these encounters depend upon the arm sweep of the contestants; they are proportioned to the height of the duelists; they run from twenty-eight to thirty-eight inches in length, exclusive of the serrated sided or saw-edge-like part of about four inches long at the larger or handle end that is inserted into a hilt and strongly fixed there when making the weapon complete for use; from the shoulder to the tip of their respective swords must measure the same in both fighters, else one of a shorter arm, say two, four or six inches less in extent, would almost be at the mercy of his opponent who could stand off out of his reach and slash him at leisure; so any deficiency of arm length is made up by using a longer rapier blade to put both antagonists on an equality in that regard.

Felderstein went up to the table and carefully picked over the case of points for awhile, balanced several up and down one after the other laid flat upon his outheld palm, in order to test their weight or heft, and finally selecting one of the longest—one of those of the maximum length allowable even for a six-footer like himself—fitted it into a light handle and screwed it there tightly, then faced the spectators, and striking an attitude made a few sweeping cuts and keen whistling maneuvers with it in the air, as though to get its peculiar motion, to thoroughly size up its manner of action and get his acute senses apprised of the way the weapon took to him and to test its suitableness to his revengeful mood. Apparently feeling satisfied with it, he stood it hilt up against the wall and prepared for the encounter.

A stuffed leather band about four inches wide, jet black, with an upper and lower bordering of silver color, and having a half-moon scooped out of one edge, to fit under the chin, he first buckled around his neck; it flanged outward at its lower part so as to come well down to the collar bones; then a large wide oval, or more nearly diamond-shaped band of the same material, heavy leather and stuffed, was fastened around the abdomen, and also buckled at his back; this too, was of black leather with an inch of silver bordering all around it. By these all the viscera, for the oval-shaped band came well up over the stomach, as well as the important jugular veins, carotid arteries, and nerves of the neck, were well protected from harm. Over his eyes he placed a pair of iron goggles, firmly held on his face by fan-like flanges on each side that covered the vital temples, and also protected the less noteworthy temporal arteries. His right arm then from an inch or so above his wrist to his shoulder he proceeded to shield, and wound it closely with a long black rope made of several strands of twisted or plaited black silk cloth. This, while it perfectly protected the arm, and particularly the dangerous blood-vessels of the axilla under the shoulder, yet allowed of the freest movement being made with it. Thus, in fact, all parts of the young man liable when struck to produce serious injury were protected, except the breast and face. To every rose there is a thorn. As all misfortunes have their compensations, so to all honors there are drawbacks.

It is considered a great disgrace to allow your antagonist to hit you on the upper three-fourths of the ear, or on the lower third, or the wings of the nose; for while scars on all other parts of the face are regarded as high honors, and are denotive of honorable warfare, those on the nose or ears are looked at something in the light of your antagonist having left his mark upon you, for the wings of the nose and all of the ears except the lower tip are composed of cartilage, and a vicious cut running through heals very slowly and badly; the blood-vessels are small and few compared to other portions of the body, and the two sides of a cut on those parts of the ears and nose usually hypertrophy greatly in healing, the cartilagenous tissue becoming three or four times as large as before the division, and look elephantine, gross and revolting. One student's nose, a wing of which had been incised through months before, had augmented in volume in consequence of the increased nutrition to an enormous size compared to the uninjured wing; it was also reddish blue in color, due to the dilated blood-vessels nature had seen fit to cause in healing the parts, while the other wing was pale and of an elegant contour. This student also had a kind of half-laughing, shame-faced look as though he felt that he only showed his countenance in the world by reason of the world's good-natured tolerance thereof. His look was engendered doubtless by the ill-concealed repulsive demeanor assumed so often and constantly toward him by nearly all the strangers he ever meets. Several ears among the fighting members were also more or less thus injured, but the marks left were extremely less noticeable than those upon the noses. One rarely looks at a man's ears, but his nose is the most prominent part of his face and the first thing one's eyes run against on a close view of him.

Finally, just as Hecht and all his crowd, who had prepared their champion at the other end of the hall, came up, Felderstein put on a thickly padded cap of the club's colors, black and silver, the body of the cap black, indicative of the color of the bird of their national emblem, the Preussische Adler (Prussian Eagle), and the band of silver in allusion to the beautiful democratic metal the immortal Frederick the Great so much loved to circulate as money.

Hecht's cap, as well as those of all his companions along with him, was, of course, of the Maikaefer club's gay colors, namely, dark green cap and yellow band. He was picturesquely encased in leather similarly to that worn by Felderstein, his protective armor being of leather, and was also dark green, with yellow borders like his cap.

Vielbeer, seeing all were ready, went over to the table, seized a piece of white chalk and going to the middle of the room, stooped down with many puffs and grunts and marked off in the center of the floor the different places for the antagonists to stand, and then backed away a few steps to the side, where he took his station as umpire. Schnurkelyah—who usually had but two locations for his canine anatomy, when his master was sitting down, snugly ensconced in my lap, and when Vielbeer was standing up, sturdily sheltered between the Baron's feet—now realizing from long experience by an observation of the preparations that a fray was imminent, and that someone was liable to get hurt, decided that he would let the honor pass him by anyway, and at once took to cover beneath Vielbeer's far protruding stomach.

Hecht, with his rapier, one of the number his followers had brought along with them, strode instantly up to his mark and stood waiting, with his second at his side, and slightly off behind him.

Felderstein also, immediately afterward stepped up to his place. "Measure swords!" sung out Vielbeer, and each duelist reached out his point and protruded it against the inside of his adversary's shoulder; they were seen to be of the same length, and then Felderstein's second, Count Luft, fell into his proper position by his principal's side, and the whole mass of students formed a circling crowd about the umpire and the four most deeply concerned. The two seconds are also armed with rapiers, but blunt ones, and stand slightly to the side and back of their respective principals. At the end of each "gang" (pronounced gahng), a round of ten minutes, when time is called, they at once strike in with their weapons and force the combatants' swords up to prevent a slashing blow from one taking effect after the other has thrown up his guard. At the instant time is called, both principals are supposed to throw their sword points to their shoulders and the seconds strike in to prevent a wound given by a blow started out half a second before or even just at the instant time is called. Also, if a wound is delivered by a principal, his second at once strikes the blades up and claims the stroke; if but a slight one, the first blood, or if a more serious one, asks for the victory, etc., for his principal. For this reason each contestant's second stands at his side a little way off and just a trifle behind him, so as to as fully as possible watch the sword-play of his champion and instantly detect if a blow falls upon the opposing warrior's person. These gangs or rounds of such and such length of time are usually fought when the combat takes place between friends, friendly bouts for amusement and exercise, and to test each other's skill, and to keep in practice; but in a duel of the kind which was to take place now between these two, where a direct insult had been concocted and intentionally given, no rounds are called, but both parties fight until one or the other gets a real serious wound or drops from exhaustion, which, of course, gives the battle, with high honors, to the other, by reason of his strength and endurance, or the merit of having more cautiously husbanded his resources, etc.

The four principal members involved stand almost like the four letters of a weather-vane which indicate north, east, south and west, the umpire off a little to one side within the circle of enclosing audience, all four in their pretty caps, their gaily colored armor, their bright, flashing blades, their stalwart figures, erect and straight as arrows, their set determined faces, the glittering hatred of Felderstein's deep gray eyes; the confident, easy elegance of manners displayed by Hecht showing in every movement and inch of his powerful form; the group of surrounding spectators enclosing them and the umpire; students from five or six different nations, and representing, as showing by their caps, half a dozen clubs of the city, all gathered in the center of the light, shed upon them by four surrounding equidistant cluster chandeliers, made the whole scene appear worthy of a medieval king's tournament in the feudal days of old, in the palmiest times of the lance and sword combats between the knights of the shadowy past taking place before the fairest of the land.

Both principals stood silent, facing each other, about five feet apart, and each with both feet together and each right arm held low against the side, keeping the rapier's blade close against the shoulder, the left arm of each bent into a triangle and held out of the way, the fore-arm horizontal against the back.

"Cross the swords!" said Vielbeer, and instantly like two clock-work automatons, both principals stepped back a pace with their left feet at the same instant that the brightly shining swords were crossed, each one's point right before his antagonist's face, and the two seconds, also, struck attitudes and threw their blunt rapiers up and crossed them right beneath the weapons of their principals who were looking each one, his enemy, squarely in the eye. At once deep silence ensued; all the directing, disputing and talking going on among the assembled students and the vain-glorious braggadocio-like blowing of Brun, who had been loudly bewailing his disappointment at not being the first antagonist, ceased on an instant, and intense quiet prevailed; the two principals were standing like statues awaiting the word.

"Los!" (pronounced lohs—let loose, or let fly) howled Vielbeer, suddenly, in a booming voice from the depths of his stomach; the seconds instantly removed their weapons, and quick as lightning Felderstein withdrew his sword from where it was crossing his opponent's, drew it back above his head, and made a terrific sweeping slash direct at his opponent's face that was parried with the greatest of ease and grace by Hecht, and seemingly without the least exertion on his part, outside of turning his wrist, much to the surprise of some of those new to the duello, who showed by their looks that they had expected, at seeing the blow made, to the next instant discern Hecht's whole head roll far over on the floor. Hecht then raised his rapier and made a feint at Felderstein who met it half way, and then blocked the real stroke by a skillful turn. Hecht continued to make feints, and struck high and low, in vain endeavoring to catch an unprotected place or get within his guard, but this Felderstein was too adept to permit; then for a time Hecht tried to draw his opponent out or get him angry, but he did not know Felderstein, who never got angry unless he wanted to, at least never so far that anyone could by the least sign see that he showed any; seeing this fail, for awhile he charged in at Felderstein's head; the latter defended himself splendidly, however. Then first one took the offensive, and then his adversary, raining blows after blows on each other until both looked like they were standing among a shower of lightning flashes; at it earnestly and furiously they went, now up stroke, now down stroke, now shoulder, now thigh, now hip, now head, thrust, feint, slash, carte, tierce, plunge, now one pressing forward, now being in turn fought backward and pressed down; faster and faster flew the weapons until one marveled how an eye could keep track of all the sword movements.

Suddenly Felderstein was seen turning off his enemy's point and swiftly striking in at him. Count Luft instantly threw in his foil and sent the swords flying up.

"A blow, a blow for my man!" he cried.

"No, no!" replied Hecht's second, quickly.

"I saw it!" said Luft.

"Never!" from Hecht's second.

"Umpire, I appeal to you," cried Luft, turning to Vielbeer.

"No strike," said Vielbeer emphatically and decisively; whereupon Count Luft, who had all this time been standing with his feet apart and right knee bent and with his rapier "struck in", holding by this attitude quiet the duelists, at once withdrew it and the antagonists resumed the fight.

Hecht well knew that Felderstein had outgeneraled

him, had flung aside his point and had cut at him unopposed, and that he had just escaped a slash by reason of his opponent's rapier falling short about an eighth of an inch, and feeling muffed, now began beating at him with all the power of his superior weight, endeavoring to break down his guard by sheer force of onslaught, backed by his heavier build. Felderstein, although in appearance slight of figure and spare looking, was very muscular, and had the fullest powers of endurance, and was not overwhelmed and routed, and did not go down before the furious pressure of his opponent's attack, which Hecht seemed to have hoped and probably to have expected, as one could intuitively divine from the momentary expression of surprise that flitted over his face. Felderstein held his own, however, with ease, skillfully bending back to neutralize as far as possible his opponent's over-weight, when suddenly by a dexterous turn of his fore-arm he threw up Hecht's sword and, in a retaliative temper of mind, made a slash at his body so viciously that the noise of the stroke-fall resounded throughout the hall. Instantly both seconds struck in and threw up the rapiers. Felderstein backed his point to his shoulder, brought his feet together and letting his left arm drop to his side, stood erect in his place, panting slightly through his dry, parched lips.

Vielbeer drew forth his little ivory measure, the seconds and a lot of Hecht's friends crowded around him, and it was found that the blow had fallen on that part of the leather armor protecting the stomach, just two inches below its top, had cut through both layers of leather, all the intervening padding, and merely scratched the skin, from which a slight flow of blood appeared while they were examining it.

The wounds in the duels are graded: a wound so deep is a stroke, and counts so much or so many points for the one giving it; a more ugly wound an increased number of points, etc., but it has to be of a certain length and depth and of some seriousness to be declared sufficient to end the fray or give the victory to the duelist who caused it. A minutely graded ivory measure is used to determine the exact status of the cut.

In an affair like that now taking place, however, a very bad wound must be given to close it, and Hecht's injury being found insignificant of course counted for nothing in this affair, and his big stomach band, which had been removed to investigate the damage done him, was now buckled around in its old position; the seconds again stepped back to their places, and once more Vielbeer shouted, "cross the swords" and "los" (go it).

Hecht was now hotly angry at being this time certainly so nearly wounded, and bitter rage, that he took no pains to conceal, was now depicted on his countenance. Had the blow struck two inches higher his breast-bone would have been cut into, and his lungs have surely given him trouble for many days. He was also much infuriated at the thought of his near defeat in the presence of his friends, by one whom he had specially determined to overthrow and humiliate, and realizing that he had met his match resolved to make a speedy end of the conflict by power of strength and superior heaviness, and he at once desperately assumed the offensive, playing for Felderstein's head. One could see by his actions that he was risking any wound on his body, was relaxing his breast guard—all his efforts being directed to strike Felderstein on the face. Rapidly as he gave his blows they were all skillfully parried by Felderstein, too cautious to fall into the trap of striking for Hecht's breast and getting in return his enemy's sword full in the face. The bait was tempting, but he saw through Hecht's scheme. The latter finding his plan fail, and realizing the depths of his antagonist, grew angry, struck wildly, lost his caution, and rushed down on Felderstein, cutting right and left, up and down, paying no attention any more to guard, just in the hope of perplexing and bewildering his contestant into puzzlement, and cutting him down. This was what Felderstein, still skillfully blocking and warding off the blows, was waiting for, and suddenly ceasing to parry the cuts, with a swift dexterous back-handed stroke and turning of his wrist, he sent Hecht's shining blade flying up above his head, and at the same instant, before his antagonist could lower his steel or recover his guard, with all his might he cut down squarely upon his enemy's face. There was a great spurt of blood, a groan of wretched anguish from the injured duelist, the clank of his rapier as it dropped from his hand, and the miserably frustrated Maikaeferian fell backward into his second's arms, from whence he sank to the floor in unconsciousness.

Felderstein never moved from his tracks, but stood with flushed face and heaving chest, staring unsympathetically at his subdued insulter until he had measured his full length in dismaying insensibility supine at the feet of his fellow-clubmen, and then backing to the wall and sitting down he shoved his cap to the back of his head, and wiped with his handkerchief the perspiration from his face.

A circle of students were soon kneeling around Hecht with basins and cloths, washing away the blood that flowed, tying the severed blood-vessels and endeavoring to bring him effectually out of his deep unconciousness, occasioned as much by the loss of such a quantity of sanguinary fluid as by the stunning effects of the blow—from which he would at intervals partly revive and into which immediately lapse again. The blade had struck the side of his head in front of his ear, and his mouth being partly open to better enable him to breath during his over-heating exertions, had cut through his left cheek from his ear into his mouth, dividing the parotid gland, and such was the force given by which the blow was struck that it was only prevented from severing his right cheek also and thus splitting his mouth from ear to ear, by being delivered in somewhat of a downward manner, for after passing through the cheek, it had glanced over the tongue and landed on the bone of the right jaw below the teeth, several of which were much loosened.

His wound was finally dressed and he reviving sufficiently to sit up, partook of a stimulant, and without saying a word, accompanied by two of his friends, left the hall, entered the cab which had been quietly called to the front door, and soon the low rumbling of wheels off into the night apprised us that the vanquished clubman and his comrades had departed.

"His beauty has been spoiled for a while and the arrogant lumps is badly injured; the game, however, was of his own seeking," said Luft, as with a glass of cracked ice water in his hand he came up to where Felderstein was sitting in a chair placed against the wall and set it down on the floor beside him.

"I am still a little too warm for that, Luft," replied his principal, "but will drink it just before the next fight. I shall rest a while and in a few moments give that 'Rindvieh' (steer) Brun the chance he all evening has so impatiently and loud mouthedly been waiting for. I am stirred up now and am feeling splendidly and have all my aggressive inclinations and guarding faculties alert and fully awake. I feel in perfect trim, Luft, and in great confidence, and if he is no better man than his partner, who got what he so well deserved, the squabble won't last long."

Brun was got by his friends into his armor, and took his position on the floor and proved himself not so good a man as Hecht by any means. In fact Brun wished himself well out of it all. It wouldn't do to back out, however, as all his friends now looked to him to retrieve their club's lowered prestige, or at least even up matters by something of a return victory. Brun, however, did not seem to feel that he cared particularly to be the one picked out and expected to balance the honors between the clubs, and looked as though he hoped some objection would be made to Felderstein's again taking up the rapier against a fresh man, in which case, the duel not taking place at the appointed time, would, in all probability, be declared entirely off. He had expected Hecht to wipe the floor with Felderstein, who, on account of his habit of usually keeping his mouth shut, had been greatly underrated, and not thinking he would have to come to blows with him; but after Felderstein's downfall would at once magnanimously let him off of his part of it; and had been blowing around among his crowd during the time the preparations were going on, of how anxious he was for his turn to come, and how he was just spoiling because Hecht's time came first, etc. Now, he looked far from anxious for the fray. However, in the presence of all eyes, and as the last hope of his compeers, he braced up, clamped his teeth fiercely together, glared viciously around and came up to the mark with a great assumption of courage and eagerness, and crossed his sword with Felderstein's.

Felderstein had heard great tales of these two young men's skill and prowess, and knowing he was shorn of his best and freshest strength by his previous contest, was exceedingly cautious and wary at first, but he soon became aware of his opponent's inferior ability as the fight progressed; and it dawning upon him that Brun was a miserable blow-hard, and had been crowing over him too soon, resolved to pay him dearly for all his insolence and offensive demeanor; and after a few moments' uneventful play to lull Brun's caution, turned away a thrust from Brun and delivered a swishing cut squarely at him, just missing by half an inch laying his whole forehead open.

This stroke produced quite a sensation among the audience from the heat with which, self-evidently, it had been sent out, and all saw that Felderstein was determined to seriously injure his opponent, and as the assembly were already somewhat appalled at the serious wound received by Hecht, great anxiety prevailed, which was painfully and, to Brun, exceedingly unflatteringly, portrayed over all the onlooking countenances. "Verfluchter Schweinehund!" (cursed pig-dog) cried Brun, blazing into anger like a flash on noticing the deep solicitude displayed by the surrounding crowd for the welfare of his visage just missed getting spoiled by a mere fraction, his eyes emitting sparks and his face assuming an expression of deep hatred, and he glared in animosity at his antagonist. He nerved himself for a desperate effort, and at once quickened his play and showered slash after slash, thrust after thrust on Felderstein, who, seeing his opponent's angry mood, defended himself guardedly and with extreme care until Brun's energetic and furious efforts began to slacken, then took the offensive himself for a short time until finally a skillfully made uppercut feint followed instantly, in the wink of an eye, by a downward slash of Felderstein's rapier, landed plump on Brun's nose, the whole lower half of which it took off; the blade, in continuing its course, also cutting through the upper and lower lips, through the chin to the bone, and sinking deep into the padded leather band around his neck. The seconds simultaneously, and quick as thought, struck up the swords.

"I am undone," wailed the "last hope of the Maikaefers," carrying his hands to his head as the blood, spurting all over his face and into his eyes blinded him, and letting fall his rapier just as the end of his nose dropped to the floor, where puppy Schnurkelyah, who had all this time been viewing the scene from between Vielbeer's legs, feeling, of course, protected there from all dangers and downfalling missiles, thinking it a piece of waste pretzel, suddenly sprang forward, snapped it up and gulped it whole, to the dumbfounded amazement of all.

"Himmel!" howled Brun's second, exasperated to fury at the second defeat of their colors. "Cut him open and take it out quick and sew it on."

"What!" shrieked Count Luft, aghast at the very idea, and instantly getting aflame. "Not for ten thousand such infernal noses."

"Cursed dog!" yelled Brun's second, now half wild, "I'll pretty soon fix you," and before anyone could divine his intention or prevent him, he seized Brun's rapier from off the floor, and drawing back the weapon, aimed and struck a blow at Schnurkelyah that, had it landed where it was intended to, would have sent the poor little innocent-minded bench-legged dachshund in a hurry to the place where all good little fat dogs go, wherever that may be; the blade's point, however, sung through the air just an inch or so above his back.

Schnurkelyah, hearing the angry, contentious voices, seeing the suspicious actions of Brun's second, and feeling from the swish of the rapier the renewal of the air above him, surmised what was happening, and giving a couple of alarmed apoplectic yelps, made a bound toward the front swinging doors of the hall, which being unbolted from the departure of Hecht and his two companions, swung open, let him tumbling out head-over-heels to the sidewalk from where he rolled down the

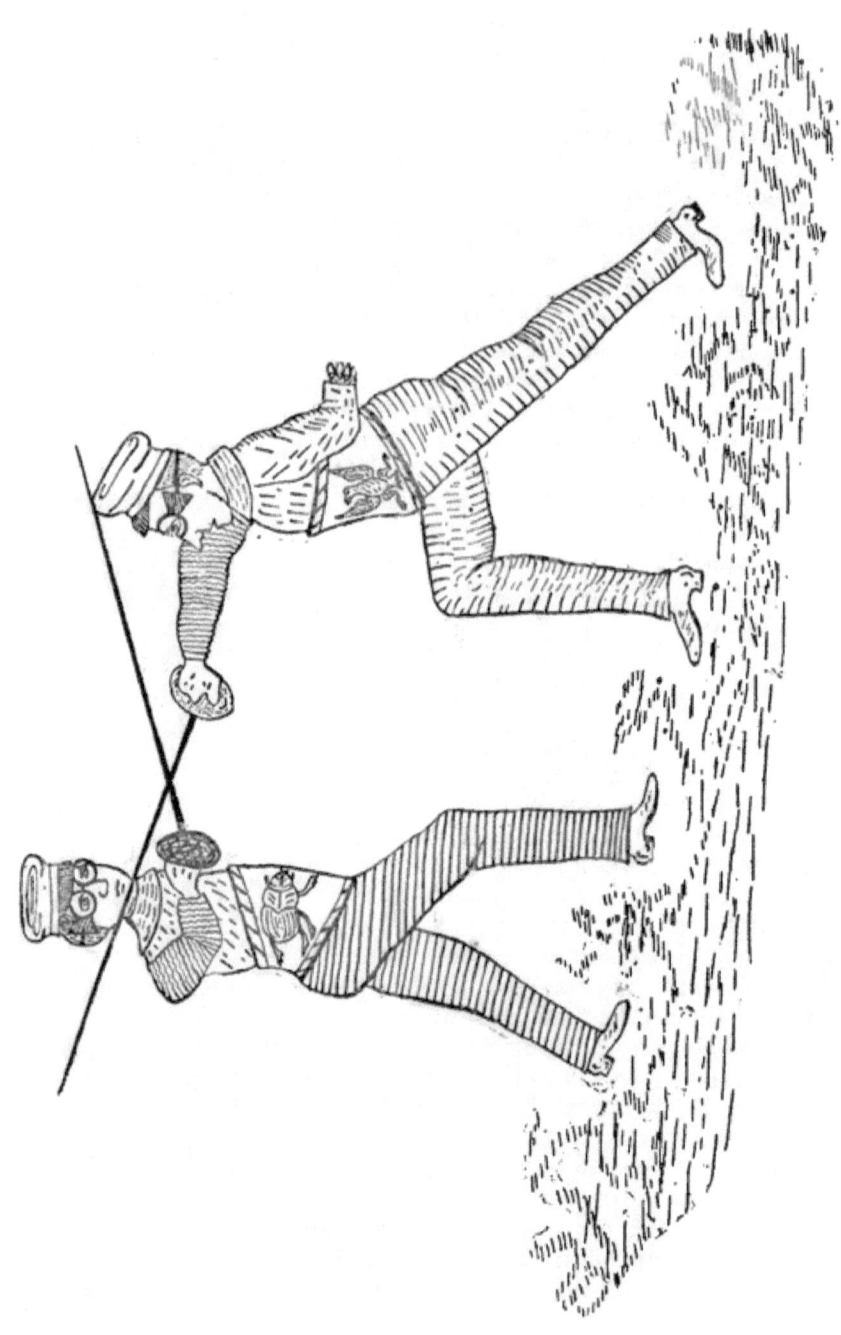

pavement like a flour barrel to the curbing, and went bump into the gutter, where he lay on his broad, fat little back, unable to right himself, with his feet feebly waving in the air.

Brun's second's blow, delivered with such vigor, and not meeting an obstacle, threw him off his balance prone upon the floor. Recovering his feet, the swinging doors closing behind Schnurkelyah hid his great acrobatic feat from view. When the second reached the door, Schnurkelyah had just struck the gutter, and the second springing out upon the pavement, and rapidly glancing all around, seeing in the dim light of early morning no dog nearer than one running along about his own business a short distance down the street, took after him with all his might, yelling at the top of his voice, "Stop him!" "hold him!" "cut him open!" etc., etc., to the great astonishment of two or three early risers already on the street who paused in their walk and stood looking in wonder after the flying figure of a man with a sword pursuing an imaginary enemy.

Vielbeer rushed to the door with Count Luft at his heels, where the former got fastened tightly between the door frames, and the greatest exertion of others in pulling and pushing failed to get him either in or out. Count Luft had flung down his foil or blunt point, grasped Felderstein's rapier out of his hand, and at Vielbeer's coat-tails had brought up against him, at the final stoppage of the rush, with such impetus that he had but jammed him in the doorway the tighter; and all the time they were putting forth all their efforts pulling at Vielbeer, Luft was getting more furious at the delay; he was jumping up and down about the room, waving his rapier about, cursing and swearing, and crying out all the terrible things he would do if he didn't get there in time to rescue Schnurkelyah.

Eventually seeing no hope of a speedy release from the hall through the door, he rushed to the front of the hall, bounded upon a table at one side of the door where the students were still at their struggles, and raising his blade with a few terrific slashes he cut through curtains, window and shutters, and leaping to the sill instantly disappeared outside and down the street.

Finally after the liberal use of a saw on the door, Vielbeer was released and landed outside on the pavement, and a couple of members on each side of him grabbing up his stomach in their eight arms galloped him between them at a gallant rate along the street after Luft, who could be seen away down the "Unter den Linden", the pride street of Berlin, just a flying along, wildly waving his rapier, his long blond hair streaming out behind him in the wind and his fearful oaths coming back to us on the breeze with ever diminishing clearness, still in pursuit of Brun's second, whose dim figure could be seen in the early gray of the morning a couple of blocks ahead of Luft, still energetically pursuing a terrified little dog, just a skinning along for dear life, far ahead of him.

Vielbeer and his supporters, were getting along finely and were making the fastest time out when suddenly, and without any warning whatever, his left leg gave out and plump the whole of them went down in a lump on the pavement, forming as pretty a mess as one ever sees. On disentangling their limbs and extricating their bodies and arising, seeing then no signs either of Luft, Brun's second or Schnurkelyah, and knowing their further efforts would be of no avail, they came slowly back to the club, in front of which the remainder, excepting those inside in care of the unfortunate Brun, of the previous fight's audience were gathered anxiously awaiting the returns. Vielbeer stopped on the pavement in front of the entrance and suddenly overcome at the thought of the probable demise of his nobly and valiantly pedigreed and ever faithful dog, pulled forth a handkerchief of antediluvian appearance and gave vent to his grief, as did several other members of the club, thinking that by now Schnurkelyah had surely been caught and cut open by the enemy.

"Poor Schnurkelyah! poor Schnurkelyah!" wept Vielbeer loudly, tears of beer as large as ounce globules rolling from his eyes.

Suddenly a feeble but familiar "bow-wow" greeted us from the gutter. There was an awe-struck ghost-creeping silence among us; a wild, scared look into each others' faces; a rush in a body to the gutter, and then a loud shout from all as Schnurkelyah was discovered still on his back with feet still paddling the air. He was picked up, carried in, put upon a table, given a vomit, and the first thing that he threw up, along with a lot of pretzels, beer and wurst, was the end of Brun's nose. It was at once seized, washed and carefully sewed on the face of the injured student, where it grew so nicely, being cut in the soft muscular tissue above the wing cartilages and below the nose bone, that no enlargement or discoloration ensued, and three months later but a dim scar remained to tell of his mishap.

A cab was called for Brun, after all the students were again assembled within the building, so as not to attract notice by their numbers, as it was getting lighter and lighter as the moments stole on. Again two companions assisted a defeated "Maikaeferian" (June-bug clubman) through the great doors into a closed carriage and took him away. The victorious Prussian Eagle, the valiant Felderstein, took off his armor, which, with the rapiers, were removed and returned to their places, the traces of the fray obliterated, the lights turned out, and, after cautiously spying out the door and still seeing no signs of the return of the two seconds, the students by twos and threes slunk away into the breaking day, like night birds on the coming of morning; and soon the bright and glorious beautiful dawn cast its enlightening rays into a vacant hall and a deserted building.

CHAPTER VIII.

ANOTHER fad of Berlin at the time was for each family that pretended to be anything, that laid claims to being anybodies at all, to have, or rather to affect a "Bayrisches Kinder Maedchen" (Bavarian child nurse, or rather, companion). These girls were from the German province of Bavaria, a southern country which lies just north of the Italian Alps. They could be seen all about the streets of the city, and were to be met with everywhere in the parks, wheeling their employers' baby-carriages, in which often nestled little cherubs, and often were found vacant. These women were dressed in the picturesque costume of their native land, which consisted of a tight silk-embroidered sleeveless bodice, shoe-laced in front over a wide white ruffled bosom, which tapered to a point at the belt, and puffed sleeves of pure white, on a waist worn under the bodice, appearing from out the arm-holes and ending in a ruffle at the wrists. The dress-skirt was short—not reaching quite to the ankles—and had four one-inch stripes about one and one-half inches apart, just above the three-inch wide ruffled lower border. An apron was worn over this. Their head-dress was at times something like a Spanish lady's mantilla, but more often it looked like our own liberty cap that we occasionally see on our old silver dollars, pictured as being held up on the end of a pole. They wore white stockings and neat slippers, looked quite captivating, and were regular soldier-heart-smashers. When a body of marching soldiers was going past (which was often) they lined the edge of the sidewalks in numbers with their little charges, and all the soldiers' eyes were strained to the sides of their heads in endeavors to get glimpses of nods sent at them; or to recognize smiles from their admiring "liebchens" (beloved ones) and "sueszchens" (sweetnesses).

It was the fad for the big families to have one of the

Bavarian child attendants or baby care-takers, and those who did not sport one lost much of their caste. So all who had an infant, turned out a Bayrisches Kinder outfit in as striking and stylish a manner as they could get up—a beautiful little carriage and a neat trim-looking girl. The families who had no baby had the nurse or child-companion and the baby buggy anyway, and sent the girls, empty-vehicled, promenading out over the parks and boulevards to keep in fashion, and waited patiently until the Klapperstorch (clattering stork) brought one, for the Klapperstorch brings all the babies in Germany. These important "individuals" are to be seen in all the rural districts in plentifulness. They have two very long, thin red legs, and are white feathered. They build their great nests on the very top of the chimneys of the houses in the country—build them of straw and large twigs, branches and vine clippings, right upon the top of the square of bricks enclosing the smoke hole; lay their eggs and rear their young therein, right amidst and seemingly not incommoded or inconvenienced in the least by the clouds of smoke that sifts up through the nest. They were often known to put out fires in the days of a hundred and more years ago—when roofs in the agricultural districts were mostly made of straw, and a spark from one of the chimneys set fire to it—by jumping down from their nests upon the blaze and flapping their wings into it until extinguished; probably doing this by instinct to save from certain destruction, by the fire progressing, their eggs or helpless young in the nest. These olden time straw roofs were now and then still to be met with in the far back districts of Germany. A law had been passed years before, prohibiting their further construction and only allowing the repair of the old ones, but the quiet, meek, light-blue innocent-eyed ruralists seemed to have gotten Americanized enough in that one particular at least to circumvent the law, for by removing one side of an old straw roof and replacing it with an entirely new covering of the same material, and after allowing six months to elapse "patching" the remaining side with a new straw covering, they succeeded in renewing entirely the inflammable roof and also in keeping beyond the clutches of the law. These straw roofs were very lasting, were made of bundles of the unweighty substance laid on and over-lapping and a second layer put on over the first one, in the space left where two bundles of straw sided together; they endured for years, and the

drizzling rains of October and November never penetrated through them.

These Klapperstorches would often fly into the suburbs of Berlin, in the district where the manufactories were situated; they would alight from out the sky and stand like statues upon the tops of the high smoke stacks and brick flue or fume pillars. On my first seeing them up there, outlined in relief against the heavens, I thought that they were sheet-iron figures set up as weather-vanes or as decorations, but one day noticing one high brick smoke stack particularly, I saw what I had supposed was a figure of a long-limbed bird suddenly draw one leg up to its breast and remain standing upon the single limb; it stood immovable upon this one leg for hours, in a fixed deeply philosophizing position as though musing upon the inconstancy or the susceptibility of variations in the essential qualities of ornithological occurrences, or else pondering upon its chances of roosting upon a full craw. On looking for it later I found it had gone—flown back to the country. This one-limb attitude is its most favorite one; its red legs are extremely long, and it has a long straight conical bill, with which it makes the klappering (clattering) noise upon the wooden eaves of the house roofs; and from this the bird derives its name of Klapperstorch (clattering stork). The sound can be heard far away, like that which would ensue from an immense woodpecker. Now and then they are seen with some colored feathers on the tips of their wings, all else of their feathery coats being white, but most often they are of the latter color entirely. And so these babyless families keep the nurse and buggy ready and handy, for some night when all is dark and still, so quiet that not even a mouse stirring is to be perceived by the ear, the family suddenly hear a great rustling and clattering coming down the chimney and the next morning a sweet little girl baby is found in the cradle. They do not tell who brings the boy babies, but I suppose the old boy himself does—gives a large share of his diabolical attention to that purpose.

Menton and I once went along with one of our club's mild students to call upon some friends of his who lived in a flat on one of the fashionable thoroughfares of Berlin. They happened to all be out in the city at the time of our appearance there, and we waited upon the edge of the sidewalk while the mild student rang the bell. He, getting no response, supposed that it might be broken, and so knocked for a short while to be better satisfied of their not being at home, which he now suspected, before leaving. Finally a lady who was living in the flat three or four stories above the apartments of the absent ones, hearing the knocking, and assuming that the caller was not aware that no attention would be given by anyone to a knock—as each set of rooms had their special bell—and thinking that he was not acquainted with the location of the bell or had not even the knowledge of its existence, leaned her head out of the window and called down to him, saying, "Bell einmal! bell einmal!" (ring awhile! ring awhile!) This expression of bell einmal sounds very much like "Belle (bel-lah) einmal (bark awhile); indeed, the similarity is marked, especially when it is rapidly or hurriedly spoken. The mild student understood very well what she meant, but he caught the comical feature of the resemblance instantly, and resolving to so misconstrue the words, he turned about to the passers-by, opened wide his mouth and gave forth several terrific barks, "Boo-wow, wow-wow, boo-wow-wow!" much to their amazement and terror.

"Nein! nein!" (No! no!) "Bell! bell! bell!" (ring! ring!) cried the lady.

"I do, madam," answered back the mild student; "I am 'bellen', I am so doing", again letting loose into a loud wow-wow, whoof-whoof, wow-wow, making fearful facial contortions and grimaces the while.

A scared crowd soon collected, but keeping away at a safe distance, about him, thinking that he had been bitten by a mad dog, and that he had the hydrophobia; but he explained to them, with a very innocent face, that the lady above had suddenly opened her window, leaned out and had very politely requested him to bark awhile, and that, although he had not the slightest idea why she wished him so to do, he never refused to accede to a lady's wishes, and had accommodated her to the best of his poor ability.

What occasioned the most curiosity among the German students about Menton and myself, was our habit of sitting in our rooms with our chairs tilted back and our feet up on the top of our study table, or high up on the wall at the sides of the room. They would often come into our apartments at night, and pause on the threshold in perplexed wonder at the sight of both of us so sitting, seemingly enjoying ourselves hugely in what, to them, appeared a most uncomfortable position. We would often, on purpose, at hearing some of them coming up the stairs, and knowing that they were bound for a brief stay in our rooms, hunch ourselves down into our far-back tilted chairs until we were really sitting upon our shoulders and necks, and with our feet away up above our heads on the wall, appear, on their entrance, to be so deply absorbed in study as not to hear their incoming. We always enjoyed the stopping of our callers, knocked clear out of their self-possession at the sight — all standing transfixed in the doorway, the foremost one with his hand still holding on to the knob, in surprise and astonishment at our artfully constructed, and to their eyes very singular, attitudes. After awhile we would, with deep drawn and heavy sighs, awaken from our deliciously recreating postures, and reluctantly slide our slippered feet, with a scrape, from their elevated situation on the wall, and arise; and with a "ha! altes, haus" (hello, old hulk), "how are you? come in" to the first comer; and then in much surprise at seeing some others following him, would extend our greeting to them, saying, "kommt herein alte kraken" (move in, old wrecks), of course seeming not in the least aware that they had any occasion to see anything remarkable at our usual way of sitting, welcome our visitors into the sanctum.

German chairs are made exclusively for sitting and not to lean in; the backs are all perfectly straight and perpendicular, and like our American parlor and drawing-room furniture have no runged braces below as our office and hotel chairs over here have, to prevent the two rear legs when it is backwardly inclined, with a heavy weight therein, from snapping off at the under part of the seat board.

We soon discovered that our method of adjusting ourselves in our places of rest, appearing to give us such happiness, had been rumored all about the University, and we learned that a great many of the students had tried it for themselves with disastrous results to their furniture. Whenever we went to interchange civilities with anyone of our colleagues and would see a chair or two minus their back legs stored away upside down in confusion in a corner of the room, we realized at once that the student had been endeavoring to find out wherein lay the pleasure of our customary manner of sitting.

One evening just about dusk a gang of half a dozen of us Prussian Eagles, with a mild student in our midst, started out to attend a play at one of the theaters. On arriving at the corner of the city's great boulevard, the Unter den Linden where it crosses at a right-angle the Friedrich strasse (Frederick street), which latter is also an important and busy thoroughfare, we all stopped on one of the four corners for a moment to look about and see if there were any more of our members in the near vicinity. We stood waiting on the wide pavement in the bright gas-light of the street lamps, and of the lighted show-windows of the stores, and as a party of ladies and gentlemen, about six of them altogether, came along down Frederick street, and just as they approached us and were about to pass the Unter den Linden, the mild student suddenly remarked to us quite loudly, at the same time pulling out his watch and looking at the time, "Yes, he comes now in an instant; keep a sharp eye, juugens (boys), for the Koenig (king) is now about to pass."

The old King of Prussia, afterward Emperor William I of Germany, always came through the Brandenburg Thor, or great arch upon which stood the famed female charioteer driving the four horses. The arch being really the end of the wayfare he invariably came through it and passed down the long great boulevard on his way coming from the old palace of Frederick the Great at Potsdam, sixteen miles away, to the new palace in Berlin, situated near the other end of the Unter den Linden, the end opposite to the Thor. He always was seen in his carriage in his military dress; his spiked helmet adorned with a golden figure of the eagle of Prussia upon its front. He was always driven past quite rapidly by his two coachmen, behind two horses, and coming in usually at night and accompanied by several attendants following as a mounted escort, produced quite a clattering and sensation as they went swiftly past over the smooth street, his white side whiskers contrasting with his black helmet and his uniform coat. General von Moltke often accompanied him; a thin-faced man whose head appeared to have shrunk down into his shoulders, and who seemed to almost disappear down out of sight within the cushions of the carriage seats.

Von Moltke always wore a soft military cap, a colored band around the rim, over which the body of the cap arose dilating to its round summit. Prince von Bismarck, the Iron Chancellor, who also occasionally accompanied his king, always wore the black spiked helmet, out from under which peered his firm, strong looking countenance. The king and his chancellor were both tall men and sat erect; were broad chested, their shoulders being nearly a yard wide in their epauleted coats. The right hand of the Prussian king and that of whoever accompanied him were continuously employed in being raised to their heads in a military saluting manner in acknowledgment of the raising hats of the populace as the equipage sped by under the control of the two plume-hatted coachmen. The conveyance in which he was driven was a landau, sometimes called landaw, a double carriage so named from the German city Landau where it was first originated or invented. The two seats were at the front and back of the vehicle and faced each other, so one could sit facing the horses or with his back to them. The cover was coach-like and could be parted in the middle at the top, and both sides thrown away from each other to behind the back of each seat, making it then an open carriage. It was so open whenever it came into the city, and on his expected arrival getting noised about, crowds collected on every corner of the great long boulevard to witness his passing, and hats and caps by the thousands went high into the air all up and down the length of the Unter den Linden as he was rapidly driven along to the palace.

"Look sharp now, boys, for he is shortly to come," continued the mild student.

"Hear you?" remarked one of the gentlemen of the six passers by, "hear you that? that the king comes immediately."

"Yes," they all replied. "So let us stop here and see him pass."

They all congregated at our side and four or five more people coming along, the mild student, each time one came within hearing, would repeat, "The king comes; he comes now—at once," as though talking to himself. The new arrivals also stopped, and finally others seeing the crowd collecting, were attracted to it in curiosity, and on asking the cause of the assembled citizens, the first gulled comers themselves now would answer that the Royal William was expected in a moment on his way to the palace. And so the mild student and his crowd, after a jam of people had been brought about, quietly slipped off, laughing in their sleeves.

We went to the theater, and soon the incident dropped from our minds; but on leaving the play-house after the close of the piece, and returning home down the same street at about half past twelve o'clock, we had it brought again to our memories on nearing the same corner, by seeing that the great crowd was yet standing there—still waiting for the king's appearance—in the same place where we had left it earlier in the night; but all were recent comers. The crowd was ever changing its individuals, but ever kept up its numbers. Old members of the concourse, after standing half or all of an hour or longer, would at length grow weary and bethink themselves of other duties (than that of saluting their sovereign) somewhat more pressing and that they were neglecting, and would give a final look down the street, and seeing yet no commotion or agitation in the distance would skip out; but new ones ever came to take their place to swell the thinning ranks. And so the gathered numbers had remained about an even hundred or so—just enough to seriously discommode the hurrying passers-by.

"What is it? what's the excitement?" asked the

mild student, rushing out from our midst and up to them, with inquiring eyes and much eagerness in his manner.

"Koenig kommt! Koenig kommt!" (King comes, King comes) replied several.

"Schoen" (that's fine). "Hurrah! then it is true, boys," loudly shouted the mild student back to our approaching selves. "Then it is so what we heard down the street, that the King is due to pass here at a quarter to one o'clock. Let me see (looking at his watch), he is due now in seven minutes; then we must stay and see him, for I would not miss it for the world. Quick! all of you; come along, boys, and we will run across the street and quench our thirst with a seltzer each, and then hurry back in time to let his Royalty have the great pleasure of seeing some handsome fellows, who will very much resemble us, enthusiastically greet him."

We all lit out over the wide boulevard, got lost to the crowd's view after getting beyond the rows of trees lining the street's center, and of course did not see fit to return.

It was three weeks later before the footsteps of the same gang of us were led to that corner again, but when they were we noticed that the large assembly of Berliners were still occupying the pavement.

"Ha! ha! ha!" fairly yelled the mild student, pointing to the waiting gathering of citizens; "just look at that! Those people have been standing there all these three weeks in expectation of seeing the King drive by. Ha! ha! ha!"

The story of the first night's joke had been told about of course, and it appeared that each evening since, some new mild student had gotten a gulled throng to collect there; and so it looked as if the same old mob was always staying on the corner for a sight of the Royal turnout.

Menton, in his conversation, amputated his r's like a good-fellow. As an illustration of his mode of speaking I can give no better example than that presented in the following old piece of early war-time poetry, as it graphically shows the exact style in which it would have been recited by him had he been singing it:

"Once on a time I fondly loved
  A young gu'l booight and fai'ah;
The sunbeams spa'hkled in hu'h eyes
  And glistened in hu'h hai'ah.

"She said that she would ma'a'a'ay me
  When the cruel wa'h was ova'h ;
Like a chicken in the cotton patch
  A-scuy'atching up the clova'h."

The last verse meaning that if the war was over she would marry him like fury, or like a chicken in the, etc., probably not willing to be made a widow too soon — all the young men being in the army.

Menton was much older than I. He had also loved and lost, but in a far different way from the manner in which Vielbeer had. Menton had been secretly engaged to marry a very beautiful young lady of seventeen years of age, an only child, whom he had met in a neighboring State. He had her likeness taken about 1860, and it was a fair specimen of the early photographic art. The picture showed her as being the loveliest type of the southern girl; tall, graceful and willowy; large liquid eyes, and aristocratic features. By one of those contra-analogies of nature her mother was a coarse brutal being, with about as much of an insight into the refined, intellectual, and sentimental nature of her daughter as a bivalve is capable of having. The girl was high minded, and extremely proud and sensitive, and as she grew up strove by every means at her command to keep from her friends, and the public generally, the knowledge of the thousand and one humiliations she was subjected to at home at the hands of her parent. Her mother had never yet struck her with a whip, but often spoke of so doing, and had purchased a cowhide whip which she kept hanging on the wall of the up-stairs hall by the side of her daughter's room, as a rod of terror to be daily and hourly seen. Under threats of direct personal chastisement her mother made her perform the most menial and, to one of lofty spirit, lowering services, and so much did the girl dread receiving a whipping on account of the consequent shame that would be hers before her companions and friends, and fearing that they would all be aware of it, and of course construe that it had been richly deserved else it would not have been given, judging naturally from their own probably kind parents' natures, that to avoid this kind of punishment she submitted to anything that her mother subjected her to. Of this the mother took advantage; of course easily reading her fears and wishes, having seen her daily from childhood, and it being no extensive matter for her to overcome the girl in shrewdness—she matching her forty years of life and experience against the daughter's less than half. It was known that at times she, a large heavy woman, would get her daughter down on her back on the floor, and placing her knees and whole weight upon the child's breast—then about from ten to fourteen years of age, with not yet wholly hardened bones—and pull her hair at both sides, and bump her head up and down, forcibly striking it upon the floor, and all the time yelling and screaming and otherwise working herself into a passion, and after fully gratifying her low nature with the delight of witnessing the child's intense terror, would, after the daughter, nearly insane from fright, had recovered her senses, threaten her with a terrible punishment if she ever dared to breathe a word of it to her father; the girl of course kept silent for fear of her complaint not rectifying matters and leaving her still under her mother's full control with the desire for revenge upon her then also added to her parent's proclivities and inclinations.

"But did her father not see the state of affairs and suspicion something of all this," I asked. "Surely in the varying demeanor of the girl toward him and toward her mother, and her different actions and behavior toward him when alone with others, and then when he and her mother were together with others; and then again when in and out of her mother's presence; surely the dissimilarity of her conduct must have been apparent to him." "Yes," replied Menton. "You or I would have noticed it, but some men not; it appears he didn't, you see; either he was aware of it and weakly ignored it, or else his dense mind noticed but a slight part of what took place, and imagined no more that just the little his superficial nature saw, leastways he did not interfere, being in business and putting his whole attention to that. One New Year's eve a large dancing party was to be given by the young people of the town to dance the old year out and the new one in, and all the young folks were agog with the oncoming event. I think the mother's actions dwelt largely on the daughter's possession of a so far superior beauty to that held by her parent that she could not forgive it; it was gall and wormwood to her; the difference in appearance between them would be remarked by friends as well as enemies, and she would be certain to hear of it, and in a pure malicious spirit showed the girl that although she might be beautiful she was still body and soul in her power, and that she could subject her to any degradation that she chose; and to make the girl feel it she let no chance pass by to show her tyrannical dominion; that although she soared above her in beauty, she would show her that she was still totally under her sway.

"The mother knowing her daughter had set her heart on going to the ball, gave out to the girl's visiting friends, on several occasions, some days before the ball, that my sweetheart had been unruly, and that she should not be permitted to attend the dance unless she first submitted to a whipping. This of course the girl would not do, and so all thoughts of the much coveted ball were given up by her; on the day of the event, however, she told my affianced that she could go to the dance that night, and without receiving the punishment; really thinking the girl would go, and maliciously gloating over the pleasant thoughts of the humiliation she would feel, and the shame that would be hers during the night among her friends, the girl feeling full to the limit that they knew she must first have been soundly thrashed before donning her ball dress, and that under her gauzy shoulders were the tinglings of a recently received lashing, and her self-respect and pride lowered to the dust; the mother gloated all day over these gratifying thoughts, life and food to her being. At night several of her young associates, already equipped, appeared at her home for her, and her father asked for his daughter, and was told by his wife that she was probably in her room dressing for the night event; after waiting awhile, and she not appearing, all of them together ascended the stairs and entered her chamber. They were all much surprised to find her in her night-dress sitting before the fire, reading. Her father asked an explanation of her absence from the ball.

"'Mother prevented it,' replied she, 'in saying that I must receive a whipping before being allowed to go.'

"'Not in the least,' sharply spoke her mother. 'I told her this morning that she could go, and that I would overlook the misdemeanor for which I had determined on severe punishment.'

"'She did,' replied the girl, in answer to her father's inquiring looks, 'but the whole town would have thought that I had received the whipping if I had gone, so I determined to remain at home.'

"'So you are not going, then; just doing that to spite me, are you?' said the mother, and securing the cowhide whip, sprang for her daughter, and seizing her by the back of her neck and tearing her night-robe from her shoulders, struck her half a dozen sharp stinging blows on the bare skin in the presence of all her companions, who had accompanied the parents up-stairs to her room. The father, grasping the infuriated woman and tearing her from the apartment, closed and locked the door, taking the key away with him.

"The next morning at daylight the girl's body was found by some negro men, who were returning from a hunting expedition, in a deep pool in a big stretch of woods some distance back of the residence. They reported the fact, and neighbors came to tell the family, who would not believe it, but on their entering her room it was found, of course, vacant, and with one window raised, and on searching the apartment they found a note on the mantel written by her and stating that she had been subjected to such public humiliation that she felt she could never again hold up her head among her friends and that she would end it all and drown her sorrows beneath the black waters of the pool."

"I wonder why she never notified you to come and get her," I asked.

"I suppose," replied Menton, "that she never took time for thought or reflection, but immediately on their leaving her alone, while the deepest sense of degradation was upon her, in a fit of desperation wrote the message, jumped from the window and rushed to the woods and sprang into the water. Women, when in deep trouble, always look upon calm, placid water in a peculiar way; its glassy stillness has a strange fascination for them; they seem to think that beneath its silent surface they will find a deeper peace, a more quiet slumber; that surrounded by its peaceful tranquility they will find a greater restfulness from the turmoil and weariness of their lives. A woman will sit for hours near by and listen to the gentle lap-lap or low swish-swash of slowly running water; they can hardly tear themselves away from the almost irresistible magic spell the sound casts over them.

"Of course, the family not knowing of my engagement to their daughter, and the two or three intimate friends to whom she had confided it keeping silent, I many miles away, only got to hear of the sad affair nearly three weeks later, when even a last sight of her was lost to me forever."

Menton here ceased speaking and shed tears. I kept silent for some time, not wishing to intrude upon his contemplation of this sorrowful happening connected with his past life. And to see men of lofty mentality weep is really heartrending; one is intuitively conscious that their anguish must be keen, from the very fact of their highly-strung natures being the more sensitive to the finer sentiments, and thus feeling the loss of one upon whom they had set their hearts the more.

"Alas! beneath the moss-hung trees, far off by the southern sea, under the green sod of his palmetto-shaded land, he has slept for thirty years."

> "The ever onward stealing years
>   Will never more by him be seen;
> Or bring a joy, a vale of tears,
>   Or regret for that which might have been."

Early one morning he and I went down to visit Potsdam. It is one of the sights of the country—the old home of Frederick the Great. Potsdam lies sixteen miles southeast of Berlin, contains something over fifty thousand inhabitants, and is situated on an island between the small streams of the rivers Havel and the Nuthe where they join.

Frederick the Great was the son of Frederick William I of Prussia, who had the famous company of Potsdamer guardsmen. He died in 1740. This latter named king had a fancy for tall soldiers, whom he formed or inaugurated into a company of giant guardsmen. All were men from seven to nine feet high and over. Every year his friends, the rulers of Russia, Austria, etc., in making him Christmas presents, sent a few—a half dozen or so—eight or nine-footers, to his unbounded delight and joy; and whenever he heard of, or himself ran across, an extremely tall man, the latter unfortunate was at once taken up and made to swell the ranks of the Potsdam company. No matter what his individual wishes or occupation might be, he was impressed to serve his majesty in such manner as his royal grace desired.

In one of the out-lying countries he once came upon a strapping, buxom young milkmaid of an enormous stature, and gave her several pieces of money to take a note, which he at once wrote, to one of his recruiting officers in her village. She took the money and note, but being suspicious, gave the latter to an educated friend with a request to read it for her, and was informed that it said for the officer to instantly take the bearer to Potsdam and marry her to so and so (the tallest soldier in his noted body of guards, the king doubtless thinking that it would be an appropriate match, indeed). The girl took back the note, and, on meeting an old bent and wrinkled hag—a centenarian—gave her a piece of the money to deliver the note, which she did, with results not only surprising to the officer, the hag and the dumbfounded tall soldier, but later on, when he came to look up the carrying out of his orders, also to the king himself.

These guardsmen all wore the tall busby head-covering, a brimless military coiffure two or three feet high, and fur covered, which, with a tall plume poised away above its top, and their own height, made a line of them a spectacle indeed.

He once, by glorious accounts of the happy life he would lead, enticed a young Irishman ten feet tall to join the company, promising, as he was the greatest in statue, to after awhile make him captain. The son of Erin soon sickened of his job, nevertheless, and longed for the land where Saint Patrick, years since, caused the frogs and snakes to cease to grow and disport themselves. Like a sensible man, however, he kept his mouth tightly shut and pretended to be immensely happy. He, at length, seemed so overjoyed at his position that the king let him go back to the Emerald Isle in order to bring over his elder brother, who, he stated, was over fifteen feet high; so lengthy, indeed, that he could take the conceit out of any two of the guardsmen standing one upon the other's shoulders. It is said that, unlike the famous cat, the native of the "Land of Go Braugh," did not come back, but, on again reaching Ireland he would ever after weekly go to the cliffs overhanging the sea, and looking toward Germany, assume a position the opposite of complimentary to the Prussian king.

This monarch's son was Frederick the Great, who was destined to become the most eminent captain of his age. He was made to undergo a very strict and harsh military training. His father did not recognize the extraordinary powers that his son was endowed with, nor realize his wonderful merits; could not understand his superior mindedness and lofty intellectuality, but mistook his flights of genius for what he chose to call "infernal nonsense", and of which he endeavored by cruel treatment to break him.

Frederick the Great, who increased the domain he succeeded to by half of its former extent, and who died leaving to his nephew an army of over two hundred thousand men, is buried in a vault directly beneath the high pulpit of the old church in Potsdam. The guardian of the edifice got the keys to the tomb, unlocked and opened the massive iron door to admit us. We both entered and stood at the side of his casket. It is of zinc and has no lettering whatever upon it. On top, lying horizontally with the length of the case containing all that is mortal of him, with end of blade toward the foot, was the great warrior's old sword. At the head of the zinc lid was a large wreath of faded flowers and leaves. A new wreath is placed there every year, and the old one removed, by the reigning king of Prussia, on each anniversary of his ancestor's, the immortal Frederick's death. We stood silently by, and with our hands gently touched the coffin, and felt the solemn reality of being within a few inches of the man of whom Napoleon, having nearly all Europe suppliant before him (standing, sixty-two years previous, at the side of the custodian of the building with upheld light, and in his other hand the downheld large keys just as we were then doing), said, "Had this man lived I should never have gotten to Potsdam."

Accounts have it that the French Emperor carried away the dead old warrior's sword, and sent it to the home for invalid soldiers in Paris, with the remark that the old veterans there would view with pleasure the weapon which had seen victory upon every field over which it had been waved. This, however, is an error as far as the sword taken away being the true one is concerned; for the authorities of the town fearing that the conqueror would secure the sword as a spoil of war, removed it and laid another one in its old place, which was the weapon Bonaparte carried away with him. The real sword was afterward replaced, and now lies upon the lid of the casket of the captain who formerly wielded it over so many scenes of desperate encounters. Frederick was a doting and tender lover of horses and dogs, and nearly all the paintings of him represent the king in the company of several tall, slender hounds. All of these faithful animals of his are buried in the grounds of Sans Souci, the royal park surrounding the palace; we visited the graves, a large, square slab marking each of the last abiding places of his horses and dogs, all with their respective owner's names carved upon them, seven dog monuments in all, placed side by side. Frederick himself wished to be laid in a final resting place in the grounds of Sans Souci along with and by the graves of his dogs and horses, beings which were ever faithful to him, saying, "Quand Je serai la, Je serai Sans Souci," the two latter words meaning "without care," and the entire translation is, "When I am there I am without care"; but to this burial, of course, the royal family would not consent. We also visited the old windmill, still standing on quite a mound, which Frederick wished so much to purchase to extend the grounds of the park, and which the owner would not sell; the king replied that he then would take it without pay; the miller appealed to the courts which sustained him, and the owner held his land and still continued to aggravatingly grind out meal right under the very nose of his irritated monarch. Many instances of the king's peculiarities are told of him here at Potsdam. We visited his palace, built of curious stones, and in an unique manner, erected just after the ending of the Seven Years War, to show that his treasury had not been depleted by the long and costly contest; also his other chateau, containing his old piano and his desk, the cloth cover of which, originally glued on to the top, Napoleon, with his own hands, tore off, and took away as a souvenir of the sovereign, who must have written many letters upon it. At all these places of interest we heard many tales of his quaint ways. It is said that if he met a person idling about the streets, he took his stick or long walking-cane and gave the shoulders of the loafer a good beating to send him about his business or to his work.

I forget now whether it was his father, the giant guardsmen owner, or "Alter Fritz" (Frederick) himself, about which the above was said; but it was the latter, certainly, who accosted a man upon the streets (it was in the time of Voltaire, the celebrated French author's widely read writings on infidelism), and taking him by the ear asked him what was his belief; the man replied, "I believe the same that that shoemaker across the street believes, the very exact same." "You do?" said the king, "Indeed! and pray what does he believe?" The man replied, "He believes that he will never be paid for these boots I have on, and which I bought from him on credit, and I also believe the same thing."

One day a person from the now capital city was conversing with Frederick, and the king finally getting angry said, as he raised his long cane, with which he always walked, and shook it savagely in the direction that Berlin lay, "Yes, I know the Berliners, they are all a set of knaves." "No, your majesty, you are mistaken", replied his companion. "What! I am, am I"? asked the king. "Yes, indeed", replied the other. "Not all are knaves; your majesty is nearly right, but not quite. They are all knaves but two." "And who are those?" extremely interestedly asked Frederick. "None others than your majesty and myself", answered the one questioned.

We were shown the old thick-trunked, extensively outspreading tree, standing a few yards from the side of the palace and near to his windows. Under the foliage of this tree anyone who considered that he had been wronged in any way had but to come and stand at a certain hour of the day to be sure of the king seeing him from his windows, asking him to step forward and granting him a hearing. And the complaints laid before him were ever thoroughly investigated and justice administered.

We were also shown the room in which Frederick died thirty years after the Seven Years War, at the Chateau of San Souci, in 1786, and the old clock, still upon the wall, which had stopped at the moment of his death.

We left Potsdam in the afternoon of the second day, and on coming into the outskirts of Berlin, stopped off to see a number of African Bedouins who were being taken about the country by a manager, in something like the style of a circus or show. They were camped in their native tents on a large field, outside of the city, out beyond the Thiergarten (pronounced Teergarten), or great wooded park and gave exhibitions in the evenings to a vast audience that daily assembled to witness their adroit maneuvers, the expert and clever feats which they performed with their weapons, and the facility with which they managed the movements of their gracefully outlined, handsome and agreeably dispositioned horses. The wild sons of the desert galloped about in their white flowing robes and hood-like turbaned head-dress, jumping up into a standing position on their horses, gesticulating with their long guns, holding them by the middle with their fingers and twirling them rapidly around above their heads, throwing them up and about in the air and catching them again while going at full speed upon their well-trained Arabian equines, making quite a romantic and spectacular appearance. Their glossy, long-flowing maned steeds were all female animals, with compact and muscular forms, with motions the perfection of agility; beautiful, slender-limbed and fleet, with proud curving necks and wide-flaring nostrils, and were as gentle and affectionate to their masters, and as intelligent almost as a human being could be, docilely obeying their riders' every slightest wish, which the latter transmitted to them by movements of the head, hands and body, or by the pressure of their knees and feet. Their colors varied through all the shades from black to purest white, and many were spotted with these two colors, while others were gray, chestnut or bay.

The male Arab steed is not so intelligent, nor is he as tractable, as the female; nor can he be taught to her heights of excellence. Six or eight of the most skillful and adept among the equestrians, taking their scimetars by the handles, threw them whirling handle over tip up into the air far ahead of themselves, and still standing and going at full tilt on their steeds would catch them again by the handles as they came circling point over haft downward. All this was going on while the audience was collecting in the grounds; and after the hour for the performance arrived and the place was full of spectators the riders retired from the field and the exhibition or scene they gave in return for the admission price, began. It represented the attack on, capture and plundering of, a European caravan while crossing the desert with camels heavily laden with valuable goods and rich merchandise. Some of the largest camels had great boxes or chests hanging, one on each side of them, each box nearly as large as an elevator cage; others were packed with bales, etc. Here came the caravan from out the far distance, getting nearer and nearer, all the camels strung along one after the other for a quarter of a mile, the camels attended by their English owners, who were bestride them or riding sideways as they saw fit. The Englishmen wore the regulation desert white derby hats with long white sashes tied around the rim and hanging down at the rear upon their shoulders to protect the back of their necks from the blazing sun.

The caravan was accompanied by several fierce Arabian-horsed Bedouin guardsmen. As the caravan came right before and into the full view of the audience the Bedouin robbers, who were all this time lying concealed among the rocks and trees awaiting the caravan's arrival, suddenly galloped out with a whoop and with furious gesticulations with their long barreled guns, and swooped down upon the outfit. The Bedouin guardsmen (in cahoot with the thieves of course, and really having posted them as to when the caravan would start out) discharged their guns in the air and made off with loud cries. The robbers plundered the caravan, opening all the bales and boxes and searching their contents; and in the last box they got into they came upon a portly merchant who had, at the beginning of the attack, tumbled out of it all the merchandise and crawled into it himself. Finally the fleeing guardsmen returned with reinforcements—came galloping back accompanied by a large party of brother Bedouin guardsmen—and on their arrival at the scene the merchants being now as strong as the attackers, a show of resistance and fight was made, a parley instituted, and by the merchants paying a sum of money to the gallant rescuers as well as to the plunderers a compromise was effected. The robbers relinquished the goods and drew off, galloping away into the distance until only a streak of dust over the plain showed the track they had left behind them; and the goods being re-packed the caravan again strung out into a long snake-like band, once more resuming its plodding way over the sands of the desert. Finally getting off into the distance and night overtaking them, they bivouacked far away. The several campfires of the caravan could be seen flickering about and lighting up the figures of the Englishmen, Bedouin guardsmen and kneeling and standing camels, and all surrounded by desert darkness, showed with great picturesque effect.

This was the close or ending of the exhibition or entertainment, and on getting out of the crowd and to where the 'buses stood in order to make our way to the city, we found them perfectly jammed with people ahead of us, of course, and were obliged to climb up and seat ourselves on the top. Here we rode for some miles through the deep woods of the Thiergarten, and all being silent and as still as could be—Germans being so untalkative, so quiet and uncommunicative when they are traveling and are all strangers to each other—we let our feet hang down over the side of the 'bus and getting lost in our own thoughts, and being sensibly affected by the dark, silent surrounding influences, we began softly to whistle Yankee Doodle. Our thoughts grew farther and farther away from ourselves and our situation, and unconsciously we gradually arose the tone of our warbling louder and louder, and finally made the darkness and gloom fairly resound to the shrill whistled strains of the soul-stirring "doodle Yank."

Suddenly at the end of a verse as we both caught our breath together for a renewal of the terrific outburst we heard, in the second of intervening silence, "Wunderschoen" (wondrously beautiful), pronounced in unison by two dozen or more voices below. Having such an appreciative audience we renewed our efforts and made the woods fairly ring. Soon the 'bus stopped at a crossing road, and here a jolly crowd of brother students, composed of Felderstein, the perfect type of the furious corps student, and ten or twelve other Prussian Eagles, all got on, having come on foot by a different route to intercept the 'bus. They all had to climb on to the top, also, and they explained to us that they had heard the whistling, while yet the 'bus was far away, and that in the calm still of the night it had sounded very lovely; the strains also having the charm of being new and novel to them. We with growing pride told them of the whole 'bus load also greatly appreciating our efforts, and were informed in return that we were entirely mistaken; that it was exceedingly impolite to whistle in company in Germany, and that we had deeply offended the 'bus passengers. We, of course were dumbfounded, for we had really taken the sarcastic remark of wondrously beautiful, made by the passengers in concert, so complimentary, as something of gratitude also for our endeavors to cheerfully enliven the weary way, that we had afterward exerted our tongues and lips to the utmost, and holding forth with all our might had awoke the distant echoes, and fearing that they would think we had intentionally ignored their feelings stated that we would now apologize to the passengers for our misbehavior.

"Apologize thunder!" ripped out Felderstein. However, he continued we would be absolutely and without qualms forgiven by the passengers if he would take the trouble to explain to them that we were two crazy Americans from a wild, barbaric, and naturally uncivilized country, where such things as manners and culture had never yet reached, and were utterly unknown—the ideas of most of them about the United States being very vague and generally being that of a whooping wild Indian land, bloodthirsty, scalping and red-faced war dancing prevailing, and that thereupon they would realize that nothing better could be expected of two such as us. This, however, he said he would not do.

"Let the insulted hundesfussen nurse their ire with all the pleasure they can get out of it and we will go you two rarely met gentlemanly-like natures, in your offers of apology, one over in high gentlemanship by now all of us new-comers also insulting the passenger audience by singing together, and your little offense will become insignificant by comparison with the immense insult which we shall immediately give them. We shall now with our united voices send forth one of the most charming songs of our fatherland, in which we respectfully request you two to join the lovely tones of your sweet voices.'' At which we all started up the refrain of the young poet Körner's (written by the light of a campfire on the field of war in 1813, during the struggle of Germany for liberty, and while wearing the trooper's uniform of the Lutzow regiment. He was killed in battle, in August, 1813, at the age of twenty-two years), commencing " Deutschland, Deutschland ueber alles'' (Germany, Germany over all).

"Wir wollen ein Heil erbauen
Fur all das Deutsche Land."

"The free land, the German land,
That was the German's fatherland."

"Yet brothers we together stand
That keeps our courage good;
Bound by one speech, a holy band;
Linked by one God, one fatherland,
One faithful German blood", etc., etc.

The crowd tried themselves, each one to outdo the other, and deafening were the sounds that arose on the still night air.

"Over all" we two "wild, uncivilized Indians" construed of course as indicating over all Europe, which is, in fact the song's meaning. We didn't consider it as including any land situated or existing any farther away than the continent we were then honoring with our gifted presence.

This furious insult so overwhelmed the lower passengers that at its conclusion deep silence prevailed. Only the low rumbling of the wheels and the soft tread of the six horses broke the stillness of the night air. But the crowd of students now having gotten their organs of music excited appeared in the mood of continuing the vocal exercise, and Felderstein the most of all; so he spoke up, "Now boys, since you have gotten the night mist out of your throats, all together now our country's soul-stirring national air, 'Die Wacht am Rhine'" (Who'll Guard the Rhine), the song of our beloved though unhappily disunited country. Let me get the beautiful refrain first. Let's see":

"Lieb Vaterland magst ruig sein
Fest steht und Treu die Wacht, die Wacht am Rhine."

"All right now, here goes, all together, one, two, three!"

    A cry ascends like thunder crash
    Like ocean's roar, like saber clash;
    Who'll guard the Rhine, the German Rhine;
    To whom shall we the task assign?

      Dear Fatherland, no fear be thine,
      Firm stand thy sons to guard the Rhine.

    From mouth to mouth the word goes round;
    With gleaming eyes we greet the sound,
    And old and young we join the band
    That flies to guard thy sacred strand.

      Dear Fatherland, etc., etc.

    And tho' grim death should lay me low,
    No prey wouldst thou be to the foe,
    For rich as thy resistless flood
    Is Germany in heroes' blood.

      Dear Fatherland, etc., etc.

    To heav'n we solemnly appeal,
    And swear, inflam'd by warlike zeal,
    Thou Rhine, for all their flippant jests,
    Shalt still be German, as our breasts.

      Dear Fatherland, etc., etc.

    While there's a drop of blood to run,
    While there's an arm to bear a gun,
    While there's a hand to wield a sword,
    No foe shall dare thy stream to ford.

      Dear Fatherland, etc., etc.

    The oath is sworn, the masses surge,
    The flags wave proudly, on we urge;
    And all with heart and soul combine,
    To guard the Rhine, our German Rhine.

      Dear Fatherland, no fear be thine,
      Firm stand thy sons to guard the Rhine.

At the completion of the song so emblematic of the people's devotion to their country, their beloved fatherland, and so figurative of their patriotic sentiments, intense quiet again prevailed, and was the more heightened by contrast to the previous resounding strains, only the same low, monotonous creaking of the wheels and gentle beat of the horses' feet on the soft earth again broke the deep silence, when suddenly from far over the dark woods, coming to our ears from away beyond, through the faintly sighing branches of old oaks and outspreading great linden trees, borne on the night breeze, like a voice from a distant world, came floating back to us, clearly and distinctly, the refrain,

> "Dear Fatherland, no fear be thine,
> Firm stand thy sons to guard the Rhine."

"What a lovely echo," Menton exclaimed, completely lost in admiration of the beautiful sound.

"Echo, thunder!" yelled Felderstein, springing up to his feet on the top of the 'bus and looking far over into the darkness; "that voice sounds marvelously familiar to me. That's Vielbeer for all the world; what in the name of all that's wonderful is he doing here at this time of night?"

Vielbeer it certainly was, for we soon turned a bend in the road and immediately saw distant lights flickering about hither and thither among the deep foliage, and then we discovered, on getting a half a mile further along in the woods, that we had run across our beloved veteran member, a great crowd of students and a wrecked vehicle, all gathered in a bunch in the road; they had broken down; a rear wheel had given way; they had lighted sticks of wood, and while endeavoring to repair the damage had heard our singing, and Vielbeer, with his rich, deep bass voice had answered, in what Menton and I mistook for one of the loveliest echoes in the world. Our 'bus was, of course, brought to a standstill; the damaged vehicle blocking up the entire middle of the road, and Felderstein at once suggested for us all to get down, haul Vielbeer up to our former place, and lay him down flat on top, and with a single strong student at either end of him for safety, proceed, and all the rest of us walk along behind, to the suburbs, which now we were not far from; this met with unanimous approval, and suiting the action to his words all but half a dozen of us at once slid off, and dropped to our feet upon the earth to put his offer into instant realization ; this the lower passengers, suddenly getting a sight of Vielbeer, whom a dozen or more had grabbed hold of preparatory to boosting him up to the down-reaching arms of the several that had remained on the top to help haul him up, fiercely objected to, and raised their united voices in loud and strenuous antagonistic protest. Felderstein insisted, and the passengers preparing to resist, grasped firmly their canes and umbrellas and began filing out of the 'bus to show fight and a scrimmage was imminent; no compromise could be thought of, for all could see that Vielbeer could by no possible means get through the door of the 'bus and sit inside ; the vehicle he had been in along with his companions was an open one with no top.

Finally, however, it was agreed to take the tongue of the broken carryall, and the two good wheels still attached, set him on the axle, and the whole crowd of students attending him behind and at the sides, except about eight or ten on each side of the tongue, which the latter party took hold of, and the balance following, after dragging what remained of the lame vehicle to one side of the road, we all set out. The angry (and "with good cause for fear") passengers resumed their seats in the 'bus, and everything now being smooth again all soon reached the suburbs. Here, seeing something going on in the distance off to the left we quitted the road and the company of the 'bus, leaving it to pursue its own way in silence, and all went over to where the strains of a band of music were emanating from what on approaching nearer we found was a concert garden, open-air theater or out-door opera café. The improvised conveyance for our ever victorious aged champion was hauled to the shelter of some trees, and out of reach of vulgar observation Vielbeer was removed from his perch, which he swore had almost cut him in two, and altogether the students entered the garden and seated themselves at one of the tables. These places of amusement usually contain a theater building, the stage open to the air and to the view of the audience who assemble in the gardens after the close of the day's business affairs. Here among the shrubbery the members of the band sit and play, and the populace meet for sociability. Restaurants are attached to these concert places, and supper can be had as well as nearly all kinds of refreshments, such as ice-cream, seltzer-water, lemonade, and so on. It is all brought to your table by quickly-stepping, genteel-looking and polite waiters, and you can sit and order supper, and eat it at your table in any part of the extensive grounds where you may see fit to select and appropriate one. At intervals acts go on upon the stage, and between them the bands play. Great crowds come to these open-air entertainments. The grounds are laid out like those of a park, and much care is taken of them, and the numbers of tables surrounded by benches and chairs are set in collections in special places about the lawns so as not to interfere with the large passage-ways, the small walks or the beds and plots of grass, trees, and flowers. We had all taken possession of a few tables, all in a bunch, and the agile quick-eyed waiters had supplied us with our ordered fizzing seltzer-water, of which we were all thirstily partaking. Meanwhile the band had ceased playing and a woman had come out upon the stage and was singing in German, and silence ensuing (from the previous hubbub of the students) caused by the cessation of the music, the tune coming from far over the mass of tables and people, between us and the quite distant stage, suddenly attracted my attention. Surely, thought I, I have heard that song before; but yet, impossible. Still the sounds were as familiar to my ears as the smell of paregoric was to my nose in infanthood. Where, where have I heard those beautiful notes before? In some past state of existence, perhaps, a faint trace of which still lurks somewhere in our make-ups. I listened attentively, and all at once as the songstress began on a new verse I recognized it. Having been searching my memory for a German song to suit the tune, it had bewildered for a moment my mind, had led me astray. It was no strain of a previous celestial life, though well worthy of being so; but was the Suwanee River—a translation into German, of which I afterward learned there were several which had been lately introduced into the country. It made me quite homesick as I listened to the old, familiar saddening song.

"Say, ain't that the Suwanee River she's singing?" asked Menton, all of a sudden, pausing in caught interest with his glass half way up to his lips and listening attentively. "That's just what it is," continued he. "Listen, now":

> "Weit unten an den fluss Suwanee,
> Fern, fern von hier,"

came the voice of the songstress.

Just then a big crowd of students, about one-fourth of whom were Prussian Eagles, and who had all been together in another part of the garden, now came slowly strolling up toward us, on their way out, being on the verge of leaving the gardens for the city. Recognizing us, they stopped for a moment, and we all arose and joined them.

O'Brien was along among this new crowd, and had been relating some instances connected with the former devastating famines that had taken place in Ireland. After the interruption of meeting us and our joining the new crowd were over, he resumed his talk, and during the conversation asked Menton why it was (as he had frequently heard stated) that it was considered impossible for a famine to occur in the United States of North America. Menton answered that he was not quite certain what was the reason, but he supposed it was because if the corn crop failed, the United States could feed the hogs with some of its doctors.

Being now in force, and feeling very courageous on account of such numbers, the crowd took the street cars, which ran to within a short distance of the Brandenburger Thurm or Thor, where all alighted, and hiring a buggy and setting Vielbeer therein, to be driven along close behind us, formed ourselves into four rows abreast, and with arms around each other's shoulders, struck up a sauf lied (drinking song) and started off down the street leading to the arch; and it being now about two o'clock in the morning and but few pedestrians upon the street, and those passing along with almost silent footsteps, and all else being quiet and still, we lifted our young, strong voices high into the night air, and Vielbeer, joining in behind with his deep, beer-voiced bass, we made the echoes reverberate:

> "Last uns unsere Flaschen austrinken
> Und rufen fuer Flaschen neu,
> Wir sind alle Preussische Adler,
> Und wir haben Geld wie Heu.
>
> Hoch soll der Adler leben, wen alles andere ist vorbei.
>
> Hoch soll Er leben,
> Hoch soll Er leben,
> D-r-e-i m-a-l h-o-c-h."
>
> Let us drink our seltzer bottles out,
>   And, waiter, fresh bottles bring,
> We all are Prussian Eagles,
>   And we just have money to fling.
>
> When all else has departed, may the Eagle still reign king.
>
> High may he sail,
> High may he sail,
> T-h-r-e-e t-i-m-e-s h-i-g-h.

This last ended in an ear-splitting prolonged yowling yell.

High above the singing voices of all could be heard the Baron's rich and deep barrel-like resounding tones.

Soon we came opposite a nightwatchman with his horn. He was standing upon the curbing smilingly watching us go by. These men parade all the streets, back and forth, the entire night. They are mainly a fire watch to guard against fire breaking out and gaining too great a headway ere being discovered; and as each hour arrives, and the district clocks strike it, they call it out in a loud, slow sonorous voice, and then blow a couple of toots on their horn, thus: "It is now eleven o'clock, my townsmen; it is time all good people were sleeping; eleven o'clock it is now. See that all fires and lights are out, my townsmen. Toot! toot!" Then at twelve the same is repeated, and so on throughout all the dark hours and until the breaking of day. They have their beats to traverse, and are very vigilant in their business, and when they see a fire breaking out anywhere, they run toward it, and to arouse the populace, shouting the word "feuer" (pronounced foyer) and blowing on their horn as follows: "Feuer! feuer! toot! toot! feuer! feuer! toot! toot!" (fire, fire, toot, toot).

This night owl (they were called so by the boys) was standing on the curbing facing us, and had his horn held under his left arm, and was amusedly viewing us passing. A mild student had noticed him while we were still some distance down the street, and had quietly left our ranks and slipped up behind him and suddenly jerked his horn away and with it ran out into the middle of the street ahead of the crowd of us, who at the sight of all this at once ceased singing. The startled watchman, as soon as he recovered from his surprise, took after him with might and main, but the student was of course the more fleet-footed, and they both kept running around and around in a circle in the middle of the wide street and about half a block ahead of us, the mild student shouting and blowing with all his power "feuer! feuer! (fire! fire!) toot! toot!" the watchman with flying coat-tails right at his heels yelling out in answer, "Es ist nicht war, er luegt! es ist eine grosze luege!" (it's a lie! it's a lie!).

"Fire! fire! toot! toot! toot! Fire! fire! toot! toot!" went the fleeing mild student. "It's a lie! it's a big lie!" kept shrieking out the close pursuing watchman.

Windows went up with banging sounds all over, up and down the street, and "was ist's? was ist's? we could hear in shrill tremulous voices emerging from the vicinity of frilled white night-caps suddenly appearing and popping out from the dark apertures beneath the uplifted sashes. "Was ist's? was ist's?" (what is it? what is it?) asked they in scared tones.

"It's a fire! it's a fire! toot! toot!" went the student. "It's a lie! it's a lie!" frantically howled the chasing watchman.

"It's the Prussian Eagle, dear women!" Felderstein

shouted out loudly. "He flies high tonight." And then gruff, calm sleepy voices would come to us from out the deep blackness within the windows in reply to the good women's inquiry, "Es ist eine masse — besoffene studenten, das ist alles, was anderes kann es sein?" (It is a parcel of skylarking students, who are three sheets in wind, that is all. What else could it be?) Soon the mild student ceased his fun, and gave back the horn to the now puffing and blowing watchman, who received it with many swears and maledictions on the head of the joker in particular, and all the students in general, and then Vielbeer again started up the melody, all joining in.

Through the great arches of the massive old Thor, right into the wide boulevard, we all swung, and down the tree-lined Unter den Linden we went; our lines stretched far out, nearly across the street; all shouting and singing at the tops of our voices; we could see the guardians of the peace of Berlin, with true German afore-thought, discretion and prudence, slink off out of the near vicinity, down dark side-streets, away ahead of our approach, and during the long march of over a mile not a policeman was to be perceived in any close proximity. On our approaching a gloomy-looking building, a few stray students were seen standing upon the pavement in front of it; they stopped us and explained that a lot of kneipers (pronounced kny-pers or cny-pers) were in the structure and should be taken home. A kneiper is a student who gets his head packed so full of the learned and doubly profound teachings of a German University that he has to go off on a spree for a few days every now and then to clear his head and straighten out the tangle in his mind; he generally goes to some appropriately selected dive in the rear of some somber appearing building and there fills up and stays for some days, drinking and smoking, his whereabouts utterly unknown to all his companions; sometimes other students, maybe total strangers to him, drop in, and they all strike up friendship and kneip together. At the end of a week or so he turns up early some morning at his rooms, wild-eyed, haggard, pale and disordered, but with a mind now wonderfully clear and eagerly desirous for the absorption of more deep teachings. Whenever a student is missed by his fellows at the University or at his club or from his rooms for a few days, and no one can be found who can tell what has become of him or explain his absence, inquiries are dropped, and even mention of the subject ceases. All know that he has been studying too hard of late, and that he is now kneiping somewhere and will show up safe and sound in proper season. These fellows had been kneiping out too long for their constitutions, explained the students who had stopped us, and were at present too weak from lack of proper nourishment to walk, and had sent word around to their friends to come and get them during the darkness; so they were brought out, limp and nerveless, and divided up among the big crowd, the members of the different clubs each selecting their own brands, and all then taking the directions of their several abiding places, soon disappeared and became lost in the shadows of the night.

In the spring Menton and I received our degrees, and (amid general rejoicing and fireworks in the evening) left the University and city of Berlin together, and on the shores of France we parted, he for his distant American home and I for the lands of the Orient, and soon the wild tossing waves of the ocean were rolling between us. I never saw him again. From the Crimea, in the Black Sea, I sent him a curiously carved meerschaum pipe, and received in return a tear-stained letter from his sister telling me he was no more, and that in the last wild delirium of his dying moments he had called my name among the rest.

CHAPTER IX.

OVER twenty years elapsed ere I entered Berlin again. In 1888 I was once more walking down Unter den Linden street and reflecting on what a change had taken place in the city since I had left just a score of years back. Whole streets of mansions and palatial buildings had arisen as if by magic, taking the places of old tumbling shacks of former days. Evidences of prosperity and wealth were everywhere; were apparent in a manner undreamed of when I was there before. And what a revolution in all Germany. Other nations had rested upon the glory shed over them by the armies of their old generals, and were slumbering deep in their night-caps of fifty years past, when, to the astonishment of the world their imperial cities, the proud capitals of their countries, had gone down before the all-conquering Prussian, and the Germanic race of Europe had once more assumed its inherent supremacy, and Germany, fair and historic Germany, the land of poetry, legend and song, which I had left divided into thirty-two principalities, states or kingdoms, all of them of tenth-class power and standing, and perpetually quarreling among themselves and with each other, had united all factions in one patriotic confederation, and now posed undisputed as the first military nation on the globe. All

Europe was copying her; the armies of other powers were teeming with officers who had been through the war within the German army lines, and were now back to their native countries giving the military organizations of their own lands a German training, a German dressing, and a German gloss. What a change from 1868, when divided Germany, with its collection of ever-fretting little weak kingdoms was the despised of all military powers of any standing!

Prince Bismarck, the admirable old iron chancellor, was making the proud boast that "The Germans fear God, but nothing else in the world." The tramp, tramp, tramp of the military was still going by, just as it had twenty years before; but now there was a prouder carriage to the regiments, and each soldier and officer in his bearing showed that he felt, as they passed you by, that no criticism on them could be made. Who is there to compare them with to their disadvantage? Monuments erected in gratitude to the victorious legions reared their proud heads aloft toward the azure sky and were towering all over Germany. A lofty mass of brown granite and bronze, capped with a gilded figure of "Victory," a winged female with a wreath held in the hand of an extended arm, had been raised on a prominent elevation in Berlin and met the eye from all parts of the city.

Germany had soared in twenty years like a rocket. Berlin, the former capital of Prussia, had emerged from "ein groszes dorf" (an immense village) into one of the greatest seats of learning and science in Europe, and had taken its place, as the capital of united Germany, among the great cities of the world. But what a wreck twenty years had made among known faces! I wandered about the stores of old, the few of them still left unmolested to make room for palaces and towering modern mansions, and only at rare intervals met a face I had known in the days of the past; a face last seen in the appearance of the prime of life, now grown wrinkled and old, with whitened head bowed in the weakness of age that the silent years, so swiftly passing, never fail to effectuate. Alas! the whirligig of compassionless time brings around its changes.

What is twenty years to science in the building of a strata! What an insignificant period of duration in the cooling of a sun! But what a great section it is out of our miserably brief lives.

The aged emperor, William I, had been buried but a few days before. I had witnessed the pageant, the pomp and splendor of the burial of this wonderful old man, who, as a boy under ten years of age and all unconcious of his exalted destiny, had fled with his mother, the sainted queen Louisa, so revered by all the fatherland. In 1806, at the invasion of the French, under the great Napoleon, the conqueror of Europe, they were fleeing for months, in vain seeking a haven of rest secure from the armies of the all-triumphant Corsican, no sooner quieted in one place than again sent flying out into the cold world by alarms of the near appearance in pursuit, of the soldiers of the immortal Emperor.

This wonderful old man, who had in childhood slept on cannon barrels to inure himself to endure hardships, and who had lived to thrice enter the enemy's capital with a victorious army — he had brought the fatherland to an unparalleled prosperity, and from what? In 1807, when his land was under the heel of the victor, the country was so impoverished that the government published for the benefit of the peasantry a list of roots and herbs that would sustain life. What will patience, perseverance and the flight of time not accomplish!

He had now been laid to rest in the magnificent mausoleum at Charlottenburg, a few miles west of the city, by the side of the two marble sarcophagi of his father and beloved mother, and the gorgeous parade was now something of the past.

Not having been able to get near the tomb until some days later, I then visited it; the building is large and lofty, is one story, entirely of marble, a flight of steps ascend to the dome-like room in the center of which rest, side by side, the marble cases enclosing the earthly dust of his parents; supine figures of them are cut in marble on the top or lid of each of the monuments — Frederick William III, the founder of the Zollverein, which made the customs and duties of the German dominion uniform, and who died in 1840, sculptured in full military costume, and Queen Louisa in the drapery, the high waisted dress of the time. A faint bluish light emitted from above through blue glass windows in the lofty dome, cast a reverential shade over the marble tombs; the late Emperor's casket, almost covered with wreaths, was lying at their heads, having been placed there temporarily.

I was walking down the boulevard slowly, having on either side of me bare trees and brown grass-plots, and thinking of the changes, when suddenly I heard just back of me a familiar "bow-wow." A dim mistiness of the past, a faint recollection of by-gone years, stole over my mind, a voice or sound out of the long ago seemed to be speaking or calling to me, awakening remembrances lost in the rapid march of time. At the same instant I felt a tug at the heel of my trousers' leg, and being unable, from some weight attaching itself thereon, to move my leg farther, was brought to a stand still, and on turning my head and looking down behind me, met the recognizing upward gaze of an exceedingly fat little bench-legged dachshund (badger dog) who had snapped his teeth into my trousers' rim and swung on to me with a teutonic grip. A surge of old memories, a rush of old associations, came and went over me in an instant. I stooped over and picked him up. Yes, it was! it was indeed Schnurkelyah (snoor-cle-yaw), hoary and gray faced as a patriarch, and, if anything, fatter still than he was in the days of yore, but still the same dear old Schnurkelyah. I hugged him fervently, right there on the boulevard, and squeezed him tightly to my chest over and over again, and he gave a half dozen gasping, wheezy, apoplectic yelps, wiggled and made desperate attempts to lick my chin and neck all over in his delight. To be held in kind remembrance, by even a dog, is always affecting, and tears filled my eyes. He had remembered me all these years; his sharp little nose had run across my track on the street and he had followed on my trail, running ahead of his companion and had tackled me.

"Himmel Reich!" (land of heaven) I heard exclaimed

by some one approaching, in great astonishment, with wide staring eyes, at the peculiar conduct of his dog, and of the stranger in thus caressing him. It was Felderstein; I recognized him in an instant, although he was now a man of middle age. I would have known those penetrating gray eyes anywhere, and that cool, calm demeanor that was still apparent in his approach, although his face showed that he was deep in wonderment.

Still holding Schnurkelyah tightly to my chest, I held out my hand to him; quick as a lightning flash he grasped the situation. "By the saints above! the American student," he cried, and rushed, German style, to embrace me, forgetting that Schnurkelyah was still in my arms and was in the squeeze between us, and only the latter's energetic squealing brought us to our senses. I put Schnurkelyah down, and together we went into the Café Bauer, and over our glasses of seltzer Felderstein related the news. Vielbeer was in the city now and at the Central Hotel; he had come up to the burial of the old Emperor; was now on the eve of his departure back to his castle; he, Felderstein, had but a few hours ago left him; had taken Schnurkelyah out for a little promenade, and was shortly to return him to his master; and I must come along for Vielbeer would be most happy to see me. And, by the way, he supposed that I did not know that Vielbeer was now Baron of a vast holding, was rolling in wealth, and lived in his ancient ancestral home on the Rhine, in grand style. The war of eighteen hundred and seventy came; the enemy's capital fell; the lately deceased aged king of Prussia had been crowned sovereign of all the German states, provinces and kingdoms in the court hall at Versailles, near Paris, by all the German States in unity, and was thus made Emperor William I of a united Germany; and that the fairy queen Elfrida's vow had at length come true in its entirety, the young prince of the year eighteen hundred and thirteen, who had fled in horror at the sudden death of his companion at the chasm, had lived to raise his country to an unparalleled prosperity and had reigned over Germany entire.

Vielbeer's uncle, Thorwald, a younger brother of the

house and who, as a young man of twenty-five years of age, had helped the aged Emperor when a prince in eighteen hundred and thirteen to get a sight of the beautiful fairy queen's much coveted but fatal crown, and who had lost his life in the gallant attempt to bring it up from the unfathomable black depths to the prince, could not of course be recompensed. He had met his rewards above, a great one of which was witnessing the "wiedersehen" (again seeing) of the aged Emperor on meeting the heavenly shades of his sainted mother, beloved father, and the colleagues of his youth who had long gone to the land above before him. But the grateful emperor while still on earth, had made what restitution was in his power to the remaining members of the family.

The confederated states had voted a large sum to recoup the fortunes of the Vielbeer family; the Baron had restored Vielbeer castle entire, and refitted it in all its former grandeur; the turrets, walls, battlements and towers had been rebuilt as in the days of old, and all the surrounding land it once owned re-purchased, and it was the home now of the noble family. Vielbeer having never married, his great, good heart having been burnt out by his fierce flame of love in his youth, had called his cousin's family, the children of the son of Thorwald's and his own father's younger brother to the castle, and this family's two sons now there, were considered by him as his heirs and the future heads of the house.

The Prussian Eagle club was long since no more. An immense stone State building now occupied its former site. At the outbreak of hostilities, when war was declared against the fatherland, the club had at once disbanded and joined the army. Count Luft had headed his regiment and had been killed at Gravelotte, along with sixty percent of his men, in a cavalry charge on the enemy's center. His body had been brought back to Germany and interred in the family burial ground, and a beautiful monument marked his last resting place.

His own (Felderstein's) father had gone the way of all humanity years before, and during my twenty years absence, two of his six brothers had died natural deaths.

One was drowned at sea off the coast of Madagascar, and two killed at Sedan, where he and another, who subsequently died from the effects of his injury, were wounded, leaving him the last son remaining and the inheritor of the title "Graf" von Felderstein. "A rather empty one, it is true," he remarked, for the death of his father, who had been in high favor at court, leaving little but his title behind him, threw the sons into the position of having their fortunes to make with their swords, their careers relying upon their own efforts.

All the beautiful mementos, trophies, and works of art of the club had been sent to the families of those who had presented them, a great portion naturally going to Vielbeer castle, as so many of them had emanated from its owner's skill in always being successful.

We remained at the café several hours discussing old times and watching the ever-coming and going throng of customers, the never-ending passing crowd on the street ever present to view through the windows. The café had a coal-black Ethiopian standing in front of the door as a drawing card; he was dressed in vivid blue from head to foot; he was at all times surrounded by a wondering, admiring audience. He was black as jet, and his face shone as though lately oiled. Little children were among the crowd, which was large, and was ever present to gaze at him, and they were tightly clinging to their parents' hands and drawing back shrinkingly in fear of the "Mohr" (Moor), as they called him.

Negroes are very rare in Germany. It is only at intervals of weeks that you meet one even in such a metropolis as Berlin. The climate is too cold for them, too damp and penetrating; their teeth chatter, and they have to wear overcoats even in July and August; and this one was as much of a curiosity as an Eskimo would be in any of our cities here. The people about him asked each other, "Do they let him go about loose?" "I guess they surely keep him chained at night," etc., etc. He was enjoying the sensation he created immensely, and when an American (knowing full well that he was a darkey from the United States) stepped up and addressed him in English, saying, "Ah there, boss, how's everything, hey?" With a shake of his head the black replied (although one could see from the light of recognition in his eyes that he understood) in French, "Par comprenz, monsieur, Arabe! Arabe! (pronounced Ahrahbuh) claiming to be an Arab (though black as coal, indeed) from the interior French Algerian colonies along the south Mediterranean sea, in northern Africa.

"Come along with me now and we will go right to the hotel and meet Vielbeer," said Felderstein, as we turned and left the richly dressed darky to his admirers, and all three of us were soon walking down Friedrich strasse (Frederick street) on our way. We finally reached the hotel, entered and went straight to the Baron's apartments, and on knocking and receiving in response an old familiar deep bass "Kommt herein" (come in), opened the door, and sitting behind a cloud of smoke drawn from a marvelously "well aquainted to our view" old meerschaum pipe, I recognized the Baron. Vielbeer (pronounced Feel-beer) also knew me at once, through his large spectacles.

"Donnerwetter" (thunder weather) "here's that American student, back again after all these years", he cried out instantly on clapping his eyes on me. He extended his fat right paw in a welcome greeting, and I could see by the humorous twinkle in his eyes that he was thinking of the same thing that my own thoughts were upon, namely, the last few times in which we had met, my final session at the University and last winter at the club, the gay times and lively scenes of twenty years ago when I was a mere thoughtless youth and his own joints were much more limber than at present. I gripped his old hand—the hand that had carried so many bumpers to his lips and to victory; the hand that had marked off so many places on the floor for duelists to station themselves on; the hand that had been ever just; the hand of a man who had never been the slave of his own characteristics, never been the prisoner of his own nature, nor the captive of his own sentiments, but had been ever right and true to justice; the hand of a human being such as is extant in one among each ten thousand — with both of mine, and was unable from emotion to speak a word for some time. Felderstein related to him the circumstances of Schnurkelyah's memory, of nosing my tracks out upon the street, and of his brilliant break for my trousers' leg to attract my attention, and Vielbeer seemed not surprised at all, but remarked that Schnurkelyah had a great deal more sense than thousands of men whom he had met.

The Central Hotel was in the near vicinity of Vielbeer's depot. The Baron was a prudent man and always got near his starting point on the last few days of his stay, to be reasonably certain not to lose his train by a mishap on account of his weight. His hair and mustache were now snow white; his hair falling almost down to his shoulders gave him something of a patriarchal appearance; he was far over eighty years of age, but still walked about erect at times and with fair strength. He at once invited me down to spend the summer at Vielbeer castle in southern Germany, remarking that I would find a different state of affairs there now than what I would have had I visited it in the days of the club, when the few acres he still owned surrounding the building barely paid him enough for his subsistence.

I accepted his kind invitation on the spot, and ringing for his valet, Diedrich, who was also his old coach-driver at home, and who accompanied him everywhere, he asked him to bring in a bottle of Rhine wine, which was drank altogether to the memory of the good old days—"the days," said Vielbeer, "although not by far as prosperous as now, that will nevertheless ever remain fresh and brightly outlined among our recollections, for they were the days of our youth, of our health and our strength."

"Baron," said I, after a while, "you have never been out of my thoughts for one whole week at a time in all these twenty years since I have seen you." He was much too intelligent a man for one to presume to flatter, and on his asking me in what regard he had been so constantly in my thoughts, I told him the truth, that in America my friends had never forgiven me for not being able to make them acquainted with the circumstances relating to the assistance his ancient ancestor Centavus Vielbeer had given

Monk Monastus in the fourth century in that interview with the Forty Saints, and that I had been pitched into weekly by friends ever since because I had thoughtlessly left Berlin that time, at the close of my final semester at the University without learning it. The Baron laughed long and loudly on hearing this, his fat sides shook, and old as he was a flattered expression of amusement stole into his face, and he remarked that I could have the opportunity of searching the archives of Vielbeer castle soon myself, and glean the whole history of the interesting and romantic occurrence to my full satisfaction. At this we shook hands all around, all four of us former Prussian Eagles, although Schnurkelyah, curled up on Vielbeer's slippered feet, looked far from being able to soar like the bird whose name had given the club its designation, and Felderstein and I took our leave.

On again finding ourselves in the street, I remarked to Felderstein that it appeared strange to me that he and the Baron, seeming to be, to all outward appearances, such bosom friends, yet Vielbeer had given me a direct invitation to visit his home in his (Felderstein's) presence, and had not mentioned even the word to him. "I see," replied Felderstein, "that you have in your twenty years' absence from the University largely forgotten the 'corps studenten' honorable interpretation of high gentlemanship. Had Vielbeer invited me, it would have been with an intention on his part to directly and deeply insult me, and so I, in my position of a retired corps student would have construed it. The very fact of his never opening his mouth to me about coming to the castle means that I am considered as a beloved brother, whose home the castle is supposed to be at any time and whenever I see fit to go there for a period. As the Baron and I stand in friendship together, the invitation would be about as one inviting his wife to come down and make a short visit to his home. I shall be down this summer while you are there; shall come to the ball of which the ladies of the castle give two yearly, one in the midst of bleak winter and the other in the season of blooming flowers."

We soon got on to the great boulevard again, and were walking down its length toward the old Brandenburger Thor or gate, to pass through it on our way to the station; when still quite some distance away, we noticed a great commotion going on about it, and on quickening our pace and arriving there, we found a mild student had played a prank at the Thor, after first attempting and failing to get off a joke on the guard-house.

Since 1870 many beautiful and costly monuments have been erected all over Germany, such as the Column of Victory, crowned by the heroic sized and gilded statue of Bonessia, in the Koenig's Platz of Berlin, the Niederwald Denkmal, and so on. Soldiers stand in duty about these magnificent structures to prevent their defacement by relic hunters and evil minded persons. A barracks was now stationed near the old Thor; it was situated in a building on the left side of the street as one approached the Gate, and was about two hundred feet from it; four soldiers also guarded the center passage way of the Thor, which is at the west end of the boulevard. The great gate itself is really in three divisions, all three being passage ways into the Thiergarten beyond; the two structures at the sides are in the shape of porticoes, are about seventy feet high and have several rows of pillars running from front to back, and thus form lofty open colonnades, the right one having several transit ways and the left one half a dozen or more; these are for the use of pedestrians. The center structure, the monument between the two side porticoes, and what is really meant as the Brandenburger Thor itself, has six eighty-foot doric columns supporting a fifty-foot high right-angled parallelogram, composed of a richly carved and decorated architrave, frieze, and cornice, on the summit of which the bronze ornament, the Goddess of Victory upon her quadriga or chariot drawn by four horses abreast, overlooks the Unter den Linden. The six columns form five passage ways or corridors, and are for vehicles, the one in the center being the widest and is guarded by four soldiers, one at either side of its entrance and its exit, which latter is also its entrance into the boulevard from the Thiergarten; this central one of

THE BRANDENBURGER THOR, BERLIN.

Page 158.

the five corridors is intended to be used exclusively for the passing of the carriages of the Emperor and the members of the royal family, the general public's conveyances having the use of the four others. A soldier is also stationed in front of the barracks mentioned, who keeps a vigilant watch and look-out for the coming down the long boulevard of any carriage containing a member of the imperial household or any high military officer, and on them approaching to within a reasonable distance, he calls out "wacht heraus" (guard, come out), and a file of soldiers, who are always ready, like a thunderbolt string out of the guard-house door, line up abreast on the sidewalk with glistening bayonets and salute the occupant of the carriage ere it passes through one of the corridors of the old Thor, then they turn about and re-enter the guard-house to await the next summons. As soon as this call "guard, come out" is heard everyone on the pavement in the immediate vicinity of the barracks steps briskly out of the way to allow the emerging soldiers a free pathway over the pavement for their coming salute, in the same manner that we do on hearing the bell of a fire engine coming around the corner, all our rigs and pedestrians at once clear the track for its passage. A mild student heading a crowd of his "pals" had come along, and just as he got in front of the guard-house door, between it and the military watcher on the curb, who was industriously looking out for an imperial personage or a high officer's carriage, and whose back was necessarily toward the barracks, just as the student was in the act of passing the entrance, the watching soldier perceived a conveyance coming, containing an occupant to whom a salute should be made, and at once cried out "wacht heraus." The mild student, so skillfully as to make it seem a perfectly unavoidable accident, at once made a wild skittish maneuver as though attempting to get out of the way, and then suddenly fell down with a smash — cane, cap, gloves, eyeglass and all — right on his stomach, flat upon the pavement, and just before the entrance, as the waiting guardsmen came flying out. The expected mess of sol-

13

diers did not turn out satisfactorily to the mild student for they all lightly leaped over and sprang around him. Being all young active fellows they easily cleared his prostrate form and without the least disorder or trouble, took their station on the pavement aligning the curb, and made their proper salutation in a highly creditable manner. Three large heavy policemen, however, had their misgivings as to the fall right smack in front of the doorway and in the direct path of the watch being so very innocently unintentional, seriously aroused, and rushed over to where he lay, fell on top of and made a grab for the coat collar of the mild student, who agilely crawled out from under them all and made off into the middle of the street toward the Thor, where the two soldier guards of the royal driveway were standing in mute awe at the audacity of anyone daring to take the liberty of so offending, or offering such insolence as to attempt something witty or sportive on, the arms of the military. The nimble and quick-eyed mild student saw at once that the two guards' nervous systems had been violently deranged consequent upon the overwhelming emotions produced by the attempted jest on some of the members of an organization which they held in such supreme awe, and were in an apathetic and unalert state, and he yelled at once to his companions, "Quick, boys; all of us together through the royal driveway! Quick, now! Hurrah! There he goes! there he goes! catch him quick! hurrah!" And the mild student darted through the wide center corridor (while all the onlookers were bewilderingly scanning about for a sight of the invisible fugitive who was seemingly being chased), with the crowd of students at his heels. Past the unexpectant guards (who couldn't understand or imagine why anyone should want to go through the imperial driveway when it was known to be especially prohibited) they all went through like a hurricane, and at once scattering out soon disappeared entirely among the bushes and trees of the Thiergarten.

Quite an agitation had been raised around the Thor at the act, and soon a large number of police officers (members of the finest) gathered, and loudly expressed themselves that if the crowd of transgressors *had been caught* they would have made "die funken davon fliegen" (the sparks fly from them).

This lark of the mild student brought forcibly to our minds the same thought of the flight of years, and Felderstein echoed my sentiments and just what I was thinking of when he remarked that he realized we were now old men in comparison to the present University student who joins the mild and corps bands, and were no longer of them.

Ah! sad is the day when we, in long after years, visit our former Universities, where we once had the proud distinction of being one of the youngest among the young, and feel that we are now looked upon as old fellows by the present students.

We wander among the lecture rooms, the galleries and halls, yet our footsteps fail to awake even an echo of a former time, and on the assembling of the classes we scan the crowded amphitheaters over—a sea of industrious, fervent zealous faces meets our view, but they are all strange ones, and are the countenances of two generations behind us.

Twelve thousand students now attend the University. The staff of professors has risen to one hundred and seventy-five, and as an institution of learning it has no superior.

We parted at the depot, Felderstein boarding his train and going up to the North Sea on some business affairs of his own. Some weeks later I went down into southern Germany and made for Vielbeer castle. I quitted the train of cars at Holtz, a town of some considerable size, and the nearest point by rail to my destination. The town was in gala attire, a "Schuetzenfest" being in full blast. It is something like an exposition, but lasting only a week. However a half year's jollification is crowded into the week. The streets and houses were decorated in all colors of flags and streamers, and long bands of cloth hanging in festoons. The "Marktplatz" (market place), a large square or plaza in the heart of the town, was the center of the show and excitement and was crowded with carousalles, shooting galleries, side shows, curiosity exhibits, target-throwing dummies, whirling wooden horses, games of chance, etc. And all about the sides of the square were rows of booths and stalls temporarily erected to contain wares exposed for sale.

I stopped after awhile before one tent, on the large painted canvas stretched before which was displayed a wild black man in his native jungle of Africa among giant trees and dense tropical underbrush, tearing to pieces an immense struggling buffalo with only his naked hands and sucking its life's blood, while immediately above him curled among the branches and partly stretched out in hiding upon a large limb, for fear of being discovered by the ferocious black and sharing the same terrible fate as the buffalo, was an enormous terrified python, capable of swallowing a horse, tremblingly awaiting the departure of the ravenous savage black lord of the forest, to skip out and shake hands with its tail in congratulation upon its narrow escape. On a red cloth-covered box at the door of the tent stood a showman, speaking in a loud resounding voice and inviting the awe-struck crowd, gaping with saucer eyes and open mouths at the picture, to enter the tent, telling of the wonderful wild man who had been captured in the dense wilderness of the far-off mysterious dark continent; a squadron of cavalry had chased him three days and nights over the deep marshes, deadly swamps and through the dangerous fastnesses of his unknown country before he was finally overpowered, and then he nearly killed and eat two or three of the troopers before he was firmly secured in chains and brought out to civilization.

"Come right along, ladies and gentlemen! pass right in and see the wonderful wild black man perform his great war dance right before you all. He eats live animals whole right on the stage. Pass along in!" etc. The crowd listening to him, wavered, scared and fearful of what the tent contained; mothers with children held them closer to themselves in fear.

Surely he cannot break loose?

"He will not be allowed to harm some of us or eat our children?" inquired several of the peasant mothers.

"No danger at all," replied the showman, "he is heavily chained and his keeper with a club is always at his elbow, prepared to wade into him forcibly if he shows dangerous symptoms of breaking his chains. Pass right in frauen and herren and get a look at the wonder of this 'yahrhundert' " (century).

We paid our fee and passed on in, quite a crowd of us for safety, with fluttering hearts and creepy feelings going up and down our spines, and while waiting for the man, whom we found inside, sitting on the stage playing an accordion, until a sufficient number of audience had collected for the wild man to be brought in, to stop his music, I noticed several boys stealthily abstract their knives from their pockets, quietly open the biggest blade and return their thus armed hands cautiously into their trousers' receptacles, ready to withdraw their weapon and do battle in case the dangerous captive should break loose ; a sufficient audience soon assembled, the accordion ceased, the musician arose and seizing a great "wendeltreppe" (wen-tle-trap) or immense spiral sea shell, using it as a horn, he raised it to his lips and blew a terrific blast upon it. At once horrible sounds, mingled with a great clanking of chains, coming from back of some hanging drapery, assailed our startled ears, and amid fearful whoops and yells, the chained wild man tore out from behind the curtain and on to the stage followed by his keeper with an immense club, the keeper took up a position between the wild man and the audience, facing the chained black and all the while made violent demonstrations, menacingly waving the club over his head at him, to deter him from promulgating any deadly rush at the onlookers. The wild man was clothed in but a short skirt of cloth covered with turkey feathers; he had a necklace of stringed feathers, strung through the large end of their shafts, hanging around his neck down on his chest, and also was decorated with several large turkey feathers stuck in his woolly hair; all else of him was naked, exhibiting his shiny black skin in all its glory. He carried a spear which he waved about while he danced and yelled ; he howled and opened his mouth to its fullest capacity, which was an appalling sight indeed, and rolled his eyes about, showing great amounts of white eyeballs, and all the while making an awful clanking noise with his chains, all of which, with his fearful grimaces, which he threw in ever and anon, was quite terrifying, especially to the younger members among the onlookers. At last he quieted somewhat under the increased energetic threatenings of the keeper with the club, knelt down on one knee, pointed his spear upward and waving his free hand toward the zenith, made his wild fetish prayer or superstitious worship and adoration of his deity in the following manner:

"Awful spirits did dey raise, hark! doom!
 Till de audience crazy wild,
Rushed and broke into de dark room,
 In a frenzy fa'h from mild.

"But at sight ob de spirits dey were dazed,
 Fa'h dey saw two jugs ob whisky,
Lookin' very jaunt and frisky,
An as do'h dey had been pretty often raised.

CHORUS.

"White boy gimme gold and silver,
 Black boy gimme pearls,
White girl wears straight brown tresses,
 Black girl she wears curls.

"Ky! yi! boss! kum! ketch, kuhnotchka, cum, hi, O,
Ise de homesickest niggah in de lan',
Yi, yi, ky, ya-a-a, O-o-o-o-o."

I at once of course recognized him as being a Sambo from my own land, and let him know by my laughter at the song that I was "onto him." He at once bounded to his feet, rushed to where I was standing in the front row of the onlookers, grasped my hand, knelt and kissed it, arose and fell over my shoulder and wept, muttered a lot of gibberish, gave a last lingering wring to my hand, made as though brushing tears from his eyes and went back to his devotions, on finishing which a dead chicken was brought in, which he grasped, raised it to his mouth, tore the feathers off with his teeth, blew them all about in the air over the audience's heads, and grasping his spear, with a last furious dance, a wild whoop, and a final demoniacal yell and a wave of his hand toward me, disappeared behind the curtains, leaving the onlookers standing all wrapped in amaze.

The keeper with the club got upon the four-foot-high platform which the wild man had just left, and explained to the crowd that the foreigner, whom the wild man had embraced, had, years ago, rescued him from death. He was once captured and was to be eaten by a party of enemies in the jungles of Africa; was lying tied while they built a fire and heated the pot, and the foreigner had crept up on his stomach for half a mile and released him by cutting the thongs from off his bound limbs, whereupon he had jumped to his feet, seized a club, and had immediately killed all his enemies and eaten them then and there, after cooking them in their own pot; and on recognizing his deliverer a few moments ago had been immediately overcome with grateful emotion and ran up to caress him, etc.

From the glibness with which he got this off, together with the fact that toward the middle of the story he suddenly found that he had left out some and went back and started afresh, I saw at once that it was a "stock act"; that, of course, he must run across lots of Americans in traveling about with his show who would recognize and speak to the wild man, and the act of rushing up to his deliverer and its accompanying explanation was a "cut and dried" part of the performance to be brought into play when the necessity arose.

On leaving the tent, the showman outside asked the outgoers what they thought of the exhibition. "Wonderful," they replied. "We wouldn't have missed it for anything." At this there was a rush by those still staring at the picture to get in and also see the great African. He created so much excitement in the town that doubts were entertained of him being really black, and hints went around that probably he was a white man stained with some kind of juice or color, and that maybe his head had been shaved and black sheep wool skillfully pasted upon it, and that the whole thing was a fake played on them; and the population began to feel insulted at the idea of a showman taking them for such ignoramuses as to try to make them believe that he had a man who was really black and had woolly hair. Their ire arose the more they thought about it, and finally a deputation of the principal citizens, including two physicians, got together and called on the showman and demanded a thorough examination by themselves of the wild man. The sharp showman bowed at their approach to the very top of the box he was standing upon, knowing the instant they had presented their case that the fact of the examination proving the wild man to be real would be noised abroad at once and be spread throughout the whole country and cause such a rush to see his captive as he had never dreamed of before.

"Certainly, my respected 'Herren'" (misters), replied he; "all of you step right in, and as many more as will fill the tent, and all free, all free, and I will let you prove his genuineness to your entire satisfaction." The committee filed in, followed by a large, eager crowd, and the tent was soon jammed. The chained African was brought out and was made to submit to an examination. The doctors put acids and bleaching chemicals on his skin, in spots all over his arms, back, and legs, but without effecting the ebony tint in the slightest degree; and on investigating his wool, of course it was found genuine, and to the astonished contentment of all. They retired with loud exclamations of wonderment that a being could be a man and still be born black as coal; they had read about and heard of such individuals from persons who claimed to have actually seen them, but the general rural public had a very misty idea of how they must look, if, indeed, the accounts of them were really true, which many of the unlearned much doubted.

As the showman had foreseen, the rush to get a view of the wild black the next few days was unprecedented, and money just poured into his coffers. All were more than satisfied. Only a few, however, marveled that the wild man had been so extremely tame, good natured and

UNIV. OF
CALIFORNIA

VIELBEER'S CASTLE ON THE RHINE.

Where shades of mail-clad
    figures lurk,
And ghosts of Ladies fair as
    Turk-
Imagined houris of the skies
    (Their loftiest dreams of
    Paradise)

Linger o'er towers, 'round
    gloomy walls,
'Mongst dark and desolated
    halls,
Where knights of old in
    shining steel,
In armor 'rayed from crown
    to heel,

With helmets plumed, for
    beauty's glance
Once fiercely warred with
    sword and lance ;
Where present travelers'
    sighs and tears
Dim echoes wake of long-
    gone years.

Encastled stream, enlegened Rhine,
What art can swell the fame that's thine?

quiet during the examination, while at all other times his keeper had to stand between him and the audience in a dire threatening attitude with a club to keep him from making a break and slaughtering the whole crowd. These few deep thinkers pondered awhile and then gave it up—they couldn't understand it.

I left the town of Holtz the next day and went by a stage route, which ran between the latter place and the little dorf of Bischen, to the last named village, the nearest one to the castle. It was about two o'clock at the time of my arrival in Bischen, from whence I decided to give the "go by" to conveyances and walk to the castle, the looming turrets of which could be seen about twelve miles away on the heights in the distance. I went along a well worn road, that I was told would bring me direct to the principal gate belonging to the inclosure of the extensive wooded park that surrounded the heights on which the great building stood. On arriving at the gate, at the end of about two hours' walking, I was met by a keeper coming out of a little house within the inclosure, accompanied by three Dutch doggers. These animals are as large as our English mastiffs—are probably the same race of dogs. They are most often yellow, but now and then grayish; their heads are very big and broad, but they are not specially vicious; they were the same kind of canines the mild students in Berlin, in 1868, had so much affected as companions and pets, decorating them with beautiful and costly collars and taking their dogships along with them upon the street, to their own rooms, and into those of their brother students when calling upon the latter, and also in their carriages when driving. They are, in fact, really good natured animals when properly reared.

The gateway was of stone in the shape of an arch, two massive side pillars supporting the half circle above. Carved on the keystone of the arch, on the side facing the incomer, was the heraldic device or coat of arms of the noble family I was on my way to visit. It consisted of a laughing fox in mid air, in the act of springing from one rye or wheat stack to another, the fox's face expressive of the highest of glee; it all being portrayed on a shield, running around the upper rim of which was the word "Auf-immer"(forever). Passing the gate and entering the great wooded grounds surrounding the castle site, I strode upward along a deeply shaded graveled drive, between woods of giant oaks, linden and other trees, for about four miles. On all sides were evidences of a gardener's high taste. When the trees finally ended I came upon the flower and shrubbery garden made upon the several plateaus, and extending up toward the heights, on the extreme summit of which, high up over all, towered the surmounting castle.

After getting past the garden I then began the climb to the building, going up winding ways cut, in places, through solid rock; up zigzag roadways, beautified on either side by trees, flowers, shrubbery and plants. The whole ascent was through a cultivated garden. The plants and trees would change at different elevations, and hardier flowers and shrubs had been set out on the heights than at the base near the valley. Up, up, I went along the same wide path, up and down which so many brave and gallant knights in iron and steel, and with proudly flying pennons, ensigns and standards, and so many fair ladies on snow-white steeds in richly decorated trappings, had ridden in the days of "once upon a time long ago."

All the surroundings appeared as in the days of old. I could easily fancy myself transported back to medieval times—the romantic days of hunting horn and falcon—and had a knight, a Baron von Vielbeer of old, clad in glittering armor from head to foot, his helmet crowned with waving and nodding plumes, with erect lance and clinking sword and bearing his emblazoned metal shield, mounted on his armored and gaily-caparisoned, fiery, prancing war-steed, come riding down from out the castle gate, and on passing raised his vizor from before his face with a strongly gauntleted hand, and informed me that he was on his way to a tournament at which the fair lady of his choice and affections was to preside by right of her being the queen of beauty and of love, and passing me descended the winding way, and finally have disappeared in the green woodland beyond, it would all have seemed perfectly appropriate to the surroundings.

As I continued my way up I realized pretty fully how extremely apt the constructor or originator of the coat of arms had been in realizing or reading the strength of the castle's position—the inaccessibility of its situation; the interpretation of the very appropriate heraldic design being that Vielbeer castle was so strongly and safely built that its capture or destruction by an enemy was considered impossible, and so even the foxes had played always and were never disturbed in their amusement in the gardens inside the outer walls and fortifications by any of the long wars of medieval days that had so shaken the country; but forever had daily gamboled about, jumping from one wheat or rye stack to another, grinning in frolicsome sport entirely oblivious of war and its meanings.

It was no easy jaunt to get up to Vielbeer castle to a light-footed man, and for one in armor and heavily weaponed, as in the middle ages, it was a stout-hearted job for a warrior alone, and if astride a likewise iron protected animal a still tougher job for the beast; the endless windings and acute angles necessary to be traversed to approach nearer and nearer were disheartening.

On arriving at the uppermost plateau, the one on which stood the building, however, the scene repaid many times over the toil of the ascent, for the view was magnificent. One could look back over all the ground he had traversed as from some peak. You could trace the passageway by which you had ascended winding away down until it almost spun out like a thread to the valley, dotted here and there with groves of trees and small villages, the clusters of dwellings looking like spots on a green carpet, for the people do not live on their farms but build their homes in little collections about six or eight miles apart; all the barns, stock etc., of the surrounding agriculturists are at the village. This custom is also a remnant of the days of feudalism, when the rural inhabitants had to live as near together as possible, had to congregate in little hamlets for protection from small bands of marauders and from which places they could receive in a body the news when large bands or armies threatened, and they could sound the alarm and all fly in a company to the castle for protection. It would not have done in those unsettled and unlawful times for single families to have resided on their farms, almost at the mercy of every wandering couplet of outlaws that came to the vicinity. So the inhabitants clustered together in little towns about seven miles apart, and paid heavy tribute to the fiery lords of the castle, the ancient Vielbeers, for protection when danger threatened, and for an avenging pursuit on bodies of evil doers, too large for a town to cope with or oppose, when sweeping suddenly down in a surprise upon them.

This custom of dwelling in little villages and going from thence daily to their outlying farms to work, driving the stock there in the morning and back home again at eventide, still hangs on to the older inhabitants, although no country is now more law-abiding than Germany; but it is difficult to eradicate old usages. I could see the little village that I had walked from easily, lying nestled among green branches, some twelve miles distant, and its tree-bordered road leading away to the depot town where I had left the cars, which place was also discernible against the green background stretching into the gray mistiness beyond, a long line of space among the trees indicating the railroad track, and ever and anon a crawling black band with a low streak of smoke hanging over it showing the passage of a train.

Just below, on the descending heights, and clear to the woods were splendid evidences of landscape gardening, the heights were laid out in plants and shrubs, trees and flowers, and now and then in looking over the surrounding inclosed forest one could see where whole streaks of trees had been removed, sometimes a tunnel-like clearing or passageway having been made through them for two or three miles, at other places merely trimmed in proper shape to open up a view to a small pavilion and boathouse on a little river, flowing a few miles away on its journey to the Rhine, or a giant path cut through in another part of the woods to unobstruct the vision of a little summer hunting cottage in the distance, surrounded by a small park of tame animals such as deer, fox, mountain goats, etc. All this on looking backward over the trail from whence one comes up to the building on the landward side.

Looking forward, on the opposite side, a sheer precipitous rocky cliff led away far down to the Rhine, the silver, historic, beautiful, beloved Rhine, flowing in silent majesty far below. Onward, ever onward past so many ruined strongholds of the dark ages, its surface dotted with boats making their way down and up stream; and opposite on the other side the lowlands, sloping away into the dim perspective, both banks, where not too perpendicularly inclined to render it impossible, in a high state of cultivation, covered with grape vines, and over and beyond them, toward the interior, the fields of wheat and rye, etc.

Both the sloping, and where at all practical, the steep acclivities are terraced and planted in grapes. A wall of stone would be built near the river, of greater or less length according to how soon it ran across or into a deep gully, and the ground leveled from its top back say eight, ten or twenty feet where another wall is erected eight or ten feet in height, and another patch of level ground made from its upper surface back to the lower part of the next wall. And so the banks ascend in receding tiers from the pure transparent stream, far up toward their summits like enormous steps. On the level places thus made the grapes are raised and carefully attended to, so that both banks for miles and miles, as far as one can see with a glass, look like a terraced garden—not a weed to be seen. The bank on the other side to that upon which the castle was situated being the lower, the building overlooked the opposite country, as it did all the land on its own side of the river.

One could easily see that the structure had been placed on a site well adapted to suit the manners of the baronial lords of the past, and perfectly in accordance with the prevailing conduct of its time. From its lofty towers, commanding a view of the whole surrounding country, the old feudal masters and their retainers could spy out all traveling caravans, journeying from one large commercial mart to another, loaded with rich goods, wares and merchandise, and swoop down upon them, exacting heavy tribute for the privilege of safe passage through their vast domains, or finding the caravan's armed escort a little too heavy for their stomachs, and ready to resist payment, courteously apologizing to the merchants for the trouble given them, and withdrawing with many left-handed wishes for good speed. Alas! human nature, hast thou ever changed an iota under any circumstances, conditions or climes since the oncoming of man?

The river was alive with traffic in merchandise, fruits, wine, grain, products of factories, etc., and numbers of gaily decorated passenger boats, with bands of music and flying flags, crowded with tourists and sight-seers, were to be seen going one way or the other, the Rhine, with its beautiful scenery, its castles, and terraced vineyards being one of the sights of Germany.

I seated myself on a stone at the end of the cliff for half an hour and overlooked the Rhine and all its enchanting surroundings, and industriously rubbed my calves to feel sure that they were still flesh and not lumps of lead; and I also had it to faintly dawn upon me that the elasticity of twenty years ago, when we students toured it every vacation on foot over mountains and valleys and into distant countries, and were almost unaware of the existence of such things as legs, was becoming a feature of the past. My aching limbs, after a twelve-mile level walk, and a climb to the lofty summit of the eminence, was a fair reminder that youth is short, time flies, and that human machinery also wears out and grows old; and as necessity is the mother of invention, and a great engenderer of trials to overcome obstacles and the need for labor, and the stimulator of inventive thoughts, I began to ponder, and wondered why so many things came out of place in this world, and why elevators were not invented in feudal days, for then it would have been no trouble at all to land any number of men and horse up or down at an hour's notice, and the shaft could have been easily protected on the near appearance of an enemy.

I finally arose, after resting, and approached the grand entrance door of the castle, mounted the broad granite steps, and advanced into the large, the wide and deep, area way formed by a high pillared and sculptured arch, about six feet above the keystone of which was a similar escutcheon or shield, chiseled in relief on the wall, having on its surface carved the same coat of arms of the family as that I had seen on the gate that gave entrance to the wooded park, the jumping fox and grain stacks, but here very much more elaborated and finely worked out. The figure of the fox had been so well dressed out in the stone that a kind of witheringly, contemptuous grin was plainly discernible on his face, and in the background of the well-pictured stacks were cut splendid representations of stone fortifications.

The entrance doors were of oak, massive, and studded all over at about eight inches equidistant with nails, the heads two inches in diameter. The knocker was of brass and in the shape of a chest handle, the covexity of the curve bulging into the life-size representation of the head of a laughing fox. In appearance the knocker looked as though a large, curved bar had been run through a fox's head just back of his ears and the ends then bent to fit into two brass decorated screw eyes, from which it hung pendant, and could be raised and lowered at will; the under chin of the fox's head rested upon a large, round piece of metal, imbedded in the oak even with the wood; the knocker was of great weight, and took a good deal of force to lift, and when brought down upon the round piece of metal it was intended to strike, with a strong hand, it made a noise that went resounding throughout the great hollow halls, along the stairways and into the rooms of the structure loud enough to awaken the seven sleepers.

I had just got through inspecting the curious knocker, and was on the point of reaching for it to "thunder at the gate," when one of the wings of the heavy door swung slowly back, and there on the stone floor of the hall stood Vielbeer, and between his feet Schnurkelyah. The baron had seen me wandering about the base of the building from his window in a tower overlooking the Rhine, and recognizing me had come down to the door just as I had put forth my hand to knock. One of the most flattering circumstances I ever ran across in my life was the unbounded delight expressed by Schnurkelyah at my appearance; he gave one upward jump, and I took him in my arms and hugged and squeezed him to me again and again, just as I had on the streets of Berlin early in the spring.

"Donnerwetter," said the Baron, and tears gathered in his dear old eyes as I grasped his extended hand and was welcomed to the castle. Here at the end of an intended two-weeks' sojourn I was urged to stay so vehemently that I realized that the request was not left-handed, and so settled down and remained the balance of the summer, as Vielbeer's invitation in Berlin had really meant for me to do. I was given apartments on the same floor as were those of the Baron's own, in one of the lofty towers, from where I could look out upon miles of scenery and fancy myself a Raubritter (robber knight) of old, spying sharply from the windows, keeping a vigilant lookout for the sight of dust raised by traveling bodies of traders and merchants, and was told to make myself at home. This latter offer has a far different meaning in Germany from the manner in which some guests in our own land construe it, as they often, on being requested to make themselves at home, do so with a vengeance, literally kick the host out and install themselves in his dwelling in great style and comfort. At home I immediately felt at once, and if for no other reason could have done so by cause alone of here again seeing all the old familiar trophies won by Vielbeer's never lowered championship that I had admired so often and that were so much thought of at the old club.

In the hall the first object I ran across was the well known immense metal and carved wood hat and coat rack that had stood at the side of the door of the principal chamber of the club-rooms in Berlin. It had been constructed by a carver in wood as a sample and display of his artistic work for exhibition at some exposition, and after the closing of the fair it had been auctioned off and the clubs of several cities had purchased it in conjunction and then had a contest for its possession, and Vielbeer had lowered all their colors with a rush, while the Prussian Eagle's banner, which he represented, still soared. It was an elegant, large-mirrored piece of furniture, was deftly carved in a decorative manner, and was a work of high art, and had taken a prize at the exposition where it had been displayed. At the first landing on the stairway and from which place it divided to take its upward flight in opposite directions was the ten-foot-high grandfather clock, its large dial staring me right in the face, and its slow, solemn, low, regular tick-tock was being sounded down through the halls in the same monotone of long ago, when the timepiece had shown the all-too-soon-sped-by hours on the interesting nights at the club.

All the trophies of the Prussian Eagle that were won by the Baron during a victorious career of half a century I again saw here, and they seemed so familiar to me after the intervening twenty years that I felt, on seeing them about everywhere, as though I was returned to my old home after an absence of two decades. All the gold and silver flagons, drinking-cups, mirrors and pictures, etc., were here, and were met with at almost every turn.

A neat little hand-elevator had been placed in the side of the building; it ran up several floors, from whence another and a much lighter one ascended to the loftiest floor of one of the towers that overhung that portion of the structure facing the Rhine. The convenience of an elevator in a towering castle cannot be overestimated.

The stable maintained was quite large, and Vielbeer's great desire and pet wish, which he had expressed so often and with such heartfelt earnestness in the days of the club, was here at last attained in near perfection; for he had his own coach and special pair, and was driven about to his fullest satisfaction. Having been deprived of this earnestly-yearned-for treat for so many years, he now laid a greater value upon it. It assumed much importance in his eyes, having looked at the vision of himself in his own vehicle through the small end of a telescope for so long, he still saw the now-gained, longed-for enjoyment largely magnified; and the baron never tired of sitting in his coach, fat little Schnurkelyah snuggled up on the cushion beside him, and following his mettled steeds over the surrounding territory, often crossing the Rhine bridge a few miles farther up the river than where he dwelt, and driving far over into the opposite country. His old coachman Diedrich, the same one who had accompanied him to Berlin, dressed in his dapper uniform, being a landmark for the whole encompassing region, for whereever he was seen driving the heraldic emblazoned baronial barouche, the inhabitants knew full well that the master was behind him in the conveyance, for the young men and ladies of the family preferred a younger, more dashing and a faster driver.

These young members of the noble house, however, had all their own driving and riding horses, and were often to be seen riding down the long winding passage from the grounds of the elevation on which the castle stood, to the level lands below, on their cream or black steeds, in their picturesque riding costumes, for a gallop over the country or a visit to distant neighbors, a great crowd of dogs always accompanying them. And it was often a gay party, indeed, that would, on getting down beyond the base of the eminence, canter through the four or five miles of towering old oaks and aged linden trees, branching aloft and rising on each side like the pillars or columns of a vast ancient structure, and trotting through the old arched gate with neighing horses and joyful barking dogs, gallop out into the wide spreading lowlands.

I often accompanied these parties, and the return at dusk or night was the most enchanting part of the affair. Entering the gate, lit by a single lantern hung on one of its pillars by the old gate-keeper, we would slowly walk our horses home, and in the calm still of the night, with no sound to break nature's harmony but the panting of our tired dogs following after us with drooping heads and tails and lolling tongues, we would listen to the warblings of the finest of songsters—the nightingales, which birds are numerous over southern Germany. Their sweet songs are heard in the woods after nightfall on every side.

Our ears would take in the strains until the beautiful notes all died away over the great masses of green foliage, and again on coming to where a vista had been cut through the trees to open a view of the boat-house, stop for a moment in the silence and listen to the rippling of the distant river looking in the soft purple moonlight like a glistening line winding along its way to at length mingle with the clear waters of the old Rhine.

Occasionally the leading riders of the party would get square in their faces the full benefit of a mass of cobwebs swung across the driveway during our absence by a lot of industrious spiders that, German like, had thoroughly labored during our ride, and like their human teutonic co-laborers had never considered whether their toil would amount to a row of pins or not, but had worked, it seemed, just for the pleasure of being able to show others that they had not thrown their leisure away, but all the time had "duechtig geshaft" (put in their level best). "Well, Claus," a good old German mother often says to her brawny son, patting him on the back as he sits with head bowed in depression on his hands, "cheer up, there is one comfort through it all, we have fallen behind a hundred dollars this year also in running the farm, but you can still have the consolation that it was not your fault, that you worked the whole year like a horse."

Or the leading riders would have a cloud of startled German "fledermause" (flying mice—bats) swirl around them, and flap their clammy wings in their faces, until at length getting near the end of the woods we could see the old castle high up and far above us, looming upon the heights in colossal proportions as a great, dark, gloomy mass, its turrets, pinnacles and towers faintly outlined against the sky, a light here and there about the edifice shining from some of the windows but accentuating the deep, silent awe-inspiring gloom that seemed to be part of its nature, and after our tired horses would climb to the summit, their footsteps enlivened by the thoughts of supper, we would also hasten the exchanging of our riding-habits in order to be soon at our own suppers, at which, among the rest of the food, a plentiful supply of wurst, kartoffel salat, and other wholesome and delicious teutonic dishes were sure to be met with, and all eaten along with the juice of grapes gathered from the banks of the Rhine.

I one day sauntered into the large gallery that contained the life-size portraits in oil of the members of the Vielbeer family from the baron's own likeness, painted some fifteen years before, to those dating back into ancient times. The gallery was a long, wide hall, situated at one side of the upper part of the castle, and was lighted from the roof; the pictures were hung along the sides of the walls in several rows, from the high ceilings to near the floor, line after line of the family ancestors and ancestresses, and with each is connected a longer or shorter narrative of former events, some noted for their heroic deeds, some for their beauty and the delightfulness of their amiable and charming personality, and others famed for their intimate association with this or that historical occurrence. Here was the painting of the baron himself, looking just about as he had at the club in Berlin; on a nearer inspection the canvas showed that it had been executed in 1872, just four years after I left the Prussian capital, and about at the period of the flush times connected with the restoration of the building; there was also one of him represented as a young man in the neighborhood of twenty years of age, about the time of his desperate attempt to abduct his peerless inamorata, Gretchen, and which ended so lamentably for him; it was the same face as the baron then wore, only the ravages of time had changed it; the features and expression were those of the now aged man, the same mild blue eyes that could be so firm, yet gentle, the identical, genial, open-hearted honest face; one would have recognized it as Vielbeer in his youth among a thousand.

Here was also the painting of his great grandfather, Commander Marverdt von Vielbeer, who disappeared that night during the terrific thunderstorm which shook all southern Germany and made such havoc among the black forest mountains; he was drawn in the picturesque costume of an officer of the army of Frederick the Great.

Here also was the portrait of Baron Crusadus von Vielbeer in his dress of the crusades, cap-a-pie in shining metal, his three plumed helmet on his head and lance in his gauntleted hand, his suit of mail being chain armor, over which a skirted vest was worn, a large cross of golden cloth being sewn on to the front of the vest, below the neck. He it was who had the romantic ariel flight along with the fowls and the devil from out the black depths of the dreaded chasm.

High up hung the picture of Gustavus von Vielbeer, the roistering young blade who helped the young architect get the plans from the cloven hoof, and to whom the city of Cologne is so much indebted for its beautiful Cathedral; he is depicted just as one would imagine him to be, young, strong, a slight tinge of good cheer on his nose and full cheeks, from high living, and a reckless "who-may-care" look upon his set "no-insolence-taking" countenance.

I stepped back from the likenesses and running my eye about took a general sweeping look at the mugs of the long lines of Vielbeers, which run for generations upon generations back; the visages grew more savage and vicious as one went back to remote ages along the ancestral line, until when I got to the delineations of those portrayed garbed in skins and armed with great, manyspiked clubs, who had had it up and down with the early invading Huns; it seemed that the fierce looking cut of their jibs alone were enough to scare off the Huns without any display of arms whatever.

Then I took up the antecedent line of the ladies of the family; here was the Baroness Marverdt von Vielbeer, nee Princess Christina Marienchen Hedwig Wilhelmina of Komwecht, the wife of the commander and the great grandmother of the baron, a very beautiful young woman indeed, and dressed in the Queen Louisa costume of a century ago.

The features of the ladies changed as I went down the line to earlier ages, just as the men's did; after some generations back, the women of the race grew less and less lovely and seemed to have rather forsaken great beauty for massiveness and strength, and as I got far back beyond the Middle Ages the Vielbeer ladies nearly all were heavy and powerfully built.

I stopped before the life-size painting of one whose weighty arms and shoulders gave evidence of great strength, and who looked a physical champion, and in whose fair face no trace of amiability showed in the least; on a nearer view of it I learned that this was Germania Vielbeer, the fair oak of the black forest. Later on I asked the baron about her, and he stated that she was the bewitching daughter of a neighboring baron whom his ancestor, the master of the house, had married in the seventh century. Vielbeer told me that she had once detected the master of the castle red handed in the act of throwing sheep's eyes at another fair damsel, and utterly prostrated at the discovery had laid for him when he returned home that night, and that they had had a terrible battle together in their lofty chamber in one of the towers; such a frantic struggle had they that the noise alarmed the entire building, and all the master's relatives armed themselves with bludgeons and whatever they could lay hands on, and gathered together at the outside of the locked door from whence the fearful uproar of strife proceeded and thundered loudly for admittance and to know the cause of the great disturbing rumpus.

The clamorous tumult eventually quieted when the fair Germania had finally overcome the master and wrapped and wound him round about from neck to foot with a lengthy rope, and then taking a great spike and a heavy sledge-hammer she ascended a huge cask standing at the side of the chamber and drove the iron into the wall, deep between the great stones, high up toward the ceiling, and then shouldering her lord she hung him by the encircling ropes at the back of his neck upon the spike, descended, rolled away the cask to the other end of the apartment, unlocked and opened the heavy door of the room to the now furiously crying-for-admittance relatives, who, no longer hearing the master's voice, were getting seriously alarmed. The fair Germania suddenly and without warning unbolted the door, which flying in unexpectedly from the outside-pressing force, spilled half a dozen of those foremost in the pushing mass in a lump upon the floor. Germania stood a few steps back from the threshold, pointed dramatically to her lofty suspended lord, and said, "Da bleibt der hund die ganze nacht" (there sojourns the hound this entire night), planted her feet firmly, and with a swing poising her sledge above and back of her head, dared all his relations — the whole house of Vielbeers — to step in and take him down.

"The tradition runs," said the baron, "that those of the crowd who were the farthest behind were the most vehement in urging the foremost ones on to the fray, and that the extreme front ones put forth much strength in shoving shrinkingly back upon the others. 'Rush in quick and grab her, boys!' shouted those at the back. 'I just wish I was in front, I know what I would do,' said one far in the rear. 'So do I,' repeated another at his side. 'I would down her mighty quick,'" etc.

Finally, however, all together made a desperate, mad rush inward, the whole excitement of an American discussion on the silver question ensued in the next few moments; there were shouts, groans, yells and dire imprecations for a spell, and then the silence of night reigned supreme; and on the smoke of battle clearing away it was discovered that the fair Germania was the only one whose perpendicular attitude remained unhorizontalized.

The baron took me to the upper floors of the tower and showed me the room in which the fray occurred and the enormous spike high up on the wall, it having been put in so tightly that no force has since been able to get it out again, and there it had remained to this day. The sides of the walls also showed where pieces of stone had been chipped off during the rash, headlong encounter, fought in the unavailing attempt to rescue the master from his uncomfortable position, "where he remained," said Vielbeer, "until near morning, for his better half, after turning out all the vanquished ones, extinguished the light and calmly retired to her downy couch and went to sleep, and only after the night had well departed and her lord had promised many times over to never again even look at the hat of any but his own gentle darling one, that she recovered from the utter prostration into which she had been thrown all along since his detection, relented, arose and forgivingly released him from his suspended place of repose."

As I got still farther along down the ancient line of the Vielbeer ladies, I came to one more picture that caught my attention—another of those charming dames among the ancestresses of the Vielbeer family, who, like the soft and winsome Germania, were noted for all of the previously mentioned traits comprised within the meaning of "a delightful feminine personality." It was the portrait of another massive woman, this time clothed in the skins of wild animals, a club in her hand, a Roman helmet upon her head, around which was painted a halo. This, the baron informed me later, was Teutonia Vielbeer, a very ancient young daughter of the house, who, when the last Roman invasion was made into Germany, and her barbaric people were giving way before the legions and fleeing, Teutonia headed the women, who, with clubs, met their running-away fathers, husbands, brothers and sons, and with blows drove them back to the struggle, where, shamed before their women folks, they had rallied their courage, and putting forth renewed efforts were finally victorious, overcame the Romans and utterly annihilated the legions, almost destroying them to the last soldier; and in consequence made all Rome howl twice in unison, "O give us back our legions!" which victory, caused by Teutonia's great leadership of the women, was the beginning of the downfall of the proud "Mistress of the World," for the wild skin-clothed nations took heart at the now gleaned fact that the armies of the invaders were not invincible; and appropriating the mailed suits and armor of the defeated, and seizing their swords and spears—all arms so much superior to their own—(that is, they took the offensive weapons of their vanquished, undersized enemy, to the last one, but of course could only use the captured protective armor when the immense thighed conquerors could get into them, which was the case once in about each hundred suits) and following up their successful conflict with the Romans, and pressing closely on the heels of the remaining legions, one after another of which the leaders at home withdrew from afar to bring them back for the defense and protection of the home city, it all ended in one conquest after another, and finally in the downfall and plundering of the haughty Eternal City itself by the barbarians—the warriors under Alaric, the king of the Visigoths, in the first few years of the fifth century.

Here was also the painting famed as a great work of art all over Europe, of the elopement of Thermusia Vielbeer. She was called in her day "The Rose of the Castle," and was courted by the great nobility of the land from far and near; and her parents had set their hearts upon her marrying a duke at the very least, but she had given her affections to a young nobleman of the vicinity who had a lovely, soft, silken mustache and dark curly hair, and who had told her that he loved her dearly. He was forbidden the castle, but came down the Rhine under the shadows of night, in a skiff, accompanied by two companions, an old man and a young boy; had left them in the boat moored to the bank at the river side, and had scaled the heights to the base of the edifice, and with unerring aim had shot an arrow with a long twine attached right into her window, which twine she had drawn in until a stronger one came up at its end, and on getting this last into her chamber, a ladder of rope appeared which she and her maid pulled into her room and fastened, and then followed by her faithful girl had courageously descended to the arms of her lover, who carried her down the precipitous cliff into the boat.

The painting shows the old castle way up on the heights in the background; in the front is the river with the skiff at the bank, and standing up near the boat's rudder, with fingers on the end of the tiller, is the old, long grey bearded man, who is looking at the fleeing ones with an expression as of deprecating the rashness of youth. Sitting near the prow and at his oars, steadying the boat, is the boy whose face is upturned in open-mouthed wonder, and whose features are delineative of being perfectly lost in admiration of the vision of loveliness which young curly hair, who is just stepping into the boat, bears in his arms; the gallant is looking longingly into the eyes of his sweetheart who is adoringly returning his gaze; he has one foot on the seat-board of the boat, the other still on the bank he is just quitting; as he carries her she has one partly bared arm thrown over adown his shoulder, the other resting lovingly and trustfully around his neck; a few paces back of them and still some distance up the cliff, the rocks and crags of which are so naturally represented, is her following maid, with head half turned from looking back to see if any signs of the discovery of the elopement were yet apparent at the castle, against the wall of which the rope ladder can be faintly seen hanging from the window by which the two maidens had taken flight. The low descending moon is just shedding its last soft rays over the romantic scene and looks as though reluctantly disappearing, as if it were unwilling to sink its face beneath the surface of the earth while the rose of the castle remained above it.

I was shown the window from which she escaped and was impressed at the sight, by the thought of the deep affection she must have had for her lover to risk the frail ladder, and also the perilous heights reaching to the river. It also shows the loyalty of her faithful maid in making the same venture to accompany her mistress. The painting is renowned, not only from the fine execution of the work, but also from the great insight the artist displayed of human nature in portraying what a smart youth the dark haired lover was, as he had taken along as his two helpers an old man in whom all thoughts of love was long something in the past, and as his other assistant a boy of an age when all women seem to him to be hallowed angels; had young curly hair have selected two stout companions of his own years to help him kidnap a lovely being, they might have been bewitched clear out of their senses by her overpowering beauty on his arrival with her at the boat, and there might have been an immediate three handed fight for the possession of her and to decide which one of the three handsome young fellows should continue the elopement with her; the ascending rocky cliff, the castle, river and the figures of life size are all splendidly drawn, and so naturally colored that one almost expects to see the participants in the affair move, so truly does the scene seem to be enacted in reality before you.

CHAPTER X.

THE ball was given one night in the late summer, by the young ladies of the family, and the dancing took place in the large banquet hall. All the surrounding landed families took part in it, and lots of Vielbeer's old friends from Berlin. Felderstein, now Graf, of course came down; also Hecht and Brun, his two former antagonists, all now meeting together in the best of comradeship, for the necessity of mutual protection had united them all — the declaration of war against Germany in 1870, and the threatened invasion of the fatherland; at the oncoming of which the clubs had disbanded and all had entered the ranks of the army in patriotic defense of their country; had endearingly joined them every one into a common brotherhood. These had come along with a lot of their officer friends and lady companions.

Hecht's face showed plainly the scar where Felderstein's rapier had made such a startling cut, but it did not disfigure him in the least; in fact it gave him something of an intense look, an appearance of firmness and mystery that his wife remarked was such a source of delight and entrancement to the ladies that she had to accompany him everywhere to shoo them off. Brun picked up Schnurkelyah and the little dachshund stared knowingly at the end of his well healed nose, as if he recognized it as having been part of his own dogship's little anatomy twenty years ago.

We spent many long hours together, we old former students, in calling to mind the occurrences of past days, and especially in reminiscences of our host's former wonderful achievements, pacing back and forth along the ridge of the precipitous cliff, arm in arm, smoking our cigars and watching the boats going and coming on the Rhine; or at times we sat on the broad stone steps leading up to the front arched area way and listened to Vielbeer, who, sitting in his old comfortable cushioned chair, pointed out objects of interest about the surrounding country and related historical events connected or associated with them.

The banquet room, which must have been the scene of many merry parties and roistering celebrations in days gone by, was floored in wide stone flags which had been covered at the time the Baron restored the castle, as he had all the floors, excepting the wide lower hall, with inlaid wood-work. The walking surface of the great lower hall Vielbeer had left, showing its immense flag stones or slabs as in the Middle Ages.

The dancing hall floor had been covered with a large and pretty pattern of this inlaid wood-work, and the walls were decorated by a series of pictures and paintings framed in a rare and costly manner ; on one of the sides of the walls, and just above the center of it, two stag heads were fixed about six feet apart, and between them, about four feet higher, hung Vielbeer's old silver-mounted drinking horn that he had always worn hanging from his left shoulder, as his badge of office in umpiring a duel or deciding a contest when appealed to by some of his club members who had got their opinions mixed in an athletic competition or in a game of some sort. On again seeing the horn for the first time, Vielbeer's appearance, as he had so often looked twenty years before at the club—standing with the horn hanging at his left side, puffing slowly away at his pipe, deeply weighing the case of each side, both of which had been presented to him with much vigor, and little Schnurkelyah wisely blinking, standing between his feet—came as vividly to my mind as though seen but the day before.

The ball scene was a vision to remember. From the ceiling were suspended eight chandeliers of curious and beautiful construction, containing lighted candles which shed their soft refulgent rays over the assembled happy crowd. Candles were still the correct mode at that time, ere electricity had been generally introduced into the households. In Germany the candles do not drip. One can be placed upon a silver quarter and be allowed to burn down to its last flicker, leaving but a fourth inch long char of wick on the quarter dollar and not a drop of tallow will be found to have run over the piece of money. One never sees a drop descending the sides of the candles in Germany. At the manufactories when a stock is made it is tested, and if it does so overflow the candle shaft while burning, the whole lot is immediately turned back into the great caldrons and remelted, something it has lacked is added and the stock molded over again. They are made in all colors and convenient sizes, and often in fanciful shapes, and besides presenting in their places on the chandeliers a magnificent effect of tastefully arranged colors, also greatly enhance the ladies' beauty by their mellow rays, in contrast to the effects of other lights which render powder, paint, wrinkles and sallow necks painfully apparent.

Large vases of wax flowers, and shell-work in the shape of pedestals, crosses, and so on, under glass covers, stood on polished top stands about the sides of the hall; lovely mirrors, broad and tall, and inclosed in carved frames reflected the enchanting ball scenes from all parts of the room; officers in all the charm of their showy uniforms, high-heeled boots, clanking swords, and stiffly-waxed mustaches, supporting on their gallant arms ladies gowned in masses of flouncing and costly material, rustling in silks and glittering with jewels, were soon whirling over the floor in step to the low strains of sweet music, in the heavenly enthrallment of the Blue Danube waltz; the low, soft murmuring voices of the women, the fairy-like whisk over the smooth floor of satin slippers, the resplendent chandeliers, the radiant young faces, the brilliant eyes, the fascinating white gauzy dresses of the young ladies, the shining uniforms and swords of the young officers, and the entrancing sound of music — the music of poetic, legendery Germany, of the land of sentiment and song — issuing from the artificial shrub thicket-hidden orchestra, gave the scene a resemblance to what one in childhood imagines the innermost regions of fairy land to be like, and awakens the thought of what must have been the beauty of those ancient pleasure gatherings in the same chamber, when gaudy colored velvets and silks were the costumes of the cavaliers of the time.

The flames from the high chandeliers shed a flattering light over all, and were reflected back from the mirrors in thousands of beautiful blazes of light; and the white flounce-attired women in the seventh heaven of bliss on the arms of meritorious sporters of brass buttons, floating about in the dizzy mazes of the dance, looked like fairy queens tripping the light fantastic toe with their brother magicians—the gnomes and kobalds of the famous black forest mountains—amongst millions of dazzling stars twinkling about their regions of wonderland.

CHAPTER XI.

A PARTY of us went from the castle a few days later and took passage on one of the excursion or sight-seeing boats, so many of which ply upon the Rhine for the benefit of tourists.

We, comprising most of the younger members of the family and the remaining visitors who had come to the ball, and whom the young hosts and hostesses were going to accompany as far down the river as the city of Cologne, where they were to say farewell, and the guests to take their departure for their homes in northern Germany. The boat was fairly well filled with tourists, mostly in parties, and many nationalities were represented. A party of Spanish were among the passengers, they having several young ladies along, the latter on a vacation tour from their studies at a pension in Hanover. The magically brilliant-eyed young women of the land of the Abencerrage and the Alhambra, paraded the deck most of the evening, and seemed to have the prettiest formed ankles and the smallest feet that walk. At night sitting out upon the deck under the moon's pale beams they sang together in their native language, and also in English and German. Among the English songs they favored us with, one began thus:

"Someone is coming when the dewdrops fall,
He will be welcome the first of all."

And I thought that I had seldom heard anything so exquisitely lovely as their dulcet tones floated softly out over the rippling water into the darkness of night, their clear silvery voices rounding and mellowing each word into something of a dreamy southern modulation. Only one who has been in the situation where for years even the tongues have been a stranger, can realize the pleasure, and how grateful to one's ears it is, of hearing an American song again. It is like the worn and thirsty traveler

STUDENT LIFE IN GERMANY. 221

among the burning sands of the desert sighting an oasis, and having wafted to his listening ears the welcome sound of a flowing brooklet.

We steamed down the current to the city of Cologne, now one of the most important commercial places in Germany, situated on the western bank of the romantic stream. Coming to it by way of the river the city with its numerous spires and towers presents a highly charming appearance. Across the Rhine, which in places still show traces of Roman masonry, it has a bridge of boats, and a grand one of iron which connect it with the suburbs on the opposite bank.

Our boat soon landed, and all visited the beautiful cathedral, the most magnificent Gothic edifice in the world, which justly excites the admiration of every beholder, and for which the city is far more famed than for its renowned perfume, "Kolnisches wasser" (cologne water).

On the outcoming of the new translation of the Bible, issued in the early eighties, the bibliologists having disowned the Evil One, and eliminated the infernal regions entirely, and therefor substituted sheol, the city of Cologne took heart, threw off the superstitious traditions that had hung around it for a thousand years, and appealed to the country, to the German public, for aid to complete the structure, on the grounds that the devil now being entirely "out of it" his vow no longer held good. All Germany subscribed heavily, the aged Emperor, William I, heading the list of those making large donations, and being closely followed by the nobility and the wealthy men of the land, and adding thereto the sums raised in all the great cities, the towns and villages, the city of Cologne itself made up the remainder needed, and thus managed to at length, after the lapse of over six centuries, complete the building, finally succeeded in rearing up into the skies the last and topmost third of the two front cloud-piercing towers, and in 1882 the structure stood for the first time finished, amid a great celebration in the old city, in which the venerable emperor and the high officials of the fatherland took part.

How far extending the new version of the Bible has been in its effects one can see from this single illustration, from this one portrayed instance. The building stands on an eminence sixty feet above the Rhine, and is situated nearly in the center of the city, and not a great ways from the river. Its cost was five million dollars. The largest of the bells in the tower was cast with the metal of captured guns, and weighs twenty-five tons, and requires the united exertion of thirty persons to send its peals out over the surrounding land. We entered the cathedral at a time when services were going on, and the long-gowned and white-surpliced clergy and boys to the number of about one hundred were standing in front of the altar facing the congregation, and singing in accompaniment to the great, sweet-toned organ; the strains of the chanting and of the music commingled would ascend aloft to the dome-like roof of the building, so far up as to be almost lost to view in the dim above; the beautiful and harmonious tones would rise on high overhead toward the interior of the roof and seem to wind about the arches, cling around the chaptrels, the tops of the pillars and columns and die slowly away to complete silence in the distance. The monks all had light wooden canes, about four feet in length, with which they beat time in the air as they chanted to enable the boy part of the choir to keep in tune, and one finally brought his stick down with a whack on top of the head of a youthful warbler who was cutting up some devilment along with his singing, just as a section of the song was melting gradually into quietude, so hard that the sound it made on the young, hollow pate, was loud enough to be heard throughout the whole church. Have boys either ever changed a jot under any circumstances, conditions or climes since the coming of mankind on the earth?

There are two winding stone stairways leading up to the top of both towers which are five hundred and twelve feet in height, and are the loftiest church towers in Europe, and after about an hour's hard work at climbing, on reaching the end of them, one has a view that is unsurpassed. The cathedral, in the midst of the houses of the town, looks like an immense hen surrounded by innumerable little chickens. The course of the Rhine can be followed with the eye both ways for many miles; the large blocks of buildings, far below us, seemed diminished by distance to children's toy-houses. Interesting specimens of architecture of the twelfth and thirteenth centuries are to be seen in many of the old streets. The moving inhabitants in the thoroughfares were mere specks; the parks and suburbs of the city, with their aligning long rows of trees, appearing like miniature play-gardens, laid out for children to romp about in, while beyond was the rolling country, beautiful hills and valleys, and far off, lying like a low haze along the horizon, were the mountains, the intervening land dotted with innumerable small patches of planted trees, and covered with the cultivated growths of the soil.

The cathedral is entirely of stone, and very solidly built. Of course, having stood all these centuries one can not expect to see anything else; it looks as well and strong now, however, as though it had been but lately erected, and after the passing of a second thousand years a visitor will see no change for the worse in the appearance of the edifice.

From here—from the city of Cologne—the last of the visitors of the Vielbeer family flitted away to their own homes, and the host's folks and I at length found ourselves alone. On getting back to the castle some days later, and after all the guests but myself had flown, I put the whole of my attention and leisure, strongly to play in endeavoring to locate the ancient archives and glean therefrom some of the great events they were reported to chronicle. I searched faithfully through all the deep dungeon-like cellars, which were so low beneath the ground and so far from the light of day that winter and summer the temperature never changes. I ran on to tiers on ties of shelves built all about the sides of the vaults against the heavy stone walls, piled high with bottles of wine, mellowing for use in the years to come. Some kinds of the Rhine vintages must be kept in the upper cellars to season properly, others in the deep lower ones, farther from the outer air, while special vintages must ripen against the walls on the sunny side of the cellar; other kinds get their bouquet from the shady corners of the opposite end of the vaulted underground apartments, etc.

In order to feel certain that I had overlooked nothing in my hunt for the valuable old records, and also to be conscious of the fact that I had German-like so thoroughly labored in my search as to leave nothing within reason undone, every now and then I opened a bottle to see if the archives might not, by some of the many mysterious, strange and unexplainable ancient goings-on about the castle, have gotten perchance into a wine bottle, and not finding them in it naturally had to then drain the contents to save it from spoiling.

However, after my patient look through the castle's cellars, and failing to find even a trace of them there, I explored the old musty vaults of the upper part of the building with the success of running across, in one out-of-the-way chamber, a great pile of old parchment-leaved books made of glazed goat- or sheep-skin. In some places where holes had existed in the pages, the sheets had been neatly repaired by another piece sewn into the place by skin thread and the restored part showed evidences of having had heavy pressure applied to smoothen it down to the level of the rest of the leaf before having been written upon; the threads were spread so flat upon the surfaces of the pages that they looked like streaks of paint. After viewing quite a number of the vast amounts of them, and so far succeeding in deciphering some as to feel certain that the ancient German characters or language of writing was started, by copying for letters the impressions left by a couple of dozen cats dipping their toes in ink and dancing the olivette farandole all over open pages, I concluded to say nothing to Vielbeer about my coming upon the archives with their hieroglyphic-like formed letters, but resolved to ask him for an account of the history of his ancient ancestor in conjunction with that of Monk Monastus, both of whom lived in the fourth century. I being pretty dubious but what his relation of the occurrences would not take near the length of time seemingly necessary to its procurance by digging it out of the records.

The archives will be a feast to some antiquarian in future years for they are almost as well preserved as on the day each one was completed. They are written in ancient German and in Latin, on animal-skin leaves polished as smoothly as our present glazed writing paper. The leaves were sewn together in books of about two hundred pages, and were in two sizes, one square, about twelve inches each way, and the larger one twelve inches by eighteen and more in the shape of the books of our day. On the cover of each, in front on the outside, was painted a picture—something representative of the work's contents; and on the cover's back was usually a decorative design or ornamental device of some curious and antique pattern, also painted. The paint was as fresh and true to its colors as ever, not even the green had faded, the fading of which color among art works, like paintings, etc., has caused such distressing effects upon masterpieces of later ages, and the painting looked as though but lately executed, and the accumulated dust of a few centuries suddenly poured over the volumes. Inside all was writing in inks that also held their own colors as well as the outside painting—better, if anything, as the inside leaves were protected. The beginning of each chapter is headed with a word, the first letter of which is made in very large size and in the form of an emblematic or decorative pattern just the same as we sometimes do today in our books, but it must have taken the writer of old half a week to finish each big letter, to trace out all the intricate curlings and circles in several different colored inks; and one must bear in mind that a false stroke or an accidental slip of his quill would have spoiled the entire leaf and he would have to take a fresh one and commence anew. The letters of the archives are well formed and are of splendid workmanship, and show that skilled hands had labored at them and that extreme care had been taken in their formation.

At the time these pages were covered with writing the

great masses of the people were densely ignorant, writing and reading unknown among them, and such things as books and written messages that conveyed the thoughts of one learned person to another were held in great superstitious awe. The monks in those times had all the learning themselves and did all this work in their stone cells and behind their cloistered walls. Sheltered in solitude and silence they often spent their lives in writing copies of the testaments and histories of the events of the times. Had they not done so we would be poor, indeed, in knowledge of ancient occurrences. A very good part of a life time would be taken up in copying the Bible, and consequently books were very rare, and were valuable, highly cherished and well taken care of.

How many monks have spent years upon years in quiet behind their gloomy walled monasteries writing these old works, found now and then in hidden places on tearing down the remains of old chapels, houses of worship, etc., one with good imaginative powers can think out for himself.

Reverently I handled this literature of antiquity — these old musty records — some of them almost concealed in the impalpable fine dust that had been collecting upon them for years. In silence I viewed the leaves speaking of long gone ages — the handiwork of men whose bones have been dust and whose very names have been forgotten for from three to fifteen hundred years. One feels in the presence of these skin pages as though time had rolled backward, and could easily fancy himself invested with the monkish gown and sandals of over a thousand years ago, reading the freshly written work of a brother monk just handed in for one's perusal and for an opinion on how truly he had depicted, as a record for the future, the recent happenings of the time, worthy or of sufficient importance, and of such interest, or so greatly far-reaching in their results, or considered deserving enough to be handed down to coming generations.

I at length reluctantly replaced the ancient writings after looking at the pictures, the illustrations of the customs, the habits, the attire, the superstitions, the wars, the tournaments, the habitable structures and the ruling forces of early years; and that same evening, on again sitting alone with Vielbeer before the large stone and grated fire-place in his room within the tower, for the early fall nights were chilly, and, taking up a little "hasen" (hare) furred robe and again lifting sleepy-eyed Schnurkelyah into my lap, as I had done so often at the club twenty long years before, I asked the baron for his promised account of the monk and his ancient ancestor.

Vielbeer slowly filled his old familiar pipe, and in a state of deep retrospective thoughtfulness, blew the smoke for some little time in rings above him, and puppy Schnurkelyah that used to be, hoary Schnurkelyah then, with such a learned expression upon his countenance that one would be justified in thinking that he had promulgated a new theory upon the internal calculus, wisely rolled his eyeballs up to the face of his old master and blinked the sleepy lids as if he knew as well what was to follow as he did in the far past days of the Prussian Eagle when we two, his master and I, were attendants at the University, and all three of us members of the famous club. Twenty years at that moment seemed to roll around again, and I saw revolve before my mental eyes in a flash as though it all had happened but the day before, the occurrences of two full decades, from Schnurkelyah's disastrous exploit at the duel to that present moment when he was again cuddling down upon my lap, his head on one paw and his face in adorable attentiveness on his venerable master's every motion.

"It was the year three hundred, and I forget what just at this 'augenblick'" (eye-wink), began the baron, "but I know that it was in the 'Vierte yahrhundert' (fourth century) that a distressing war broke out in the Rhine countries of Germany. A fierce renunciation took place against the authority of the chieftain of the southern provinces. The uprising was put down at length, however, but only after such a desperate resistance on the part of the insurrectionists that the conquering chieftain swore a great oath that he would put to death every man, woman and child—every last one of them—except the burgemeister, the priest, and a half score of the most prominent officials and citizens, whom he would allow to remain unmolested to suffer the pangs of remorse for the fate their exasperating actions had drawn upon their innocent families and the other inhabitants; that outside of these he would leave none spared of all the dwellers of the then small dorf (village) of Cologne, situated on the western bank of the Rhine, and from which place so much assistance was lent to the rebels and which had been the means of conveying, by reason of its important position upon a great navigable watercourse, so many supplies to the warriors of the side they had joined that it was thus specially designated and selected by the conqueror to feel the full effects of his anger.

"Now at that time my ancient ancestor, Centavus Vielbeer, was the "burgemeister" (burgomaster) or governor of the village, and had been one of the first among the chief magistrates of the rebelling towns to march out at the head of a lot of sturdy followers to the scene of the conflict in defense of what he thought was right, and had, of course, returned to the village after the defeat, with his now but a handful of war-worn and grizzled warriors, most of them suffering from deep and yet unhealed wounds. But he was a veteran to the full, was the burgomaster, and as soon as the first inkling of the fate in store for his native place reached his ears, he at once made earnest preparations to defend the dorf, threw up embankments, and had great trees felled and rolled about in lines around the village, and was getting in good shape for a stubborn defense and a desperate resistance that all were unanimous in their determination to make.

"'What!' my ancestor would say to the toiling inhabitants, as the great log-defensive fortifications grew thicker and higher, 'What! I surrender calmly, and hand over our citizens, our women-folk and children to slaughter, while I and my men have a drop of blood left to battle with? I, the descendant of the great chieftain, Unus Vielbeer, who in the first century made four journeys to Rome to engage in the gladitorial fights, and in the great contests on the grand opening, in the year eighty-one, of the just completed Coliseum there, at each time he was pitted in mortal affray against numbers, cleaned out the whole amphitheater, and who became the guest of all the Roman emperors from Vespasian, who invited him down to take part in the great demonstration made on laying the foundation-stone of the Coliseum in the seventy-second year, to the successor of the great Titus, under whom the exhibitions reached such a high stage. Yes, indeed, and who was time and again the guest of the emperors, and of all the nobility of Italy, and who was only prevented from going back a fifth time by the fact that he was a very prudent man, and because, on his fourth departure from the great Roman capital he had carried away with him as his bride the Princess Clotilia, the beautiful young daughter of a brother of the then emperor, along with sundry gold and jeweled candelabra, goblets, flagons, and other vessels of valuable metals that he had managed to lay hands on, and which he had deftly and snugly placed in a good strong sack, thinking probably the practical western thought, that as they had so many, and he had none, he would divide the things up a little so that both would have some, and feeling also pretty certain that they would come in handy in setting up housekeeping on his arrival home with his lovely and youthful bride, who had fallen so desperately in love with him, had become so infatuated on account of his great prowess and exploits, that she was willing to elope from her home and from her city, the center of power, civilization, culture and refinement of the age, to spend her life with him as chieftainess of all the German barbarians who lived south of the Schwarzwalder, and by whom she became to be so much loved. Never shall a descendant of such a gladiator, to say nothing of the daughter of the Cæsars, even entertain the thought of such a thing! Pile this log a little higher, you heavy feet! Lend a hand here, some of you fellows, and let's give this tree trunk another boost! that's it, altogether, now!' etc., etc.

"Thus spoke my ancestor Centavus, the burgomaster of Cologne, while directing and assisting his men in building the defenses, and the troop of oncoming minions who were to do the base work of vengeance of their lord would have met a warm reception indeed on their arrival, as all was soon staunchly fixed for a big fertilization of the German soil surrounding the village, with the three phosphates of ammonia, magnesia and lime, as well as a couple of oxides and several other substances proceeding from the decomposition of bones, and the vile minions would have furnished the osseous material, when monk Monastus, the spiritual adviser, just returning from a distant mission of mercy, cool-headed and strongly intellectual, knowing the futility of resistance as but more deeply exasperating the conqueror and making the final slaughter of the women and children certain, when, by submitting to be taken without a blow might at least speak well enough with the swearer of vengeance to eventually cause him to spare the weaker sex and the younglings, at last so far prevailed upon my ancestor, the fiery burgomaster, to accompany him on a mission to the forty saints to plead with them to intercede for the village with the conqueror, and in some manner induce him to forego his terrible threat.

"The saints succeeded so well that the chieftain sent, along with a guarantee of their safe return to the village, an order for the monk and the burgomaster, demanding their presence at his court, and on their arrival before him asked what they proposed to, in recompense, should he consider to overlook the misdoings of their dorf, and their kinsmen. Many plans were put forth and offers made by Monastus, but all were scornfully refused. Finally the long-headed and observant monk noticing that the chieftain's wife, who sat beside him, was not so young as she used to be, by any means, but that she was striving by every method possible to show to the world that she was, craftily working into use his great insight into, and knowledge of, human nature, responded that they both, the burgomaster and himself, would journey into the far East, a land wrapped up in the vast unknown, in search of something for each, the chieftain and his wife, and bring back to them a present that should be certain to please them—for the lady some rare and costly bauble, or decoration, perhaps, the wearing of which would but enhance, if such could be possible, her many charms and peerless beauty; and for the chieftain some weapon may be, some implement of war that would be, on presentation to him, as an offering, in allusion to his great military skill and knowledge.

"The monk was well worthy to have lived at a much later day of the earth's existence, however, so well poured he sweetness into the willing ears of the two occupants of the seat of power that each was but too eager to urge the consent of the other, and the two from Cologne were about to withdraw after gaining the consent of the chieftain to delay the accomplishment of the threat until their return.

"'But restrict the time,' spoke the spouse, quickly, to her lord; 'they may remain away for years, and (emitting a barely perceptible sigh) time is ever passing.'

"'True,' answered her lord, 'and it is well that thou mentionest it to me, else they might have stayed away altogether and we be holden to our word of tarrying vengeance until they return, which may be never. No laggard in mind is this same monk, I now discover; no muddle-brain is he, and well thou speakest. I will grant a trace of years, thrice twelve months from this day; if the contract is not fulfilled, thrice over vengeance will I take in recompense for the delay.'

"With that he arose and dismissed the monk, my ancestor, his state advisers and the great assembly that had congregated to hear the conference. Light in heart, indeed, did the two return to their village, to their kinfolk and their fellow-men, the monk in elevated spirits, because he knew humanity's frail hold on life; the chieftain might not live to wreak his will, and he also, held well in mind the vengeance-allaying influence of time. Burgomaster Vielbeer in happy mood, because he had, while on their long journey together to and from the seat of power, as well as during the discourse that ensued on their arrival there, gained such an insight into his companion's capabilities that he felt confident, long ere thrice twelve months should roll away, that the monk would certainly euchre some great somebody out of some great something, and he rested his part of the cause upon, figuratively speaking, his companion's broad and respected shoulders.

"So the two men now made high preparations for the journey into the far East in pursuit of the wherewith to fulfill the contract, and had many pairs of serviceable sandals made, and good, thick, warm-lined clothing prepared, of well-tanned, sewn animal skins. Vielbeer stood by the village smith and directed the welding of a good, stout blade, which the maker used so much skill upon that after it was finished the burgomaster loudly spoke its praise. Monastus selected the articles which he thought most appropriate and necessary to take along, and early one bright morning, with a bag heavy with gold, which the monk took charge of and which he wore well concealed from view at his belt beneath his gown, after taking farewell of all, and with many tearful wishes of good speed, and prayers for their welfare and safe return from the inhabitants, the two pilgrims shouldered their packs, turned their faces toward the rising sun and soon disappeared from view over the wooded hills and beyond the limits of their native territory, while yet the mournful and sad good-bys shouted after them by the villagers, as long as the two were within their sight, were cognizant to their sense of hearing.

"They followed the bank of the Rhine to near the river's origin in the upper mountains of the Swiss canton of the Grisons, and there leaving this guide for their footsteps, and widely circuiting south of the Brege and Brigach streams which arise within the trackless depths of the black forest mountains, traveled through the valleys and in the paths which led over the peaks of the Tyrol, until they reached the source of the Ober Inn, the third or most southern one, which with the two above-mentioned are the three long tributaries forming the headwaters of the Danube, and at this locality purchasing a boat, laid in it their packs and went down the swift current of this ramification to where it flowed into and mingled with the waters of the beautiful blue stream along the course of which they floated to the Black Sea, and there securing passage on a small sailing vessel were finally landed upon the northern shores of Asiatic Turkey, from whence they journeyed to the capital, the monk desirous of an interview with the ruler, in hopes of making a barter for something rare and thus accomplish the object of their mission.

"They eventually arrived at their destination, and after a few days spent in rest and recuperation from the effects of their long and wearisome journey — for they had been just fourteen months upon the way — and after furbishing up their sword, buckles and buttons so as to present the most favorable appearance possible, they prepared to seek an interview with the Sultan, and having sent word to the Grand Vizier that they were two pilgrims and had journeyed hither on a mission from a far Western land, soon found themselves admitted within the palace.

CHAPTER XII.

"NOW, just twelve years before monk Monastus and Burgomaster Centavus Vielbeer from the distant West had arrived at the palace of the Turkish ruler, there had appeared out of the mysterious East, from far India, away beyond Afghanistan, and coming through Persia, and down over the Zagros mountains into Asiatic Turkey, an aged man, his back bent nearly double beneath a burden which he carried, and who was supporting his frame with a staff as he plodded slowly and wearily along. His hair and beard were both snowy white, his hair long and falling in thick masses about his shoulders; his beard, which he kept confined by the girdle about his waist would, if allowed its free sway, have dragged upon the ground; his outer covering was a single garment—a heavy gown—that reached from neck to heels, through two apertures in the shoulders of which protruded his long, bony arms clothed in the sleeves of what might be a jacket he wore beneath; on his feet were sandals of good and strong make, and over his head he wore a pointed hood to protect him from the direct rays of the sun; his eyebrows were also snowy-white and protruded thick and grizzled from out his face, and beneath them, deep in their sockets, were two glistening eyes that seemed ever to be looking for something they could not find; his clothing, though dusty, worn and tattered, was of good texture, and had been of worth in its day, and his conversation was that of one well learned in the advanced arts and the lore of the age; his bundle was cloth enwrapped, and bound about with many thongs, one of which in the form of a broad band coming down over his head to about his breast, was the means by which he held it secure to his person. That he had journeyed many miles was by his appearance betokened, and all who saw him agreed that he must have wandered from some far distant land ; at times he would pause, free himself from his burden, and staff in hand, sit down upon the edge of some wayside boulder to rest, while the little children of the neighborhood, attracted by his strange appearance, would gather around him in awe and wonder at his curious garb and lengthy whitened beard, and marvel if he was of the times ere the world was made. He would often coax the youthful ones, both girls and boys to him, by means of beautiful tales of the wondrous accomplishments of the great genii who live in the magic land of impossible workings, so enchanting to the ears and dear to the hearts of childhood, and after getting them around about his aged and stiffened knees, would clasp them yearningly to his breast, closely caress and pet them as though they were his own lost ones whom some miraculous intervention of nature had brought back to him. Then he would ask them to gather for him the reeds and flags and rushes growing about the marshes along the wayside, and on them being brought to him would fashion for the little ones head-dresses, armlets, necklaces and bracelets of so unique a pattern, of such dexterous workmanship, showing such high knowledge of, and acquaintance with, the advanced arts, and such skill in manipulation that convinced the elders at the homes to which the children returned in glee to display their charming gains, that the aged one was of those marvelous artisans of the far East, of whom returned travelers of their own country, who had gone forth journeying in their youth and returned as old men, spoke in such high praise and of whose manufactures and works they had given such incredulous accounts that the friends and companions of their childhood were certain that their long wanderings or lengthened stay in those distant oriental lands had seriously affected their regard for veracity.

"Such was the skilled workmanship of the trinkets that he had made for the youths that the shop-keepers bought them from the children and exposed them in the bazaars as wares for sale ; and they found ready purchasers, and one and all of them were anxious to secure his services for the manufacture of articles for merchandising about the country. And many offered great inducements to detain his footsteps and acquire the use of his accomplishments and reap the benefit of his handicraft. But all were refused. 'I cannot tarry', said he; 'I am very old, and have many long distances to go ere I can stay my ever-weakening footsteps, or arrest the increasing tottering of my limbs. I must not tarry; I dare not delay, else it may be too late. I must on, on, ever onward'. Saying which he would arise, resume his burden, and wander again forward, soon disappearing from the view of the regretful lookers-on, ever toward the setting sun, ever westward. His footsteps were far from rapid, and he made but slow progress, and the fame of his workmanship spread far and wide and preceded him by many days. His passage was ever blocked by crowds of wondering villagers; by gathered bodies of the lords of the land, along with their fair ladies, who offered large requital for decorative trinkets to adorn their gentle persons; by throngs of children begging for an hour's stay to form them baubles; by numbers of dealers and traffickers making their propositions to secure his services more tempting by the display and tender of gold. At length the rumors, flying about, repeated from one mouth to another, and losing nothing in the telling—told from one village to the next, and from large towns to cities—magnified and exaggerated as they grew, they finally reached the ears of the Sultan in such shape as to lead him to believe, if what he heard was true, that the strange old wanderer could cause to arise from out of a no more costly substance than weeds and underbrush the most beautiful objects, by merely looking at them. So the Sultan sent out couriers to intercept and bring the old stranger to the palace, and on the messengers arrival with him had the aged wanderer brought before him in the throne hall, where seated upon his jewel-bedecked chair of state, and surrounded by his ministers, counselors, viziers, and high state officials, he questioned him about his work, about his intentions; inquired from whence he came and to what land he was journeying, etc. Said the Sultan, 'Surely, one so aged as thou hast little yet left to get from life. According to thy appearance any day may see thee depart into the hereafter, the bourn from whence there is no return. Nay, each single hour even, may be thy last one upon the earth, hoary and gray as thou art. Why journeyest thou so impatiently, old man, and in thy extreme dotage at that? And what searchest thou for? For if rightly I divine by the gleam of thine eye, thou seekest for ought precious and dear to thy soul.'

"The questioned one removed his hood and bowed low before the Sultan, and then brushed back the white hair from his forehead, displaying a brow lofty and noble. 'Your eminent majesty,' replied the stranger, with faltering voice and tear-bedewed eyes, 'has unconsciously wounded me deeper than one couldst imagine possible to be conveyed to another by such unintentionally sharp and far-striking words. From thy speech I glean that I appear to eyes outside mine own as being of an age so great as to cause marvel that I yet breathe the medium that keeps the warmth of life within my being. Aged am I, your majesty, and far beyond that reached by any of the companions of my youth; they have grown old with me and have dropped away like the forest leaves in the time of the end of the year, long, long ago, and I still remain to witness the rapid flight of time. Old, indeed, am I in the frame that thou seest before thee, in the physical bulk that appearest to thine unobstructed eye; whitened as the snows of the mountains is my hair and beard; weakened is my arm and tottering my footsteps; but all is thus only outwardly; all is so but apparently to the view of my fellow-men. I am still as young, lighthearted and gay as in the long-past days of my youth, so long ago now as to seem to me to have been lived or spent in some previous state of the earth's existence. My body has grown old, but my spirits, my aspirations, my pleasures, fancies, joys, desires, tastes, imaginations, hopes and loves, all remain as in the time of young manhood. Exchange but my frame for the one of a youth; transfer my inner being to that of a person of but twenty years, and both my physical and mental state, my material and spiritual being, the substance of my human form and the incomprehensible consciousness of life; the outward anatomy, and the master power that governs all its actions; both, both my exterior youthful appearance and my inner self will be in perfect keeping, one with the other, in direct harmony each to each, in one single accord will be the condition of my corporeal and my immortal constituents. I am not old except in body. I could run and play as in the days of my youth. I could join in the friendly combats and trials of strength and endurance with gusto and great pleasure; could enter along with youthful companions in the chase over hill and dale with enjoyment. With elation and joy could I once more love, court fair dames as in the halcyon days of long ago, and with rapture again have little children, with cunning small hands, clasp my own and climb about my knee. With unalloyed happiness could I again go out into the world of traffic of my native land and battle with the striving throng to gain for my own ones the comforts, necessaries, and even the luxuries of life. The desire I still have within me; the wish and will, the energy and spirit of youth is now, and ever has been mine. But alas! the body has grown old, has weakened and stiffened, and has become vexatious to move; the ghostly principle of life within me is fresh and aspirant, but the outward frame has gotten aged beyond the power of expressing the spirit's desires. Love has ever been the high longing of my life, as it is of all nature, could we but read it properly there. Dissolve but two chemicals in water separately and then unite the solutions thus formed, and the two formerly combined substances of each, though probably having been connected since time began, now part entirely from old associations and rush in loving attraction and marriage each to a new comer, all four elements having torn themselves away from old interests, from all ties of long ages of friendliness, acquaintance and close companionship, and formed two entirely new unions. My children have long since grown old and passed away; their offspring have also aged to the end of their allotted time, and gone the way of all mortality; the posterity of these latter are too far removed to be ought but strangers to me, and I also feel that they are so distant in blood as to no longer be connections in kinship of mine. I would grow young in body once more as in the years of my young manhood; love and court again, and lead a fair young damsel to the altar, and begin life anew. I seek only youth in body, for my spirit has ever been young, has never aged through all the time-wearing experience of my frame. I heard in our far distant Eastern land, for I have been years upon my expedition, of a fountain of perpetual youth existing in a country beyond a great body of water, a sea so wide that months were necessary to traverse its breadth, e'en in the fleetest sails; this fountain bubbles high into the air out of the earth, and one has but to lave in its pure, clear waters to rehabilitate the flesh aged by the passage of time and useless from the wear and clog of years, and emerge therefrom in all the glory of youth— of marvelous youth, upon which is ever so great a premium set—to rise out of its waters in all the pride, strength, suppleness and beautiful physique of man's early years.

"'This land in which exists this wonderful fountain is inhabited, I am told, by a people of great wealth; their cities are built of precious metals, costly marbles and rare spiced woods; the domes of their houses of worship adorned with glittering jewels of incomparable splendor and worth; their streets are of silver, their pavements of gold. The country is of so great a size and of such untold wealth that no monetary considerations have any value there. In order for one to be enabled to enter the far interior of the vast domain and reach the charmed fountain, he must bring along with him something of a great degree of utility or else of high excellence in the shape of art, something new or novel or applicable to the usages, needs and conveniences of the inhabitants' far advanced state; something such as an invention of usefulness to mankind or a capability of workmanship, a skill in handicraft, a cunning in the art of constructing new devices to serve the pride, sentiments or wants, or flatter the vanity of the dwellers there by showing that one has come from afar with the best of his land's out-turnings as an humble offering to such lavish greatness as exits in the country containing the marvelous fountain. I was told that mariners, storm-tossed and spent, have been cast upon their shores, but were quickly dismissed with but glimpses secured of the external parts of the land; but they have returned home over the seas, and related about the richness and wonders of the interior, of which they had gleaned much in hearsay during their but too short stay on the strange shores. Oft have I searched for the sources of these rumors; long have I wandered in days of the past from one city of my land to another, in the hope of getting interviews with one or more of these returned shipwrecked mariners, but ever the trace by which I had followed led to nought, all ended in hearsay. One city had heard of such a returned sailor, with his wonderful tales of the land beyond the great sea, but upon being closely questioned, the inhabitants stated that the news was brought them by visitors from a distant sister city, and on my journeying to that one, they replied that they had heard it from some other way-off place. All, all my inquiries and searches, all ended in disappointment; none could give more information than that they believed the tale was true, and that in order to visit the fountain of youth one must have in his possession something considered of sufficient value in the eyes of the inhabitants of that thrice-lucky land to tempt them to allow one to journey inward and make his way to the magic fountain, and in its waters forever renew his youth. So, at last, I concluded to waste no more time in making useless inquiries, but start at once for the distant land. An art or a craft I have, and long years of usage of my fingered limbs in dexterous handicrafts have stood me in great stead. After years of patient trials and long calculations, after again and again desponding on meeting failures, seemingly at the very threshold of success, after great lengths of time in ceaseless midnight toilings and in tireless industry and perseverance, I have been successful. An art or craft I have discovered, to make two articles held in the highest esteem throughout all the world, useful fabrications upon which more time is spent in manufacturing, in searching the world for new devices, in penetrating the interior of the earth for better substances to formulate their parts, in fashioning new designs of them to please the eye, humor the fancies of the owners, and in inventing new methods of constructing them, than upon all else together existing among the arts of the races on earth, one of each I have discovered, one for each sex, and I rely upon the pleasure and satisfaction, one at least, of my inventions, will give to the high authorities of the land, of the far-famed country that I now am on my way to, either to the governing lords or their fair ladies, to speak and plead for me in my desire for permission to depart into the land's interior, and for an escort along to the wonderful fountain of perpetual youth. I have here in my bundle the materials and substances, tools of hand and contrivances, many of them of my own invention, to make both articles. Long have I toiled under the burden of the bundle ; oft have I fallen in weakness and been overcome by fatigue upon my way; but I have ever gathered together my remaining strength, arisen and come on — ever facing myself toward that far western land said to so surely exist beyond the great water. Every moment now is precious to me, and I must away. I have already delayed my departure too long, having spoken my case at far greater length than first intended by reason of my being carried away by your majesty's enwrapped and flattering attention, and by the all-engrossing silence and deeply appreciative listening of your assembled court. I bid you now farewell,' said the aged one, once more taking up his bundle, bending beneath the weight of it, covering his head with his pointed hood, and seizing his staff.

"'Ere the morrow breaks I must be far away and well upon my route to the Christian lands that border the immense sea — the lands which have torn themselves from the faith of their fathers, now since many years, and who have set their faith upon the teachings of Jesus of Nazareth, claiming Him as the Son of the All-seeing One, sent on earth to redeem a fast spiritually perishing mankind. He of Nazareth has now been crucified for over three centuries, but the faith that he taught, it is said, is spreading over all the domain, from your majesty's land to the vast water, and thence upward to the frozen zones of the bleak and sublime north. Ere the suns of another long year roll over my dotaged head, as thou callest it, I will be well upon my way among the people of those Christian countries where, if no more evil befall me from the worshipers of the Nazarene than there has in my wanderings up to the present part of your majesty's land, I have hopes of soon witnessing my safe embarkation upon the rolling waves of the mighty ocean.'

"'Well, good-by, old man,' replied the Sultan, 'and well may you, on your thoroughly imbecilic journey, fare in the Christian lands; aye, the teachings of the Nazarene are God-like and noble. I have nothing to say against the teachings; far, far from it. I have heard of them and have studied them over carefully. Than the teachings of Jesus of Nazareth there is nothing purer on earth. "All things whatsoever ye would that men should do to you, do ye even so to them." What can be sweeter than that? The teachings are God- and Heaven-given, but much I doubt, from what I have heard of these Christians, that they follow them. That they pursue a course the very reverse has ever been my experience in all that I have had to do with them. Take my advice, given from dearly bought practical acquaintance with them, and on thy trip through these Christian lands, in some parts of which I understand that such, to their view, insignificant things as principle, honor, and character are as little known, even the words as destitute of meaning to them as our writings are to our fattening kine, on thy journey through them, old man, speak little of the worth of what thou carryest in thy bundle, and look well to its safety; rely not too much upon the honesty of those who speak too freely of Jesus and their endeavors to aid His holy cause, else they might consider thy goods, but feebly protected by thine weakened arm, as being valuables necessary to enable them to extend His faith to new countries, and without thy consent, and e'en against thy vehement protests, abstract them from thee in His name, as a course needful to Christianize others. But stay, venerable and most worthy sir! Stay thy eager footsteps but for a moment longer; that what thou seekest in far distant lands and which may be, and in all likelihood is, non-existent there, perchance may lie here right beneath thy now weary feet; it is like the child that in pursuit of the beautiful butterfly which ever eludes him, tramples the fragrant lovely flowers to the earth as he rushes by with eye uplifted to the air; "it is distance that ever lends enchantment to the view." Those stories and tales of that wonderful land are but mythical, have no foundation, except in the imagination of idle gossipers; of one fact I can assure thee, that no vessel has ever penetrated beyond the dismal sea's wild waste of waters to such an extent as to find evidences that land exists beyond, and shipwrecked mariners, cast away upon a strange rich shore would be objects of too curious interest to be expelled, to be at once compelled to leave by the inhabitants; they would be from too strange a land of such different customs, manners, dress, and appearances to be treated inhospitably by a rich and powerful and advanced nation whose desire is to secure the paramount, for themselves, of all existing arts. The sailors would be questioned and well treated in hopes of gleaming from them unique, curious and useful and worthy crafts of the sailors' own land which now they could be certain existed over the sea, and would have adventured across it here to us; the mariners would have fared well by them in their expectations of learning of manners of civilization that they could adopt, if found as being improvements upon their own; and they would visit this land in great force of numbers, bring the castaways back with them to gain our good will along with a knowledge of our devices and superiorities over themselves by eye-witness; the tales are false, the aspect of them show it so. I feel assured that you have never in all your search caught up with one who got the story from an original cast-away himself.'

"'It is all but too true,' sadly replied the aged one, pausing in hesitancy, with deep pondering gaze at where his staff rested upon the floor ; ' it is but too true, and in the reasoning light that thou presenteth it to me, I much fear it is but a chimera I pursue ; that it is unreasonable on the face of it I now begin to perceive. I fear my aged brain has been getting back to the fanciful days of childhood when we grasp all tales that are marvelous and impossible as certainties, be they but beautifully colored and charming to our ears.'

"'Stay with us, then, skilled sir,' replied the Sultan; 'remain and make thee thy home amongst us in the palace; ply thy art here and we will do our utmost to recompense thee according to thy desire. Thou art old and unlovely to the sight of youth, yet wouldst thou be young and love again. That showest not, as thou sayest it does, that thy aged brain art getting back to the fanciful days of childhood ; on the contrary, it speaketh still of much wisdom and human-like yearning. Thou art not alone in thy desire ; far from it. We would all be young and love again ; would all be fair and strong and pleasing to the eye ; would all once more return to the days, the enchanting days of youth, the hours ere we ceased to be a light in the eyes of our opposite sex. That wish of thine, hoary sir, is but in keeping with the desire of us all ; is common to entire mankind, and showest that truly thou speakest, thou, with others, art not old except in thy and their own wintry frames, to renew which we here, right amongst us, here at the very palace thou hasteneth to flee from, have discovered the secret, lost since the days of Solomon, my great ancestor ; lost by reason of not being understood and explained and thus forgotten. Solomon was aged far greater than thou, who art but a child in years compared to his ; but the means by which he attained his many years, although plain to us now, have lain unread in nature throughout all the centuries since his time. As to whether King Solomon held all his years in the appearance and elasticity of youth, or carried them mainly in the expression of middle or of hoary age we now have no means of ascertaining ; all that has been lost in the dim mist of past time. But reason thou, why did his skilled physicians order him many wives, all without exception youthful and gay? Well they understood, the olden day medical advisors, that the aged absorb vitality from the young, who, in their exuberance of animal life and overflowing spirits, can well afford to lose much. So as the years rolled on over the head of Solomon and he began to feel the departure of youth and sought his physicians, many young and frolicsome wives were ordered him, and from the pages of history we gain that he accepted his prescribed medicament without a murmur, and in the daily companionship of his wives grew young again and lived far beyond all the allotted days of man. We will do the same here for thee; thou shalt have a harem of young beauties, the fairest of this and all surrounding lands; thou canst take thy pick and choice of them, select those most pleasing to thine eye and fancy. We all know that when aged men marry, that all their companions remark they seem to have grown young again; that a score of years appear to have fallen off their snow-capped heads, and that the sprightliness of youth seems to be in a measure returning. It is so common to hear of this that it is worthy of higher note and inquiry than has been given it by the wise. Mine own learned and all-enlightened doctor, he that thou seest sitting on thy right, looking so well and strong and apparently in the prime of middle age, is in reality of years fewly inferior in number to thine own, but he has pondered deeply upon the methods pursued by his colleagues in the ancient time of our royal line and has himself studied out the meaning of why Solomon's physicians gave the prescription they did; to his deep researches and his ready grasping of the hidden meaning of parables of old, I owe my own life; for when born, a puny, feebly vitalized being, with not the strength to suck in sufficient atmospheric fuel to sustain the barely flickering flame of life, his great skill and wisdom, his aptitude in mental readings of the customs of old came to my aid. Bullocks, young and teeming with animal life, were brought to the palace and slaughtered, their sides cut open and lower body eviscerated, and I, naked as when born, instantly inclosed in the cavity thus made and well folden in except my face for breathing, all done at the moment life in the bullock became extinct and while still warm and reeking with animal energy upon which my pores fed, the weakling absorbed the vitality from the immense body surrounding him, and after half an hour another was slaughtered and myself moved from the first without an instant's delay or loss of time to the second one so prepared; and so on, day after day, in each several trials of this kind were made, and the puny infant throve and grew strong from imbibed animal vigor and in late infanthood and early childhood was already the equal in health and strength of its companions. My physician shall also be thine, hoary one; if old men marry and become so young again with one wife as to occasion remark, then shalt thou marry a couple of dozen and become twice twelve times young once more and that should be youth attained; secured by sufficient backward turning of years, to satisfy even thee. Thou shalt have the pick of the maidens of the provinces for thine own, a part of the palace shall be set aside for thee and thy family; thou and thine canst have the freedom of the extensive gardens surrounding the vast parks of the palace; thou canst wander with thy wives, thy family, through all the flowered and vine-entwined bowers, the mossy crags, the cultivated groves, the miniature artificial woodlands; canst glide over the rippling waters of the glassy lakes in pavilioned vessels, sail about over their silvery surfaces accompanied by soft strains of music from our own royal bands, sit with thy wives in the shaded alcoves of giant towering monarchs, and canst watch the happiness of sweet-toned and brilliant-plumaged birds joying about their nests suspended aloft, the arching and surrounding branches about which are interwoven with the scarlet linonia and the slender stems of the winding, clinging ivy, and see in their delight and happiness and content of mind but a reflex of thine own, and as the sleepy brown shadows of calm, contemplative eventide descend over the woodland thou canst cast thine eyes o'erhead and catch glimpses through the softly sighing branches, of the heavens, illuminated by the same serene resplendent moon of the Orient, the same evening stars of the East, that have looked down upon the beauty of the Queen of Sheba in the days of the wise King Solomon; and in continued association with thy family, catch their youthful spirits, awaken again within thee the latent energy to romp, dance and play; in truth, by being constantly among them and within the area of their emanating animal spirits, within the circle of their outflowing youthful refulgence, they yielding up animation and thou ever aquiring it; thou shalt absorb in vast quantities their invisible sublimated radiations, their delicious, thrilling, feminine aura, and shalt detect thyself grow young again day by day; wilt find thy frame lose its stoop and become erect, thy tottering limbs grow firm, thy slow and weary footsteps get strong and elastic, and thy heavy drooping head rear itself aloft and face the world once more in all the pride of conscious strength and power.'

"The wanderer wearily stroked his brow, and slowly and sadly shook his head. 'But love,' said he, 'love, the subtle influence that moves the world, will not be mine. Unpleasing is my aged and hoary looks to the eyes. What woman of mature age would espouse such as I? And thou speakest of me in the same sentence with the love of maidens; alas! I fear thy majesty talketh wildly.'

"'Fool thou, old man, to brush aside my words so lightly; thou still holdeth in mind the damsels as they were at the time of thy youth — of a gone-by period. New women have sprung up since then. Little thou knowest of the gentle sex of the present age as thou well showest by thy remarks. Young men can take their choice from among the fair ones of the world, and full conscious of this, have, in consequence, but little appreciation of the worth of the sex, common, from the superabundancy of numbers, to their boyish eyes. Young men can choose from the plenty, and so value none; and their wives are not held in the esteem and regard by them by far, compared to that which the husbands of older years do hold them. The life partner whom the young man selects is but little, if any, in his regard and affections, above numbers of the plentifulness of her kind he could have gotten for the asking, and she is treated by him accordingly; often slightingly, and rarely held as anything much of a treasure; but as for older men who feel the charms of youth departing in the frost-touched hair and in the wrinkles of coming age, and who are cognizant of being crowded into the background by younger and stronger arms, they desire but to gain one youthful wife whom they may love and cherish, and having secured her hold her dear, as a jewel far beyond an estimation of value. It is a well known fact that elderly men make by much the kindest husbands; and the far aged husband is ever lavish in his expenditure and love for his youthful bride, while the young — the married youth — it is rarely that he is not at war with his espoused one. Women know this well. It is often but a choice left them between being "an old man's darling or a young man's slave." Thou here shalt have wealth, station and position, and if thou cautiously and slyly causeth it to be hinted about that the bride showing thee the greatest love and devotion shalt be left the richest pretty young widow upon thy naturally early expected demise, I speak that thou shalt receive love and affection sufficient and galore to suit even thy accumulated yearnings of a century or more. This will we do for thee, old man; and in return, so that thou needst not feel that thou art accepting charity from strangers,' continued the lofty minded and noble Turk; 'thou canst make for us the two wonders which thou sayest thou hast alone discovered the method of constructing. Take thine own time and ply thy craft as suits thee, at thine own will and at thy leisure. Go not from us, withered dotard that thou art, but view it in this light, that what thou in phantasm seekest among the clouds exists in truth and will be trodden down by thee and passed over here beneath thy departing footsteps.'

"The aged one consented. Let us not judge or blame him. Who wouldn't; indeed, how could he refuse, or resist all the aural sweetness that the Sultan had poured into his ears? and the greatly aged are notoriously lacking in the capability of resistance to words that awaken the thoughts and memories of siren voices of the fair sex.

"'I recognize the weight of thy words,' he replied, 'and am convinced that my wish to believe in the existence of such a shadowy land containing a fountain of such coveted virtues, has overbalanced my judgment, my powers of reflection and my strength of reasoning and comparison. Here, then, will I remain in the palace of your majesty, and the highest skill and most painstaking care my aged frame is yet capable of shall be brought into use at your respected service.'

"So the Sultan gave the proper directions, and the old artisan, releasing his bundle into the willing hands of attendants, bade a present adieu to his majesty and then to all assembled, and following his guides departed from out the royal presence."

CHAPTER XIII.

"NOW, just two years previous to the arrival of the wanderer with his burden, the Sultan had selected as his favorite wife a beautiful Albanian girl, lovely as a dream, and at the time that he had made her Sultana, though but sixteen years of age, yet in the full development of all the charms of delightful young womanhood. Her luxuriant glossy black hair, when unrestrained, fell to her feet in broad silky waves, nearly concealing the perfect formation and snowy whiteness of her arms and shoulders; her eyes, large, liquid and almond-shaped, were as black as the deep recesses of the earth where the shades of ancient night ever rule, and contrasted, when she smiled, with the dazzling whiteness of her teeth, and the lustrous orbs of sight, at times shown with such intense feeling as to resemble glowing metal, and beamed with an expression that seemed to search one's inmost soul. She was tall, shapely and pliantly graceful, with face and hands fair as the Nubian lotus bloom, and white as the floating lily of the old Egyptian Nile; a true and unsurpassed daughter of the Southern Orient, where languishing, passionate beauty is regarded as the charm of womanhood in the same manner that amiability and gentleness are considered the types of loveliness of the women of the North. And who shall say which is the more attractive, the more worthy of fondness and devotion, of tender attachment and affection, the more irresistible, the more lovable.

"No one had ever charmed the Sultan so; no one ever gained the influence over him as she; none ever been held in such great adoration by him as the fair and peerless Albanian; her very appearance suggested to beholders that she was in all her being and in every trait of her character 'innately fit to be a queen.' But two years later than his marriage with her, and at the time of the appearance of the aged wanderer on his westward journey in search of the fountain of everlasting youth, the Sultan began to tire of his favorite, and at eighteen she appeared to him to be getting old ; for women in southern provinces develop early, and correspondingly fail in the same swift manner ; and the Sultan, comparing her with younger members of the harem, noticed that their cheeks were peachier, their natures more guileless, more new and novel to him; that to them he held the great charm of mystery that long intimate association with the favorite had somewhat dispelled, that they hung upon his sayings and delightedly listened to his recounts of experiences and adventures with unfeigned pleasure, admiration and attentiveness. Whereas, in relating the same to the favorite, he could see the weariness gather in her lustrous eyes at the oncoming repetition of something she had heard dozens upon dozens of times before. The effects of novelty were being thrown over him by the new and younger members of the household, and though still much devoted to his selected one, was ever and anon commencing to cast eyes about elsewhere. Although it was some time before this was generally observed in the palace, that there were sentiments shaping that might eventually result in the displacing of the favorite, you may believe that she was by far the first of all to take notice of it herself, and many a day was spent by her in retrospective sadness, and many a night passed in the contemplation of prospective resignation, upon a tear-stained pillow. All this, of course, did not add to her beauty. Her large, liquid eyes became cold and dry; her face appeared drawn and worn from the sleepless hours of darkness, and finally it was generally remarked about the palace that his eminence could not be expected to be faithful to one who allowed herself to get haggard and old when there were so many fresh and blooming young girls about.

"It was just at this stage of these sad proceedings that the aged wanderer had arrived, and certainly the report of his appearance and reception was soon noised to the inmost chamber of the palace, and you can be sure was quickly carried to the ears of the desponding favorite; and, woman-like, on learning that an exclusive art, known alone to himself, for making two articles, one pleasing to one of the sexes and one to the opposite, was claimed by the wanderer, she immediately sent a messenger to see that, after his nourishment and rest had been consummated, that he was instantly requested to attend her presence. The aged one, on learning the bearer's message, replied, "Rest and nourishment to the fiends! a single glance at the eyes of the Sultana would be sustenance sufficient to make amends for the physical loss of a month's unnourished travel; take me at once to her supreme presence. Although I am aged my spirit is young and has never learned patience, never been taught cool, reflective observance of slow and vexatious formalities. I go with you at once; e'en now my soul chafes impatiently at the delay.'

"On entering her presence, the beautiful favorite was revealed reclining on a richly cushioned lounge, and surrounded by the groups of her young ladies. As her insignia of Sultana she wore a sparkling ornament, interwoven at the front of her jet black tresses; a crescent-shaped collection of emeralds, diamonds and topaz, the appropriately arranged jewels, vividly colored in green, white and gold, were gleaming above her alabaster forehead like triumphant stars exulting in their location, so near to the matchless beauties that lay beneath them.

"The hoary artisan again uncovered his head, as he had done before the sovereign, and once more brushing the thick whitened locks of hair from his elevated and stately forehead, bowed long and deep in dignified reverence at the throne of supreme beauty.

"'Be seated, venerable sir', spoke the Sultana in a low soft voice, with a musical cadence that sounded in his ears like the whisperings of the angels he had heard in the far distant years, when smiling in his sleep, an infant in the cradle. 'Be seated', again spoke the consort of the Ruler of Asiatic Turkey, as an attendant placed a downy seat beside him, into which he immediately sank his stiffened bones. 'I learn that you are to remain

THE SULTANA. Page 256.

among us and become one of our household, an agreeable knowledge to me, and all of us, let me assure you; and I also hear that you have, contained deep within your breast, the secrets of two handiworks of your own invention; that you alone have acquired and now possess the knowledge of making two objects that are the most desired by humankind, and best of all one of them for each; one to delight the lord and another to bring joy to the heart of the lady. You will pardon my womanly curiosity in that I sent for you in my eagerness to learn what it was you have discovered to so please our sex. As for the other, the one for the masters of creation, let it pass for the present; they can well take care of themselves, of their own affairs, and of what pleases them. Speak, O, reverend sir! I await in great impatience.'

"'My inventions, most lovely moon of the oriental heavens', replied the wanderer, 'for the fair and gentle sex, is the craft of constructing for them a garment of whatever size, shape, style or fashion they may wish and direct, of building it of a substance—a stock of which I have brought along with me from my far distant home— a fiber, an asbestos of the purest dazzling whiteness. Such prettiness, such a feathery, velvety, fairy-like appearance does the substance of which it is composed give the garment, that the being clothed in it shines out as the peer of all beauty in the world. She has but to present herself to have all fall down before her, deep in admiration, glorified veneration and exalted regard, as though she were a deity. All gaze at her in rapture, from the young to the aged. She is adored with a sacred reverence extended to none below the celestial ones; she becomes a being of such perfect loveliness that all other women fade to insignificance beside her. She need only appear to view and all hearts are her own. This substance is so peculiar, this material out of which I form the apparel is of so strange a nature that it is indestructible, and a chief merit in the favor of a finished garment is, that on its becoming the least soiled it can be placed in a fire for a few moments, and on being taken from out the flames it will be found restored, absolutely uninjured, to all its former beauty and its pristine supra-snowy whiteness.'

"The fair Sultana, who had all this time been listening with intense interest, with wide-staring, penetrating eyes, her breast heaving with gasping respirations, at his conclusion arose from her divan, threw herself full length upon the floor at his feet, and looking up into his face with tear-streaming eyes implored the aged one to at once commence the garment.

"'Let the invention of the lords wait, venerable sir', she said, 'let it be until afterward; they have so many joys and pleasures, so many of nature's immense resources to apply themselves to, to beguile their hours and play to their fancy; and we women so few, so restricted are we by customs and habit that we almost get into such a state as the child, heartbroken at the loss of a little something so dear perhaps to it and to us, but its equivalent not being worth a second thought to our masters, they having such a vast command of distractions at their disposal to turn to at a moment's notice. Begin at once, venerable sir', continued the fairest gem of Turkey, the princess jewel of the Orient, still prostrate before him, clinging to his knees and still with uplifted imploring face, from the liquid, black lustrous eyes of which tears yet flowed. 'Leave not the room, but let me order your bundle brought and set at once, in the presence of us all, to work. Your every need and wish shall be supplied. Say nothing to my lord of what you are constructing; he shall remain in ignorance of it all until completed. I confess to one so intelligent as thyself, what thou must naturally have perceived at once from my demeanor, that I fear thy sudden demise, and thou canst not realize unless thou wert indeed the Sultana herself what thy early loss may mean to me. Thou art old and thy life is nearly spent. I am young and have all the years before me to be passed in happiness, contentment, and in the power of doing good, or in melancholy grief and despondency. Consider that, and overlook my rashness, but let me beg of thee, commence the garment at once.'

"'Your supreme loveliness has but to request to be

obeyed', replied the gallant old man, and with something of the old-time grace of his youth, with a remnant or trace of the elegant and courteous manners of centuries gone by, he arose, assisted the Sultana to her feet, and with the air of a school of politeness, now long lost in the forgotten ages, escorted her back to her cushioned rest.

"The bundle was brought; all obstacles removed from a large space in front of the Sultana; a great rug was spread over the mosaic floor; the aged one placed his bundle in the center of it, untied the thongs that had so well done their duty during his long expedition; unwound the cloth, displaying a large heavy bag which he opened and emptied therefrom what was needful, and sitting cross-legged in the center of the rug, facing the favorite, seized his curiously-shaped tools, and his delicate fibrous masses and started work.

"'As it may be days before my master can select and arrange for thy harem, and as every hour is precious to thy ageing and weakening frame, I will arrange to supply thy needs of vitality at present by surrounding thee with some of my young frolicsome and spiritful ladies, that thou mayest at once begin imbibing animal magnetism, and lengthen the days of thy skillful, and extend the period of thy welcome, presence among us upon this earth.

"So she inclosed him about with three or four rows of young and blooming girls, teeming with humor and gayety and overflowing with life; and the old man had much need of their services, it seemed, as the work progressed, to hand him his several tools, to hold portions of the garment, to pick from his fingers the superfluous and curious strands and fibers that he wove into delicate textures, to bring him drink and food, and to remove and again place on him light shawls as the coolness or warmth of the air seemed (so incomprehensively to others) to effect him. Much need of their varied services he continually had, and they, in high pleasantry and earnest, helpful mood, gave all assistance in their power; lent the willingest of hands and hearts, for none knew better than they that the displacement of the favorite, through whom they held their high position, meant the complete although faultless downfall of themselves.

"The languid afternoon waned, the work went forward, the eyes of the old fabricator grew sparkling, his frame became more erect, his long depressed spirits arose, he became lively and kissed several of his nearest helpers in appreciation of their quick-witted services, and he finally lifted his voice — raised it aloft — and loudly sang love songs of old in the height of his elevated exuberance and delightful ecstacy of mind.

"The days and weeks and months wore on silently and rapidly, and the garment progressed under the deft hands of the artisan and his surrounding bevy of youthful helpers, who lent no mean assistance after their first few days' careful observation of his methods of interweaving, fiber separating, sewing, etc. The dress advanced to nearing completion with marvelous rapidity. From earliest light of day and far into the night of each turning of the sun, sat the Sultana silently and intently watching the growing of the work, never opening her heart-shaped ruby lips except in directing the fashion and style of the garment; and when it was finally finished it was a marvel of beauty to behold; and on the Sultana donning it and emerging from her dressing apartments to before the old manufacturer to see if aught else were needful thereon for his skillful hand to apply, before his final dismissal as artisan from her presence, all her ladies acknowledged that no fairer vision was ever presented to human eyes upon the face of the earth; and when she appeared invested with the raiment before the Sultan, he instantly fell down upon his knees before her in an attitude of adorable supreme veneration, and while still upon his knees uplifted his hands and raised them out wide before him and vowed that the houris of paradise would be deep sufferers by comparison.

"That had now been twelve years before Monk Monastus and Burgomaster Centavus Vielbeer had arrived upon their memorable mission, and the beautiful Sultana was now thirty years of age; but during all the period of time that had elapsed from the completion of the garment to their coming, she had held to the fullest the affections of the Sultan. He had had no eyes for any but her, no thoughts but of how the execution of them would be likely to please or displease her; no wish of the favorite could he refuse, no expressed desire proceeding from her that he left a stone unturned to fulfill. So supreme had she all these years reigned in his affections, so entirely had she held full sway in his heart, that all had bowed in the acknowledgment that such an idea as of a rival arising was something never even to be entertained. Beautiful and lovely, indeed, she appeared, and celestially radiant beyond all manner of description; and in the throne-room and in the departments of state, among deeply important papers and his country's affairs, whenever the sovereign was seen to sink into a state of thoughtful introspection and a heavenly expression of intense rapture pass over his intellectual and noble countenance, his observant ministers all knew that thoughts of the peerless Sultana were passing through his mind.

"Now the aged wanderer had been growing more youthful all along during the term of his duties for the fairest on earth, and at the completion of his undertaking for her supremeness, looked so spry and buoyant, so middle-aged-like and energetic, that on meeting him again, for the first time since his tottering departure by the assistance of his staff, and along with his bundle, from out the throne-room, he looked so well and fine that his majesty supposed it must surely be the old man's grandson come in search of his wandering ancestor, the resemblance between their principal features being so greatly marked. On learning that it was indeed he, on being assured that it certainly was the same aged wanderer who had been spending the days of the many passed weeks in the reception-room of the favorite, the Sultan was dumbfounded at the pleasing change wrought, and after inquiry discovering that the fair possessor of his heart had at once applied to the hoary guest the prescribed treatment of their all-wise medical counselor, and had continued it with such happy effects until his recent dismissal, upon the fulfillment of his task; he decided to make no further delay but at once assign to the artisan his part of the palace, and his score of loving damsels.

"This being arranged satisfactorily to all concerned (for truly as had the Sultan prophesied of all those fair and youthful maidens whom the wanderer selected out of the great number his majesty one day caused to congregate before the artisan, none refused to abide with him; not one withheld the soft connubial hand), and the espousals over, and their celebration by all the court in a fervent and appropriate manner completed, the old fabricator and his household enjoyed to the utmost the immense romantic gardens, parks and luxurious and dense woods that surrounded the palace.

"In the long sunny days growing vivacious and cheerful, with elastic steps and encompassed by his frolicing, dancing household, he and they would pass the fleeting hours as happy as they were long—their footsteps gliding along through entrancing rustlings of fallen leaves, they would ramble through groves of ancient and towering trees, fragrant with the jasmine and mauria, and musical with the songs of beautifully feathered warblers. At times they would wander among the flowery gardens, and gather roses and leaves and weave garlands and ornament themselves in great profusion with nature's never equaled productions, or play at hide and seek among the trees and shrubs of the cultivated semi-tropical forests, which in places were reflected into double by the placid waters of artificial lakes; flitting about and hiding behind giant palm trees which reared their widespreading heads far aloft as though expanded into tabletops upon which to set a feast to dwellers in the Turkish skies.

"The artisan grew younger and younger, and as his strength increased he turned his mind to the construction of the other article, of which he alone possessed the knowledge of making; bent his thoughts upon producing the second object, the one that now should so please the Sultan. He presently spent hours of the nights deeply employed in his workshop, forging metals, hammering iron, beating copper, and cutting and polishing rare jaspers and ivory; and on-lookers coming up silently in the darkness would stand by, respectfully and with veneration, and watch his seemingly tireless work, and many of those who curiously paused and who had seen the hoary, slow-moving and tottering figure as it entered the throne-room that former day, bent beneath its burden, now marveled at the change as they would see a form in the midst of the workshop appliances, towering up in all the grace of power and strength, raise an enormous hammer aloft, and with an easy swing above his head bring it down and smite a metal band held firmly upon the anvil, a blow that would have commended itself well to a far younger man.

"At length the object for his majesty was completed by the artisan, and on its presentation to his eminence was seen to be an article of defense, a something to wave over the field of war, glorious war; a sword, with blade of marvelous flexibility; a sword of curious design and of costly worth, for its handle and scabbard were richly inlaid with precious stones and metals, rare marbles and other beautiful minerals, a sword of master workmanship. So thin and sharp was the blade that the lightest downey feather blown into the air, and wafting gently upward and about in the atmosphere, and finally slowly settling, being allowed to alight on the blade's edge, would at once be divided by the force of its own weight pressing down upon the sharpened margin of the wonderfully fine tempered metal ; so thin was the blade, of such a mixture of ingredients of different qualities, and yet so strong, that it could be rolled like a band of parchment from its tip to its handle, into a small close roll that the hand could encompass, and on being released uncurl itself and spring back again as straight and true as a line.

"That the Sultan was delighted goes without saying ; and that the entire court was charmed, and felt that the wanderer had far beyond their wildest expectations requited his promise, no one need for a moment doubt. His majesty and his people all felt confident that they had in their possession two things of such high workmanship, uniqueness, strangeness and wonderful value, that no even fancied improvement on them could be suggested but what its adoption would detract from their merits. And as the wanderer had brought but sufficient material with him to construct the two articles now finished, he ceased his labors from necessity more than wish, and with his youthful family continued to grow young, tarrying among the verdant hills and glossy glades, walking through the great masses of flowery shrubs and green foliage, or wandering in merriment with his gleeful and sportive young wives, hand in hand, along the margins of the waters of the clear, fascinating lakes fringed with rare water lilies, and the semi-tropic vegetation of a southern clime; a land where the icy winds of desolate winter ever sleep amid the fragrance of roses and the perfume of the orange blossom, vanilla and vine.

CHAPTER XIV.

"NOW, Monk Monastus and Burgomaster Centavus Vielbeer on being admitted into the white marble palace had not long to wait ere they were ushered into the throne-room, the very hall, forsooth, in which the aged wanderer had entered, his staff in his shaking hands, his limbs weary, and his back bent beneath his burden just twelve years before, and they now stood before the throne of the sovereign of Asiatic Turkey, in the same space upon the richly mosaic floor that his fatigued feet and his treasured bundle had occupied so long ago.

"The Sultan had grown much older since then in despite of complying with his physician's prescription in ever surrounding himself with youthful beauties, and plentifully besprinkled with gray was now his formerly raven-wing locks; and although his voice still was clear, his frame yet erect as the mast of a vessel, and his eye as firm, glittering and penetrating as of old, still it could be noticed that more than half a score of years had passed and gone into the vanished period since first the aged wanderer had stood before his imperial presence. The now Sultan, the present man, the feeble, puny infant that was, had not received from heaven that cast of strength, that stamp of the principle of animation necessary to robust existence. Nature had not intended him to live, it seems, but was defeated by the wise healer of corporeal afflictions; great vitality had not the Sultan to enable him to withstand the ravages time makes in one's appearance, the progress of years he exhibited, but his vital tenacity, his adhesiveness to existence, his attachment to nutritive activity was great, and one could well note that although the years had told upon his frame, they had but done so in apparent sincereness and not in reality.

"However, as all losses have their compensations, much deep wisdom had the Sultan gained in return for the loss of his unbesprinkled hair. He was now seated in his ivory and gold chair of state, and richly dressed in the silks, velvets and furs of his official robes, while about his person, from various parts sparkled the light, radiating from jewels of an empire's ransom. Immediately surrounded by his fair young beauties—his reign being long before the days when the ladies' faces were hidden from view—and more distantly inclosed (back of and toward the sides of him, in a half circle, of which he was the diametrically central point), by his viziers, ministers and court, he awaited the opening words of the far western visitors who were standing before him in the soft skin and leathern garb in which they had left their village on the Rhine over a long year before, the monk in his cowl and waist-girdled gown, and Vielbeer in his heavy leather trousers and jerkin and feathered hat, and carrying his worthy sword that had stood them in such good stead all along—without the damage of a nick or dent—hanging at his side from his broad leathern belt.

"Leaving Vielbeer standing in his tracks, gazing in wonderment at what he saw, the monk advanced, removed his cowl, bowed low, and approached near to the foot of the broad and costly rugged steps leading to the waist-high platform, erected upon which stood the throne whereon the Sultan was seated, and in the language of the court introduced himself, spoke his own name and that of his companion, and designated the whereabouts of the remote land from whence they came.

"'Bring forward thy companion, armed as he is, and introduce him to me; I fancy his appearance well,' replied the Sultan, in answer to the monk's opening words.

"'His majesty sayeth he likes the looks of thee and that thou mayest approach his imperial presence and still retain thy weapon; a great honor to thee, indeed, I must mention,' said the monk, turning to the burgomaster.

"'Oh! he doth, doth he?' replied Vielbeer. 'Imperial, presence be hanged! Much sorry am I that I cannot return the compliment he maketh me, for the looks of him I like but little. Much he appeareth to me enveloped, as he is, by all these young women, as an infernal, sly old villain; and as to his doing me such high honor in allowing me to retain my good sword, why, what would be done with it? for I would not lay it aside; and by all the forty saints whom I shall ever hold in such reverence, I should like to behold the one or the many to take it from me,' continued the burgomaster, getting warmed up and withdrawing the weapon from his side, and raising it high up in front of himself, he cut a few terrific slashes with it through the air right before the astonished gaze of the Sultan.

"Ha, ha! ho, ho!' continued Vielbeer, doth he think that had he merely spoken the words that I could not approach armed would have caused me to be dispossessed of my faithful and true weapon? Let him but give his slaves such an order, and after making hund-wurst (dog sausage) of them, I will grant him a swipe from crown to foot that shall make two Sultans of him, and his harem can divide the spoils between them. Ha, ha! ho, ho!' loudly laughed Vielbeer at his own wit, throwing back his head, shaking his fat sides and portly person in boisterous guffaws, and bringing down his open hand upon his leg above the knee, in great glee, with a forcible and resounding slap.

"'What!' replied the Sultan, with flashing eyes, arising from the throne, grasping the jeweled handle of his scabbarded scimetar (which hung at his left side), as though to draw the blade, and making a step or two forward. 'What! does the infidel giaour first threaten and then make sport and ridicule of our imperial person?'

"'Nay, nay! your majesty; nay, nay! quite opposite; indeed, quite opposite; quite the contrary,' hastily interrupted the monk as he perceived Vielbeer instantly clutch firmer his sword and his face harden and set in sudden dangerous anger and resentment at the Sultan's aggressively suggestive demonstration. 'Nay, quite otherwise. He sayeth', continued Monastus, 'that he is so appalled, dumbfounded and overcome in finding himself in such an august presence as thine own that he cannot find his tongue; it cleaves in admiration, reverence and awe-stricken wonder to the roof of his mouth, and he meaneth to express by his sword-play that should any offer to do harm to but a single hair of thine imperial eminence's head, that he will spill the last drop of his sanguinary fluid in your supreme majesty's defense.'

"'And really sayeth he that, and meaneth he the rest?' By the infernal, far looketh he from it,' replied the Sultan, resuming his seat with the faint suspicion of a smile lurking about the corners of his mouth. 'His attitude and expression lendeth a far different meaning to his utterances, conveyeth quite another impression to one's mind, and wert I an infidel giaour as thyself, Monastus, thou slick-tongued monk, and speaking in thy language and using the phrases and vernacular dialect of thine own land, I would make answer in response to the reverential explanation and artful, gratifying construction thou makest of thy valiant companion's remarks regarding my sacred personage, that thou wert "way off" in thy highly pleasing interpretation. Cannot find his tongue, indeed! Cannot lose it, surely thou meanest. His tongue cleaveth to the roof of his mouth, doth it? It cleaveth there tightly, perchance, but only so in the middle, and swingeth with much freedom at both ends. However, I admire largely his brave, warlike spirit; and also I feel that much have I this moment gained in respect for the length of thy head, Monastus, for I plainly discern that thou pickest with a sensible eye the companion to accompany thee through dangerous traveling on thy missions; a little rash is he, it is true, but when controlled, balanced, and in conjunction with thy deep head, thou two maketh a wondrous combination indeed. Well do both of thee appear to have come through thy long, long, adventurous ramble from thy native lair.'

"'Hold thy peace, burgomaster,' now bade the monk. 'The Sultan meant no offense when he spoke about allowing thy armed approach, but a high honor to thee surely, for thy very appearance, massive, great and powerful, conveys a threat of injury or harm to all beholders. Thy warlike mien has indeed been well to our advantage along our route, it is but too true, for evildoers seek not to work their base designs when there are prospects of resistance and a combat, but await the opportunity to direct their mischief upon weak and unprotected ones. Ever the best method to insure safety and peace is to be well armed and seem strong as though spoiling for a conflict as thou by right of thy very build looketh so remarkably; but, remember now, what we stand here for, bear in mind the cause wherefore we undertook our long journey; come forward now and let me bespeak thee to his eminence in proper manner. What hast thou to criticise customs and manners of other lands, when those of our own are yearly changing; what surety hast thou that in the centuries to come, these satined, jeweled and gauzy lace-apparalled Turkish women whom we now consider so bolden in allowing so much of their arms to be seen, and so much of their shapely lower limbs to be displayed to casual view from out the end of their silken puffy trowsers for he who runs to see, and who dress in such thin soft-clinging garb as to exhibit with every turn of their well studied movements and poses the graceful curves of their divine forms, may so greatly change their ways and usages as to even shield their faces from all gaze, and regard it a high breech of decorum for themselves to even set foot within their country's state and reception halls, and our own gentle women, the fair sex of our blessed Christian lands, grow bolden and rough, unwomanly, arrogant, and disagreeable to our minds; and what knowest thou but that in the far off years to come, say perchance in the twentieth century, our own lovely fair ones may become new women to our sorrow, and so mannish that the male shall be considered the gentle sex? More of thy own now well and heavily covered form, for instance, so lightly clothed as these women are, we would not like to see, for fear of the ensuing nights' ghostly and frightful dreams produced in consequence and occasioned by a view thereof; but regarding the picturesquely arranged attitudinizing display of these lovely women, as is by their custom allowed and commended, comely to the organ of vision do they appear, thou mayest not fancy the seeming brazen effrontry of it, Vielbeer, but consider that we of our own land are not all the world, there are others. What hast thou to utter censure on, others can well do the same of the (to them) curious modes of thy land, and speak in much ridicule of them. How seemest it to the people of strange lands thinkest thou, the customs of the non-abstemious minded worthies of our own Christian countries of repeatedly treating one another at the places where wine is sold by the gourd sip or by the flagon, and causing each and every one to beswill his brain in vast quantities and whoop about in ungodly doings as a result thereof, whereas, had each been left to his own free will and unhampered devices he would have bargained but for a drink or two, or at most a flagon? Or else what think they of our own pure Teutonic people sending at great cost our learned, and we had hoped wise, men to sit in council and legislate for the nation, and the greater part of them making such inane laws and in such vast numbers that nobody gives any attention to them, except to pay heavy fees to employ learned counsel but to break them again; and our people all send thankful praise to the forty saints that their great law-making assemblies sitteth in council not weekly, but only once in a good twelvemonth; how thinkest thou that these Christian and moon-blossoming ways of doing seem to their view, seemest it not to thee that our ways but dimly interpreted and not clearly understood by them, look as unseemly to their eyes as their (to thee) unusual customs do to thine?

"'Remember the anxious ones whom we left and whose hopes are built upon us; let not a momentary passion influence thee, Vielbeer, and cause, by some rash act of thine impulsive nature the defeat or failure of the object of our mission, and be the means of the death of our townsmen, our village's helpless women and the innocent babes at home, for when thou calmest from thy passion, and cool reflection comes, and reason which thou loseth in thine anger again assumes its sway over thee, thou wilt from the fullest depths of thy great heart regret it; the awful specter of remorse will ever haunt thee, Vielbeer, and the reasonings of long, weary years shall fail to allay it; and the grim reaper, death, whom thou now vieweth with horror, wilt thou then welcome and consider as thy greatest friend, as being the only alleviator of thy ceaseless gnawing anguish—the only one to relieve thee from the ever-pursuing frightful phantom's near propinquity, the only one who can free thee from the thrice hellish apparition's presence. Come forward now, and as I introduce thee, bow, and scrape thy giant foot in respect to this great Eastern nation of which his majesty is the noble representation, and thee and I together, with thy shoulder touch on my left to support my courage, through my lips wilt we plead our cause.'

"So Vielbeer came forward and made a large and stately bow, and swept, with a noise as of rushing thunder, his left sandal backward over the beautiful mosaic floor at the throne of the monarch; and standing both before him, the monk made known to the Sultan the object of their mission and the reason for it, together with all the harrowing circumstances which had led up to it. The Sultan, a wise and intellectual ruler, deep in learning and the desire of knowledge of strange lands, listened attentively throughout the monk's well presented recital, and at its close inquired of Monastus if the vengeful chieftain was a Christian.

"'Y—e—, n—o; that is I think—, I really know not,' replied the lightning-witted monk, instantly seeing the trap laid for him.'

"'Then canst thou tell me if he doeth that in the name of Christianity as something that will give great pleasure to his God?'

"'I fear that he is no—, that is I hope that he is no—t, that is I mean, perchance, he is yet no Christian,' confusedly answered Monastus.

"'If he be a Christain and thy mission go astray, and he wreak his vengeance, doeth he it to better keep in hand with the beautiful teachings of Christ? Surely among the Ten Commandments given by your Deity and taught by Jesus of Nazareth, which the professors of

Christianity claim to take as their standard, I learned naught of this—nothing of slaying innocent women and children, but much of forgiveness and leniency to misguided ones. Deeply have I thought on the teachings of the founder of this new religion, and far from the chieftain's construction of them have seemed their meaning to me. However,' he remarked, and a humorous twinkle appeared in his eyes, ' dire, indeed, must have been the Christian chieftain's desire for vengeance not to have been smoothly talked out of it by thee. Certainly we will do all that lies within our power to aid thee. Thou two shalt have the run of the public rooms of the palace, of the buildings of state and the freedom of the museums of the city. Thou canst wander through the apartments of the palace as freely as among the bazaars of the streets, and select thyselves, after plenty searching and deliberation, what thou thinkest will be proper to barter for, and what will appear to thee certain to fulfill thy part of the obligation for which thou two have wandered so far on such a noble mission ; all the aid within reason will I lend thee.' And with that he dismissed them.

CHAPTER XV.

"NOW, it was not long, certainly, before the two, in their search (for two rare objects that surely must not fail to please the powers at home, the chieftain and his wife) through the marble home of the Sultan, the state structures and among the spacious bazaars, and in their passing hours of recreation amidst the alluring scenes of the surrounding highly-cared-for grounds — not long, indeed, before they got much inkling and breeze of the story of the aged wanderer and of his rejuvenation; his growing backward into a more puerile condition, and of his astounding fabrications; and they were finally given an opportunity to see them, to behold the Sultana in her garment, witness her supremeness—appearing like a white-robed goddess from the celestial realms — and to observe the unique workmanship and the merits of the famed sword. Monastus at once saw that these two articles stood out so prominently in being the objects that would, beyond question, enchant the two rulers at home, that nothing else they had seen was worth entertaining in comparison with them, and he held a long consultation with the burgomaster as to the best means of securing possesion of them, as bartering for articles so priceless was felt would be held as absurd, even were their resources many times greater.

" 'Surely,' spoke Vielbeer, 'one so crafty as thou canst promulgate some scheme to wheedle them away from the owners. Canst thou not present them with some of the things in thy bag—curious to them—and by stories and tales wondrous to hear, of the greatness, wealth and glories of our own far western land, and by leading them to think that we at home, that our people hold them and their country and their arts in but little respect, and so work upon their feelings and so pique them that they will send the articles along with us as just slight tokens to our land of some of the minor everyday and not much esteemed works of theirs; that they feared to send aught of much value, in that we might lose it, etc. Surely thy head that hast carried us so safely and securely through so many dangers the past year, and which contains such a subtle mind as thine will not slump now at working out a method such as this.'

"'When it comes to artfulness loth am I, Vielbeer, to match my capacity against that of the Sultan; however great an opinion I naturally may have of my own capabilities, the depth of them but enables me to perceive the greatness of his majesty's own. To use an expression of our own western land, Vielbeer, which heaven grant that we shall see again with our journey's object accomplished, the Sultan is "no slouch." If I am a shade more crafty than he in anything, it may lie in that, that I can bethink me of the way to handle him. Trickery and guile will not do here in this; to so intellectual a one as the Sultan, its application would but work the opposite of our wishes; his keen insight would at once peruse the method employed by us like a plainly written page, and feeling we had ill-requited his benevolence, trust and generosity withdraw from us as undeserving the graciousness of his good will and earnest wishes for the success of our pilgrimage, and retract from us, to our incalculable disadvantage, his beneficent confidence and esteem. In this case not craft but candor is of paramount importance or marvelously much do I mistake the nobleness of the Sultan's rare qualities.

"'Let us go to him and ask for the loan of the sword; let us get an audience with the Sultana, let us approach her first and speak of the endangered sisters of our town, let us plead the cause of the innocent babes at home, now nestling in confidence of protection at their mothers' breasts, all unconscious of their impending doom, hovering on the failure of our undertaking; and I warrant the Sultana, from what I discern of her lofty nature, and unless much I misconstrue the reading of her ideal and divine character, will not only relinquish for a time the garment, but will add her pleadings to our own at the feet of the monarch, for the loan of the sword.

"'But now that I think more of it, craft must also come into play; it is passing strange that I can advance the interests of no cause entirely without the use of some artifice or duplicity. Ah me! well let it be so, but the deceit must only be employed after reaching our own land, for we must arrange a plan to gain them away from the clutches of the chieftain and his consort after the ban is removed from the village, after the curse of vengeance is appeased, and for that purpose, indeed, will I bring forward all my skill in shrewdness, to that end devote my entire adeptness in trickery and deception. We will explain the entire arrangement to the Sultan, that the young vizier with his youthful wife must accompany us home; he hath, thou hast noticed as well as I, but a single wife, for although it seems that the number of women one can take in marriage is not by their laws so limited, yet still do I observe that the system of a plurality of spouses is not general among them; that by far the vast majority of these Turks have but one partner of their bosom, but one sharer of their joys and sorrows, she being, it seems, all-sufficient for them to handle; they appear to find in swinging a single wife that their hands are largely full and to spare. The vizier and his wife must accompany us on our return home with the two treasures, and on the inventions of such inestimable worth being offered to our rulers as fulfilling our obligation and our part of the contract, and on their being accepted of course beyond question, and the anathema of retribution hanging over our townspeople removed, to also present the vizier and wife as care-takers of the two wonderfully constructed articles which were sent (we will state, to allow no opportunity for suspicion to arise) by the Sultan and Sultana, as gifts to the rulers of our land—the vizier as "Gentleman of the Sword" to see it ever kept in proper state, and the vizieress as "Maid of the Garment" to attend its donning, doffing, and insure its safety and protection from injury. After the ban is removed and all is clear before us, we will assist the Turks in carrying away the loaned objects, and attend them back to the western shores of the Black Sea, where at the near end of two years the Sultan can have a vessel in waiting to bring them back here, and we return again to our domiciles.'

"'Great art thy thinking powers and well planned out thy schemes, O, penetrating and far-seeing monk! In all thou now sayest I fully agree with thee. In not one particle can I add a word or suggest a variation from thy originally formed idea and the method of thy contrived procedure,' remarked the burgomaster fervently.

"So together they first sought the Sultana and urgently laid their entreaty before her for the loan of the garment for somewhat over two years, and the description pictured by the sly monk of the tiny, cute-handed little sucklings, all unconscious of evil, clinging in full trustfulness and nestling security to their mothers' perhaps soon lifeless bosoms, so affected her that she shed dewy tears and promised the garment at any time they requested to take it. Next went they to the sovereign, and again Monastus explained his outlined plans and spoke for the sword, mentioning the already secured consent of the Sultana to relinquish, for the time desired, the bewitching snowy raiment, and dwelt long and fully on the promise of its certain and safe return within two, and perhaps a half longer, years.

"Again the lurking smile stole on to and played about the finely chiseled mouth of the Sultan, just as it had on his first interview with the two when the burgomaster rashly drew his blade and presented a dexterous combination of slashing strokes in the air before his very nose, and the monk had so flatteringly interpreted his companion's threatening demonstration. Again the humorous gleam shone from his deeply penetrating eyes.

"And so, spoke he: 'Monastus, thou hast already wheedled my wife out of her fine dress, and now comest with thy oily language to me to relieve me of the care and cumber of my valuable sword. Yet much of truthfulness and faithful willingness and good and firm intention to carry out thy promises, do I detect in both of thee. Certainly thou mayest have the sword to take along with thee as well as the garment, and if not returned, in a length of moons within reason, after the lapse of the specified time, better by far for me than for thee and thine, for I will then come and take them, and in doing so casually wipe out all Christendom; it will be but giving me a good cause and excuse to invade and plunder, to conquer and pillage, to subdue and sack the land.'

"All this last the monk did not see fit to translate to the burgomaster, having knowledge of Vielbeer's heat and his quickness to take offense, and fearing that he might resent the words, the imputation that all Christendom was only allowed to exist because it merely suited the whim of the ruler of Asiatic Turkey for the present, and that whenever his caprice led him to think otherwise he had merely to make the attempt, to succeed in yoking the necks of all that portion of the world in which Christianity prevailed. This was conceit, Monastus full well knew, that, uttered in the burgomaster's hearing, transposed in language of Vielbeer's understanding, would again cause him to lose his self-possession, fire to anger and unreason, and mayhap greatly endanger the burgomaster's own as well as the Sultan's imperial person, and quarrel just as all their hopes were consummating, so he held his peace and said nothing in answer to Vielbeer's expectant, inquiring look, but raised his eyes to the Sultan's own laughing ones, and there saw that he had again been highly complimented, for he read in his majesty's twinkling eyes that he knew full well his high opinion of the monk's discretion and prudence would not be lowered by Monastus' oversetting, to the inflammable burgomaster, in their native tongue, his eminence's joking speech.

"So the Sultan caused the sword to be brought, and well wrapped in oiled and costly goods, and handed it himself to the two grateful visitors in the great throne-hall, before all the assembled court, and the Sultana entered with her young ladies and the spotless raiment and assisted them in carefully bundling the dress to save it from harm during its carriage so many leagues toward the setting sun, and then, although the travelers were strangers from a Christian, hostile and religiously antagonistic land, and although the relinquishment of the garment might mean the loss of all to her; the loss of the appearance of youth, the loss of beauty, of husband, love, position and power, yet without the faintest tremor in the tone of her soft, silvery voice, and without the mistiest shade of moisture in her lustrous, black and soulful eyes, and with an expression of the angels upon her face, with her own hands she placed the embundled garment in the grasp of the two now departing visitors, and bade them God-speed—God-speed for the sake of her imperiled sisters of a distant land—for the sake of the innocent little children clustering and clinging about their parents' knees—for the sake of the babes nestling in confident helplessness to their mothers' breasts; and they both bowed low in reverence before her. And the Sultan at that moment arose in his grandeur of character and showed that he was not a man, but in his ability to appreciate true and noble womanhood, a gift from the gods sent upon earth, for he fell upon his knee before her in an attitude of exhalted adoration, just as he had done on her first donning the garment twelve long years before, and taking her hand in his own raised it to his lips and kissed it, arose and embraced her before the great assembled court, and stated to all, that she looked more heavenly at that moment, a thousand times more seraphic and celestial, than in all the years since the magic dress had been in her possession. And then after making their farewell obeisances to the monarchs and then adieus to all, the two—in company with the youthful couple, comprising the young vizier and his bride, who were but too delighted at the prospects of a visit to strange and wondrous lands—went out of the sight of the Sultan and wife and into their dreams forever.

"Ah, the changes of time! What will they not work? What will honesty and candor, patience and perseverance not accomplish? The two travelers, jaded and worn, dusty and travel-stained, down-hearted and melancholy, had but a few months before entered the Asiatic capital afoot, heavy spirited, sore-soled and weary. They departed from it in his eminence's luxuriant carriage, behind six cream-colored Arabian steeds, which, caparisoned in harness refulgent with gold, silver and gay-colored trappings, drew them along from out the gates of the palace on their journey home.

"They had come to the capital in a worn and fatigued state, as one who has been for more than a year journeying afoot, can well describe and imagine for himself. They had gone from it with light hearts, their mission having succeeded beyond their greatest hopes and expectations, and they had now but to look forward to the Godward sent thanks of their anxiously waiting villagers and kinsmen, so sure to be given upon their safe return with the object of their expedition accomplished. They were conveyed to the sea, and all four of them embarking, white sails were flung to the breeze, and the rolling waves plowed, and soon were all standing with light hearts and buoyant spirits upon its western shore, near the same place where not so many months before the two travelers, on their way to the East, had stood alone with downcast spirits and heavy hearts, and had sadly and wearily looked out over the vast expanse of desolate water before them. From here, from this part of the shore, at the mouth of the Danube, the blue waters of which could be noticed flowing far out into the sea, where the vessel was to meet them within two years, and failing their appearance, await a space of time not beyond reason, they followed the route backward, reversed the order of their outward trip from home, by this time pursuing on foot the path of the Danube and again crossed the Tyrol, its vales and mountains, upon the snow-capped summits of which the two Turks did much shivering in consequence of their thin warmblooded structural organizations, so much better adapted to the languid summer afternoon clime of their native land than to resist the constitution-wrecking icy blasts of these azure-piercing and perpetually snow-covered elevations; much shivering did they both, the two from the land where luscious figs ripen and where roses ever bloom, and the vizier vowed as he snugly shrunk into himself, deeply among his wraps, loudly vowed from under his embrowned blue nose and from between his chattering teeth, that should a country be discovered that in summer would at no time be too warm, would never become so sweltering as his own land grew in the mid-season of fragrant blossoms, and that in the winter failed by far to get as cold as did these Christian wastes in the season of snow, that should such a country be uncovered it must surely be a portion of paradise fallen upon earth.

"Leaving the Tyrol back of them, they traveled through the northern portion of Switzerland to the headwaters or source of the Rhine, this time descending its course and in a small boat which needed no rowing along the swift upper course of the river, but merely good steering to keep it from running into the banks, and to continue it safely on its way in midstream; it was not a great length of time after entering the boat before the holy monk and the worthy burgomaster, along with their two guests, anchored right before the noses of their townsmen, having faithfully performed their all-important errand and safely returned to their home, which, after their long absence looked most inviting and attractive to their gaze, and having yet a good many weeks' time to their credit.

"Of the unbounded joy that their presence occasioned, of the praises to the All Ruler above, given for the success of the mission and the two pilgrims' unharmed backcoming I need not dwell upon or even state, suffice it for me to mention that the merry jaunt, accompanied by thankful numbers of the villagers, was made to the royal abode of the chieftain, the articles and their attendant Turkish care-takers presented, as answering their requisitions of the dorf of Cologne's part of the obligation, and the Turkish guests, the monk and the burgomaster with all their accompanying train of followers had the heartfelt satisfaction of seeing the offering accepted by those in power, with unconcealed delight, and the ban of vengeance which had been lurking over their town like some most deadly poisonous vapor, at once removed, and in exhilarated spirits indeed did the villagers return to their homes, their wives and little ones, now again to breath the pure air of freedom.

"And after the months had rolled on into the past, and

the vizier and his wife grew weary of strangers, of new scenes and the harsh roughness of a northern clime, and longed for the mellow twilight and softened shades of their oriental home, they quietly and without the least boisterous or noisesome ado abstracted the garment and sword at dead of night when all but their two stragetically maneuvering and worthy selves were deep in the blissful, recuperating, refreshing and unconscious depth of slumber, and flying from the seat of the chieftain's court, and meeting Monastus and Vielbeer at an appointed rendezvous long previously agreed upon, all fled rapidly to Cologne, from whence, after a hasty refitting, they all four once more followed the course of the Rhine, now all afoot. And when the chieftain found out the theft, which he did the next day—after vainly searching for his sword, on his furiously excited spouse early in the morn acquainting him with her discovery of the disappearance of her half of the two offerings, and rightly construing that the strangers must, being but little acquainted with the form of the land, naturally seek out, in their flight to return to their own country, the same paths over which they came —he hastened his emissaries straight to the village ; and on their arrival at Cologne the minions of the chieftain were given by the townsmen the instructions left them, to mouth out, by the monk (Monastus being well aware that a scrupulously regardful and conscientious attention to the minutest details was most necessary as a fundamental element in ensuring the success of their scheme, having, ere he departed, carefully and thoroughly enjoined them in the manner they were to enlighten the oncomers, and having furnished them with the requisite information they should impart to them); and they were to the effect that the two Turkish personages had been seen in the vicinity lurking suspiciously about late one evening, having in their possession bundles and wraps, and mistrusting that all was not regular, and fearing from indications presented that they had absconded from where their duties lay, in some deep, shadowy and not altogether just, sincere and rightful manner becoming to the noble confidence and deep trust the monk and burgomaster had reposed in their honesty, and much alarmed that all was not right, and that the Turks were making for their palm-shaded home on the olive-clad shores of the slipper-shaped sea, Monastus and Vielbeer had immediately rushed to their preparations and at once set out to follow them in hot pursuit, which fully explained the absence of all the four; and with that tale sticking deeply down where it had been shoved into their throats, the emissaries had to be content, and returned and made their report to headquarters; and the chieftain, his wailing spouse and all, awaited with great anxiety the outcome.

"Hot, indeed, must have been the pursuit of the fugitives; so hot and blasting that it seems to have burnt up and obliterated entirely every trace of their trail; to have absorbed away into the elements every impression produced by their footsteps or passage, for over a good year later the monk and the burgomaster returned and gave out that the fleeing unbelievers had, to all appearances, vanished from off the face of the Christian lands, and in desperation at last the pursuers, despairing of ever coming upon a vestige of their track, had hastened to the shore, where the fleeing ones must embark, and they had arrived there after prodigious running only to see a white sail upon the melancholy sighing waves of the Black Sea, slowly disappearing from view in the distance over the restless waste of dark and dreary waters, and on them loudly shouting, violently waving their hats and arms aloft, dancing wildly up and down upon the shell-strewn beach and making furious gesticulations, had only the satisfaction of seeing the Sultan's flag, the silver moon of the Orient upon a dark green background, run up to the masthead, slowly and gently unfold to the breeze and display itself, to their far-strained eyes, in the expression of a saluting 'good-by for ever,' and then the proud flag, white sails and all, grew dimmer and finally faded off into the sea's far-away deep blue-hazed horizon beyond their range of vision, and with that tale all concerned had to be content.

"'That a deeply sly finger in the disappearance of the

garment had that self-same monk, much confident and satisfied am I,' pensively remarked the disconsolate chieftainess on one occasion to her noble lord.

"'Never doubt it,' replied he; 'that monk, in his deviltry, is more than some, he is a little hundred.'

"So the villagers, in thankfulness to their benefactors, erected the stone chapel for the monk, as expressive of their deep love for Monastus and their undying gratitude for his services in their hours of sad need and distress. And when his holy body was at last without life—when it became freed from his immortal soul—they reverently and in profound sorrow laid all that was mortal of him to his last rest in the little secluded garden alongside his house of worship, amidst the flowers and trees, among which in moments of thought and recreation he so loved to pace to and fro; and there his dust remains undisturbed. For close on to nine hundred years later, in the middle part of the thirteenth century, the crumbling chapel was torn down and over its site, and that of the grave in which he was taking his eternal rest, was reared up into the blue vault above the magnificent cathedral.

"And my ancestor, Burgomaster Centavus Vielbeer, was presented with the portion of the unused money brought back from the long voyage by the frugal monk, and also given a sum added thereto, with which he came farther up the Rhine and purchased this site and all the land surrounding, and thus laid the foundation of the fortunes of this noble house and for the future knighting into barons of his long line of descendants who later became so illustrious as to shed glory over all Germany, and for the erection of this castle as a stronghold becoming the extensive lands of the baronial estate; and, German-like, well and thorough, as evidently you can see for yourself, and as the state of the edifice gives witness, did the builders in stone do their work upon the construction of this fastness," concluded the baron.

"The night is now far spent," said I, "and however much I would like to hear about the wonderful exploits of the burgomaster of Cologne's ancestor, Chieftain Unus Vielbeer, who paralyzed all Italy on several occasions in the first century by his astonishing deeds in the Roman amphitheaters, still I fear I must forego the pleasure. They were achievements of a surprising nature I can but think."

"They were indeed", replied the baron. "The never-equaled feats that he performed in the Coliseum were the marvel of the Eternal City for two centuries, and the beautiful young bride that he carried away with him was the cause, by her disappearance, of much wailing and gnashing of teeth for years by all the young men of the Roman nobility."

"I must, however, renounce the hope of hearing it, and I suppose for good and all, as I leave your charming and most hospitable roof, baron—under which I have spent no happier months elsewhere since the enchanting time of childhood—in the evening of the morrow.

"Nay, nay" replied the baron, "you will come back again to see us from your far distant home; say that within ten years from now, say that we shall see you again."

"Yes, dear Vielbeer" I replied, "it can be; I may come back again; such is possible, but will I find you still here?"

'Why not?" responded the snow-haired, patriarchal baron. "Why not? I am but eighty-eight. My sainted mother was over a hundred and six years of age ere she departed this life, and my grandfather dwelt upon this earth well up into the far nineties. Eighteen or twenty years yet I easily could survive, and I feel somehow sure that you will come back, almost feel certain of it—something seems to tell me that I shall see you again."

With that in my ears I bade him good-night, and retired to my own apartments, opened the lofty tower window, and took one last look at the far-gone night-time appearance of the scene; the low-hanging crescent-shaped golden moon, in all its lovely splendor, just sinking to rest over the distant vine-clad hills of fair and historic Germany, the land of poetry and lofty sentiment; the brightly twinkling stars shining from out their black firmament, as beautifully and calmly now, as they had in the days of old over the many never-to-be-unearthed villainous misdoings carried on under cover of the night; one last look down upon the silver Rhine shimmering in the moonlight, flowing past in all its lovely majestic grandeur, in legend-awakening sublimity. And then I closed the tower window and packed my grip, and late the next evening, just before the shades of darkness began to fall into the vaulted chambers of the great somber building, I took my departure. They all gathered about the door, in the area-way under the immense sculptured front arch of the building—the one which had the Vielbeer coat of arms of fox and stacks so truly and nicely carved above it—to see me off and bid me good-by. Schnurkelyah came down the steps, slipped on the last one and landed plump upon his broad back on the old, well-worn rock pathway, in which position he remained wildly and furiously pawing the German evening breeze until one of the young men, descending after him, protruded a foot and gently turned him over. Immediately giving himself a jelly-like shake and an apoplectic sneeze, he ran after me, as I left, for about the space of a hundred yards, and seeing none of the family follow, turned himself and returned to the door, nervously dabbled around about for awhile, and then with a whine paddled after my footsteps again to about half his former distance, and on then looking back and once more seeing none of them following devised that I was leaving, and giving a loud lamenting howl again went back to the arch, and then as I got farther and farther away down the elevation and into the distance and deepening shadows, and turned once more for my last look, I saw him give a few spasmodic runs of ten or twenty feet or so each time, toward me and back again to and up the steps, leading from the arched area-way to the ground, and at last, as if in broken-hearted resignation to the fact that I was going for good, he faced my departing form, reared back upon his haunches, and with his nose lifted toward the zenith, and giving vent to a last long mournful wail, I saw him turn around, run up the stone steps, dive between Vielbeer's legs and disappear within the fast gathering gloom of the massive doorway, and thus, in almost the final view I had of Schnurkelyah his heels were again up and his head again down. So with a last wide-circling sweep of my hat around in the air in response to their waving handkerchiefs in the distance, I bowed my head on my chest and turning my back on the castle again left behind me a home, a dejected dog, and the kindest of friends, and once more wandered sadly out into the wide world.

The following verses by a friend are illustrative of my inmost feelings at that parting long years agone:

AUF WIEDERSEHEN.

"Good-by", we say, but do not mean it so;
    The voice is trem'lous with the halting word—
    Our hands unclasp, the last fond sigh unheard—
Our ways part here and may not meet below.

"Adieu", the soft lips breathe with hidden pain;
    There is no wish express'd, no joyous hope
    Expands within life's mystic horoscope,
Nor love looks into eyes which love again.

"Farewell", we sigh, and go where duty calls;
    The word so idly spoken may not be
    The crowning piece of an eternity,
Nor ever lie where fate so rudely falls.

"Good-by," "Adieu," "Farewell," all bring us pain;
But Love will softly breathe, "Auf Wiedersehen."

www.ingramcontent.com/pod-product-compliance
Lightning Source LLC
Chambersburg PA
CBHW032053220426
43664CB00008B/978